Mexborough:
a Railway Juntion to Anywhere
& its Steam Locomotive Depot

Michael Brearley

Typeset and Printed on behalf of the author by
Shadowline Publishing Ltd,
the print publishing division of the Convecto Media Group
First published 2008
ISBN 9781-904706-25-0
Cover Photograph: The lines in the foreground fan out to serve Mexborough
Motive Power depot. These lines were the only way to enter and leave the
depot. In the background can be seen the water softening tower and on the
right is the turntable well with the shed shunter's cabin behind. Courtesy
National Rail Museum.

Contents

		Page
	Acknowledgements	*v*
	Preface	*vii*
	Abreviations	*ix*
1	Early Developments of the railway network around Mexboroughbetween 1845 and 1864	1
2	Manchester, Sheffield & Lincolnshire Railway 1864 to 1899	9
3	G.C.R. days pre Grouping 1923	29
4	L.N.E.R. days after Grouping	41
5	Mexborough Locomotive Depot – Shed Code 36B	48
6	Mexborough's Footplatemen – Cleaners, Labourers and Passed Cleaners	69
7	Firemen – Tasks & Tales	84
8	Driver Reminiscences	90
9	The War Years	101
10	Ron Fareham – Thoughts on entering a working life	113
11	And Quiet flows the Don - R Fareham	123
12	The Busiest Branch? – R Fareham	139
13	Moving the Coal to Manchester – R Fareham	152
14	First Impressions – A personal view of the Thompson B1s – R Fareham	165
15	Locomotive Notes – R Fareham	176
16	The Sheffield Division of British Railways – R Fareham	216
17	The L.N.E.R. Club	221
18	The Railway Mutual Improvement Class – R Fareham	228
19	Dieselisation and Closure	236
20	Wath Manvers Rail accident in May 1948 – A sequel to the book.	249

ACKNOWLEDGEMENTS

This book would not have been possible without the help of so many retired railwaymen and I wish to record my thanks and appreciation to the following in particular, all of whom served a life long career on the railway, for their generous and significant contributions:-

Joseph Raybould – for his statistical information on the Mexborough and Wath depots. He produced an interesting booklet on this which was printed locally by Cheswick Printers Ltd in 1996, and I am grateful to him for permitting me to use this as a reference book, much of which is reproduced in Chapter 5. He has also contributed many photographs. Cedric Lockwood, Richard Case, George White, Dennis Porter, Alf Hughes, Vic Parkes and Wally Smith.

A special thankyou is extended to Mavis Fareham – her husband Ron who sadly passed away, worked 44 years on the railways. His knowledge and dedication inspired him to write many articles on all aspects of the industry; some of which have been published. Mrs Fareham donated his diaries to the archivist of the Great Central Railway Society, and permission was given for me to refer to them. She has also been helpful with photographs and other relevant information. Other Contributors to whom I am very thankful are:-

Bryan Longbone – A former employee at the Redbourn Iron & Steel works at Scunthorpe whose work was connected with water softening and with his interest in railways was able to give me information and insight into the water softening plant at Mexborough. He wrote a book in 1996 entitled "Steam and Steel, An Illustrated History of Scunthorpe's Railways". Whilst researching for his book he came across snippets on Mexboro' Loco taken from GCR and LNER minutes in addition to details from the late David Jackson files (he wrote the biography of J. G. Robinson, who made a significant impact as Chief Mechanical Engineer of the Great Central Railway from 1900 to 1923, and co-authored the "Great Central in LNER Days" volumes). He was happy to hand these over to save my time in "reinventing the wheel", so to speak.

Ray Melbourne – A signalman He was also a keen photographer and with his cine, filmed himself working in Thrybergh Junction Box in 1967.

Chris Hawkins, - of Irwell Press Ltd and the editor of the British Railways Illustrated magazine for sanctioning me to reprint some of Ron Fareham's published articles in this book.

Giles Brearley – My brother, Accountant and Local Historian for his encouragement and the loan of his laptop computer which has enabled me to write this book in solitude, in Susan's conservatory without the usual sound distractions which emanate from when working in my own home. I also appreciate his loan of so much material from his own extensive library collection which has been relevant to the topic of this book.

Bob Gellatly - Editor of the Great Central Railway Magazine who loaned me from the Society's own collection, many of the photographs I have used in this book.

Mike Hartley, Chairman of the Great Central Railway Society for arranging the reference to Ron Fareham's diaries. I was keen to include a photograph of one of Mexborough's B1s in this book, but they proved elusive to find until Mike offered me some photographs from his unique collection, which includes photographs of every B1 engine built.

Freda Bickerstaffe for her descriptions of the Sunday newspaper scene.

Alan Lambert whose grandmother was a Hillerby, for offering me information which I thought was relative to this book.

Pete Sargieson – Trustee of the Tony Peart private Railway Collection for allowing me to photograph some Mexborough totems.

Ken Wyatt, John McNamara and again, my brother Giles, for spending their time, doing valuable proof reading for me.

Finally, a thank you must go out to those many local people who have had a connection with the railway either by family, interest or hobby whom I have met up and down the district and who without appreciating it, have made significant little contributions.

PREFACE

One could ask why I would publish a book about Mexborough Loco Depot when I have never worked on the railway. The answer really, is that ever since I started trainspotting on Mexborough station, in the late forties, I have never lost interest in the railways. I have, as an adult, over many years read specialist publications written by railwaymen, so dedicated to their work, some whose careers started at Mexborough, who committed so much of their railway experience and knowledge into words. Some were offered as articles for print in railway magazines, others were published as small books. To the people who didn't work on the railway or who were not real enthusiasts, these articles might well have come and gone unnoticed. I have attempted to collate information gleaned from many of their works and thus been able to set out for everyone's interest, the development of Mexborough as a railway centre .

I have also been very grateful and priviledged at receiving published and unpublished records from the family of a very distinguished railwayman who worked at Mexborough depot, and with their permission, I include his works in their entirety. Although the depot is long gone, there are still many drivers, firemen and other operating staff in retirement who have vivid memories of their working days on the railway. Railwaymen were my heroes, gritty working class men remembered in their denim overalls and waterproofed topped caps and as time is passing I have in the last three years tried to visit as many as I can. What I have attempted in this book is to collate their personal accounts, experiences and anecdotes and combine it with a general historical account of the role the shed played. I have tried to refrain from technicalities, a steam engine is a complicated machine and railwaymen can soon immerse one in jargon. Where I have to touch on technicality, I have attempted to put my own layman's interpretation to it. A more difficult task has been one of locating photographs. Mexborough did not have glamorous Pacific locomotives, it was purely a freight locomotive depot and it has seemed like for every one hundred photos taken of say Kings Cross, Carlisle or Crewe, there has been just one taken of Mexborough. The majority of photographs used are over 40 years old but they can still be appreciated now that we have the wonders of computers to sharpen them up.

Having spent so much time on Mexborough station, I was always aware of the presence of the locomotive sheds to my right. In an hour's trainspotting, I might collect 4 numbers but "over there," were lots of engines, lots of numbers so tantalisingly close. I desperately needed those numbers but how to get in; it always seemed like no mans land. There was no access to the depot for road vehicles and the only access for pedestrians was by means of a footpath under the railway, through the tunnel at the eastern end of the station and along the river side. As soon as I set off under that tunnel, I felt that I was trespassing, but of course, I wasn't. The problem for me started on arrival at a small insignificant little door which was the entrance to the shed yard. If you were brave enough to enter, you often suffered the wrath of a foreman; there were just too many around and you were sent scarpering. I soon learnt that my best chance was on a Sunday morning when there were fewer men around but a colossal number of engines. Going through that door, you left the smell of the River Don and the feeling of freedom behind to run across a few railway lines; muck, ash and grime all around. In a flash you made a bee line for the shed proper, which was entered by turning left and going down a narrow passage – more like a tunnel – and there in front of you were silent, yet awesome locomotives towering above you like huge giant beasts. I had never been so close to a railway engine before without standing on a platform. I was overawed by these sleeping giants. Oil, smoke and steam smelt wonderful and to this day, I still cherish those many memories of Mexborough Loco Shed.

Finally, I would add that Mexborough became a very important depot employing, in the fifties, over 700 men. It served 29 collieries. As one driver put it, "it was situated on a junction to anywhere". That is to say, to Barnsley, to Banbury and the South and South West, to the East Coast, the West Coast, to Leeds, to London, to Manchester, to Nottingham, to York, Newcastle and Scotland. Because of its size and central location it had an important role in the war years which I cover in a separate chapter.

I conclude the book with another chapter on the story of the Wath Manvers Railway disaster in 1948. I wrote this book in 2000 and emanating from that has been other stories which I can now unfold.

ABBREVIATIONS.

BR .... British Railways
CLC .... Cheshire Lines Committee
CME .... Chief Mechanical Engineer
DMU .... Diesel Multiple Unit
ECML .... East Coast Main Line
GC .... Great Central
GCR .... Great Central Railway
GE .... Great Eastern
GN .... Great Northern
GNR .... Great Northern Railway
GNER .... Great North Eastern Railway
GWR .... Great Western Railway
H&B .... Hull & Barnsley
L&YR .... Lancashire & Yorkshire Railway
LMSR .... London Midland & Scottish Railway
LNER .... London & North Eastern Railway
LNWR .... London & North Western Railway
MIC .... Mutual Improvement Class
MPD .... Motive Power Depot
MS&LR .... Manchester, Sheffield & Lincolnshire Railway
NRM .... National Rail Museum
POW .... Prisoner of War
ROD .... Railway Operating Division (of the Royal Engineers 1917-
1919).
SRBWH&GR ..... Sheffield, Rotherham, Barnsley, Wakefield, Huddersfield
& Goole Railway
SYCR .... South Yorkshire Coal Railway
SYR .... South Yorkshire Railway

CHAPTER 1

EARLY DEVELOPMENTS OF THE RAILWAY NETWORK AROUND MEXBOROUGH. 1845-1864

Most of the historical references in this chapter are extracted from a book by D L Franks entitled "South Yorkshire Railway".

By 1840, Railwaymania was dawning. The new concept of travel & transportation by railway saw literally hundreds of schemes put forward by groups of industrialists, and lobbyists, who had formed themselves into various Companies. That year, there were no less than 23 schemes, for instance, projected to put Doncaster on the railway map, but by the opening of the next Parliamentary session, only 10 of these schemes had presented bills. One of them was by the South Yorkshire Coal Railway, another by the Goole, Doncaster, Sheffield & Manchester Railway. Both these Companies wanted to use the Don Valley to reach Doncaster from the West, but rather than jeopardise either's existence by refusal of the Select Committee, they agreed to amalgamate their schemes; the lines to the NE of Doncaster to be opened by the Goole Company and the lines SW of Doncaster by the South Yorkshire Coal Railway (SYCR). The Goole Company's proposal, incidentally, was to connect Thurgoland with Goole going via Stainborough, Worsborough, Wath, Adwick on Dearne and on to Doncaster. The SYCR's proposals were very different. They wanted to connect the South Yorkshire Coalfields with existing and proposed lines of railway as well as with the canals and navigations of South Yorkshire.

Neither of these proposals however, were to get off the drawing board. The reason for this was that in the same session of Parliament, a Bill was introduced to connect Sheffield with the Manchester and Leeds Railway. Powerful Wakefield interests from the Banking, Mining and other Industries were backing this proposal The route was to edge the then belt of active coal mining as well as the heavy industry of Sheffield & Chapeltown. From Barnsley this line became the Lancashire & Yorkshire Railway. This Bill succeeded but opposition to the South Yorkshire Coal Railway (SYCR) through North Midland influence was very strong; a sort of resentment that other little companies could emerge and muscle in on the "honeypot" of the day. The SYCR Bill was thrown out. Nothing more was ever heard of the South Yorkshire Coal Railway.

When the North Midland was opened in 1840, there was a renewed agitation for a line to Doncaster from the neighbourhood of Swinton, but nothing material resulted. A public meeting had been held in Doncaster in 1840 to whip up enthusiasm for the North Midland scheme but there was some strong opposition and the local newspaper reported that the scheme "languished, stagnated and died".

At this juncture the "Railway King" appeared on the scene of conflict as to whom was to provide Doncaster with a railway from the west. Mr George Hudson attended a public meeting at Gainsborough on 13th April 1844, when he put forward a plan for a line from the North Midland at Swinton to Doncaser, Gainsborough and Lincoln. George Stephenson was present at the meeting and gave his advice as to the best and easiest route. Later, on 12th July 1844, the shareholders of the North Midland authorised the Directors to go ahead with the scheme, which was to be capitalised at £1,000,000, and on 31st July 1844, a survey was actually made on the west side of Doncaster, carried out by Mr Stephenson who was accompanied by Mr Hudson himself. It was not to succeed.

Schemes galore were being promoted. One to be eventually successful was the South Yorkshire Railway, only under a longer title. An imposing committee was formed under the Chairmanship of Earl Fitzwilliam, and a prospectus was issued. The committee obtained the services of William Cubitt as consulting engineer and Messrs R&E Baxter of Doncaster were appointed as solicitors. Thus, for the second time a South Yorkshire Railway was formally introduced in Parliament, on 7th April 1846. However, it failed to obtain powers that year. One that was successful was the Huddersfield and Sheffield Junction Railway (Huddersfield and Penistone) who got powers for a branch to Darfield from Denby Dale; which, of course, was never built. The Swinton and Lincoln Railway backed by the North Midland was thrown out by

This locomotive was one of two built at Mexborough in 1861, SYR No20 later becoming MSLR No 171. It spent most of its working life allocated to Mexborough shed. A second engine was built in 1862, SYR No 22 later renumbered MSLR No 173.
Photo from "South Yorkshire Railway" by D L Franks.

Parliament. The imposing backers announced the intention of renewing the application in the shape of a curtailed version; a line from Swinton to Doncaster. A battle of railway giants was beginning!

That same summer, a public meeting was held in Doncaster to examine the merits of the two chief contenders for the Don gap to Doncaster from the west. The meeting decided to back the South Yorkshire Railway scheme. A lesser and new scheme was also considered at the meeting, known as the Sheffield, Rotherham and Doncaster Railway, proposed by a Mr Fisher of Doncaster; but these were not adopted. Finally, in the welter of all this conflict, Parliament decided in favour of the S.Y.R.

To go back a little in the matter of date, it must be recalled that when the 1846 Bill of the S.Y.R. was thrown out, the promoters did not let grass grow under their feet. Before May was out of that year a special meeting of the shareholders of the S.Y.R. was held at the London Tavern, Bishopsgate. At that meeting, it was decided to represent their Bill, but equally important, was the ratification of the agreement to purchase the "lines south of Barnsley" from the S.R.B.W.H&G Rly. Also the Goole, Doncaster, Sheffield and Manchester Company failed to obtain powers. This company and the S.Y.R. held a joint meeting of shareholders in September 1846, when it was agreed to amalgamate their interests. The 1846 new born name was "The South Yorkshire, Doncaster and Goole Railway Company", other titles incorporated such additions as "..... and River Don Navigation" ....the mess resulting only in adding confusion to confusion. In a subsequent meeting the shareholders had agreed to purchase the River Don navigation and, also, the Dearne & Dove Canal, which was a separate concern.

The successful S.Y.R. Bill failed however, to get powers for branches from Mexborough to Rotherham, and from Worsborough to Penistone. Parliament laid it down that the Railway Commissioners were to determine the terms on which the South Yorkshire was to run from Swinton to Rotherham upon Midland Railway lines, and also the terms on which the Midland were to run to Doncaster over S.Y.R. lines. The Commissioners ruled that the Midland should have powers to run to Doncaster, and establish a goods yard there, whereas they refused the S.Y.R. permission to run over Midland lines to Rotherham. There was an element of injustice and bias in this because it was the Midland opposition which influenced the Commissioners. S.Y.R. got no compensation for this. The only good thing was that the Midland were refused powers to build their own line to Doncaster.

And so, after all the delay, a spasm of impatience gripped the good people of Doncaster. Almost before the ink was dry on the Bill giving authority to the S.Y.R. to proceed with its schemes, efforts were made to induce a speedy completion of the work. Doncaster Town Council petitioned the House of Lords that the period of seven years allowed for the construction of the line be reduced, but the prayer did not have much effect, it being explained that it was in the interests of the promoters to complete their line as early as possible. By October 1847, reports were being made in the local press of the commencement of work. Starts were in hand at Balby, Hexthorpe, Warmsworth and Levit Hagg. The ceremonial first turf was cut in Warmsworth Field; it began the cutting which aroused the correspondents of the day to eloquent description of the cutting as "of fearful aspect" and "frightening character" and "awesome". Earl Fitzwilliam, the chairman of the S.Y.R., stated at the half yearly meeting in February 1848 that they hoped the line from Doncaster to Swinton would be opened the following year.The early part of 1848 was a busy time for the officials of the S.Y.R. and not least because they moved the Head Office from Doncaster to Sheffield. On 21st July there appeared in the press an advertisement which stated that the South Yorkshire, Doncaster and Goole Railway would hold meetings at the Star Inn Conisborough and the Red Lion Mexborough, for considering rights on common lands and wastes, and the compensation to be paid. About the same time, reports appeared of the progress of work at Foulsyke Tunnel (Conisborough).August brought news on the financial side of the Company's affairs. A statement was made that it was expected not more than £15 on every £20 share would be called. The engineer's report stated that rails, chairs and sleepers had been contracted for at a low price. Wagons and Plant had been obtained at very reasonable cost. (there was no mention of motive power here). The construction work did occasionally meet with some

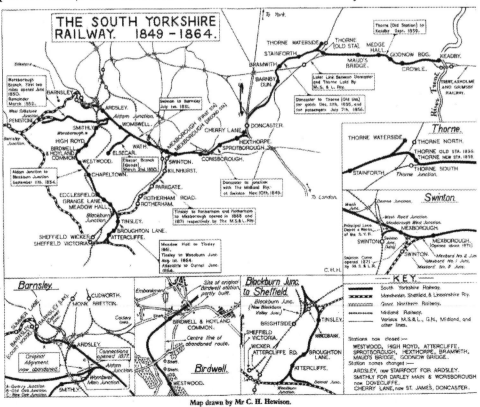

Map drawn by Mr C. H. Hewison.

reverses. On two occasions the railway embankment pushed the river bank into the water near Doncaster and seriously affected navigation. There was also a subsidence of the embankment at Rainbow Bridge over the Don, near Conisborough which effectively doomed the forecasted completion of the line as September 1849, which was also to coincide with the Great Northern's own expectations of reaching Doncaster. Two reports did counter this delaying event; one was confident the line would open for "the races" (early September), the other, an inspired one, gave a date - 8th October 1849.

The date just mentioned, passed, but on 29th October 1849, an experimental trip was made from Doncaster to Swinton, through Mexborough (but with no station). It started from Cherry Tree Gardens; a separate station to the main GNR one, and which was really nothing more than an alighting point in a Mr Crowcroft's garden; a market gardener. No press were invited.

The locomotive was a small 0-4-0 which had been used for the ballasting and the train comprised of two 1st class coaches loaned by the Midland Railway and one open truck fitted with seats loaned by the Great Northern. The train was met at Swinton by the Earl Fitzwilliam. In the report of this run, it was stated that the Midland Railway would provide the passenger service from Sheffield to Doncaster and the public opening would be the 3rd November 1849. This was delayed until the 10th until the new Mexborough station, sited near the South Yorkshire Hotel on Rowms Lane, was ready. The first station; a small platform affair, had been built at the Ferryboat crossing but the difficult access very soon rendered it obsolete. Anyone who used to go down Ferryboat

Mexborough Station circa 1910 looking East. Courtesy of G H Brearley.

Lane, cross the canal swingbridge and take the "penny" ferryboat across the Don would realise how impractical this station approach was, and it would be quite easy to miss a train if one had to wait while the swingbridge opened for a barge or the ferryman had to walk down to his boat.

An advertisement appeared in the local paper on 9th November which read as follows:-

The public are respectfully informed that under an arrangement made between the Midland Railway Company and the South Yorkshire Railway Company, the Railway between the Swinton Station on the Midland Line and Doncaster will be Opened for Traffic by the Midland Company on Saturday next, 10th November and that until further notice, trains will run between Sheffield and Doncaster as under, meeting at Swinton, trains to and from the North, Derby, Birmingham, Gloucester, Bristol and London. For particulars see Time Table.
Leave DONCASTER: 9-30am; 1-00pm; 4-30pm (express) and 7-00pm.
Leave SHEFFIELD: 8-00am; 11-10am; 2-15pm and 5-45pm.

BY ORDER,
Joseph Sanders,
General Manager, Midland Railway   *Derby 7th November 1849*

It should be mentioned that the opening of the South Yorkshire Railway did spell the doom of a one time flourishing trade. From the opening of the North Midland a Doncaster firm ran a service of horse buses, meeting all trains at Swinton. It can still be observed how the railway provided for this service by the ample approach to the old Swinton Station which can be seen today. The bus service died within a matter of weeks.

A water bus which ran a passenger service to Doncaster was also effectively displaced by the railway.

Platforms were provided in 1850 for the villages of Balby, Hexthorpe, Sprotborough and Warmsworth. Conisborough already had a station, a sparse little wooden platform with two wooden buildings on it; one occupied by SYR staff and the other by Midland staff.

The most impressive section of this line, (and probably to this day), is the Warmsworth rock cutting with its 70' sheer vertical walls of limestone. In the early DMU (Diesel Multiple Unit) days, it was possible to sit towards the front of the train and look ahead and take in this impressive engineering feat. In the modern diesel unit, there is no forward or rear looking view and a quick perception of it can only be obtained by looking out of the window at the cutting walls, as they flash by. Incredibly, the platform for Sprotborough was located in this cutting at the point where the Warmsworth to Sprotborough road crosses the line. It was reached by a flight of 66 steps; covered, but badly lit with small windows. On the platform was a small wooden shelter which served as a booking hall and a ticket office. Being so ridiculously located and with so precarious an access, it closed on 1st January 1875.

A line west of Mexborough was opened up to Elsecar on 2nd February 1850 and the local paper made much of the fact of the first coal to be conveyed to Doncaster by train. The train consisted of 20 wagons of 6½ tons each and came from Earl Fitzwilliam's Colliery at Elsecar. Coal soon began to move on the S.Y.R. to Doncaster, where it was handed over to the G.N.R., much of it bound for shipment at Boston. Shortly after this, the line was opened to Worsborough, which meant that more coal would be flowing along the line. The flow of coal traffic from the Elsecar branch was also augmented by a new seam from Darley Main which opened in 1850. [This was a private colliery located in Worsborough on the fringe of Wombwell woods. It was a deep pit and did not enjoy a particularly good safety record; 6 men had been killed in an underground explosion on 29th January 1847. All the collieries in the immediate vicinity were served by the Dearne & Dove canal until the railway came]. The SYR was then serving 14 pits on the Elsecar and Worsboro branches. In 1851, a line was opened up from Aldham Junction (came off the line to Worsborough between Wombwell and Stairfoot) to Barnsley, thus making passenger services possible from Doncaster to Barnsley. Four trains per day were run in each direction. They were run by the GNR using their engines and stock. As customary with the SYR, there was no official ceremony and complaints followed about there being no stir of excitement. It was in this period that Mexborough was to get its first engine shed. It was a single road structure situated in the cutting below Whitelea Road close to the latter day Mexborough No 4 signal box.

By 1860 the SYR felt the need for a better equipped line and in a Shareholder's meeting of August that year, authority was being sought for numerous capital projects. These included alterations to signals, points & lines at Hexthorpe Junction, new sidings at Mexborough and new waiting rooms at Conisbro, Mexbro,Wath, Wombwell, Barnsley, Crowle and Keadby. Estimated overall cost £7,780. At the next Shareholder's meeting in 1861, there was another list of capital expenditure projects. These included, one locomotive, 100 wagons, 1x3rd and 1 composite carriage, a warehouse crane & sidings at Mexbro, Elsecar and Thorne and sidings at Barnsley, Crowle and Keadby. Estimated overall cost £14,860. It was felt that the way forward was to amalgamate with the Manchester Sheffield and Lincoln railway. The MS&L had entered Barnsley from the west in 1859 with a branch from Penistone, via Silkstone, Dodworth & Summer Lane to a station, later to become known as the Exchange. And so, in 1864, the Transfer Bill of the South Yorkshire Railway passed the Committee of the House of Lords and the Company was leased by the Manchester, Sheffield and Lincoln Railway; it was not legally absorbed until 1874.

The minute books of the South Yorkshire Railway Co. have revealed the following items:-

S.Y.Ry. Board meeting of 17-8-72. "The M.S.&L.Ry. asked the S.Y.Ry. to construct an engine shed at Mexborough, and siding accommodation. The question was adjourned until the next meeting for the production of plans and estimates.

A further meeting of the S.Y.Ry Board on 31-8-72 states
9"Estimate for Mexborough Engine Shed £47,186." Carried.

Nothing further appears in the S.Y.Ry minute books regarding Mexborough Shed. However, on 30-7-1873, the following entry is written:-

"Extraordinary General Meeting of the South Yorkshire Railway Board and Shareholders" – Proposed: "The sale of the S.Y.Ry. Co. to the M.S.& L. Ry Co." – Carried.

This was the end of a small railway. It had started from narrowly conceived beginnings, it had had a stormy life and troubled relationships with its neighbours, yet it left a line with considerable breadth of vision and potential for a cross country provincial line, to launch its drive into fields never thought of by its pioneers. Scunthorpe could not have grown to the importance it has today without coal from Yorkshire. It was the South Yorkshire Railway that supplied the coal. The Trent bridge carried vast quantities, the Worsborough Branch provided vast tonnage, this line was opened up to the West and was the link for supplying vast quantities for the Lancashire mills and the liners sailing from Liverpool. Coal came into the first title, coal was its life, coal was its bargaining power and coal turned the little; almost a tramway; into a force to be reckoned with by its big connections. Lesser men and their Companies have succumbed under pressure from London and Derby.

SYR figures of tons of coal carried:-

1855	421,755
1856	723,289
1857	878,816
1858	960,010
1859	926,069
1860	917,799
1861	1,016,659
1862	905,429

CHAPTER 2

MANCHESTER, SHEFFIELD & LINCOLNSHIRE RAILWAY 1864 - 1899

The South Yorkshire Railway, after their merger with the MS&L were keen to develop their own independent route to Sheffield and so in 1871, a line opened which led south from Mexborough via Swinton Central, Kilnhurst Central, Parkgate, Rotherham, Tinsley, Broughton Lane, Attercliffe to Sheffield Victoria. At Thrybergh, a junction was put into the line to give access to Silverwood colliery and on to link up with the Hull & Barnsley/Great Central Joint Committee line at Braithwell Junction.

This determined that the second built Mexborough station on Rowms Lane had to be abandoned, for it was now wrongly located on the junction for the Doncaster to Sheffield trains. The MS&L therefore built a third station for Mexborough in 1871 and to this day it serves as the present passenger station. It had 3 platforms, the third being formed by making the down platform and its waiting room an island site. The up platform had a fish dock at its eastern end, but it was abandoned in the sixties and filled in. A wooden structure was then erected on the site around 1970 for the W. H. Smith newspaper group. Stations similar in architecture to Mexborough were built in the same period at Conisborough, Wath, Wombwell, Silkstone and Woodhouse.

In 1875, the lines were quadrupled between Mexborough West Junction and Mexborough No 2. With further increases of coal traffic on the Worsborough, the MS&L, in 1880, extended this branch further westwards

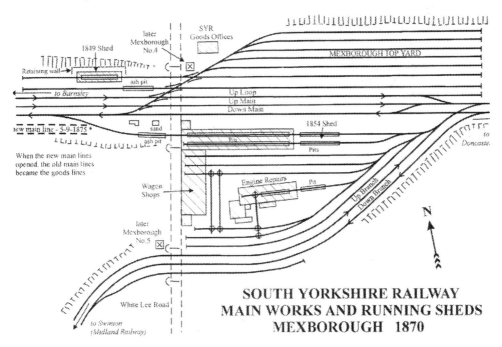

SOUTH YORKSHIRE RAILWAY
MAIN WORKS AND RUNNING SHEDS
MEXBOROUGH 1870

to link up with the existing route from Barnsley to Penistone at Silkstone. This remained a goods line for the whole of its life; it had steep gradients and was the reason why a very unique locomotive, the Garratt was shedded at Mexborough.

The second locomotive depot was actually built in the triangle of land between the lines to Swinton LMR and the lines to Wath and Barnsley. This same land is now occupied by Grove Environmental (Recycling) Ltd who operate a scrap and waste paper disposal business. It was only a small depot, having just four roads to stable locomotives.

A new depot, the third, which served until the withdrawal of steam, was built in 1874 and the former depot became used as a wagon repair works operated by Samuel Gittins & Sons, latterly known as Burnett's Wagon repairs. It closed in the seventies. The new depot became the 2nd largest on the GCR, consisting of 12 shed roads for minor repair and maintenance purposes; 3 fitting shop roads for heavy repairs; 2 ashpit roads; a coal stage road, a turntable road and 3 "cripple siding" roads known as front, middle and back roads. The term "cripple" originated from when these sidings were used for storing broken or crippled wagons awaiting repair. They had become redundant by the time the new depot was built.

Photographs of those early days on the railway are scarce, but here are some of the newspaper reports of that time, giving graphic accounts of incidents on the railway. Many of these conjure up impressions in far greater detail than the photographs of those days could ever do. I start with an extract from the Railway Review, dated 6th January 1882 concerning an accident which occurred near the first loco shed site on 31st August 1868. It concerns the accident of Alfred William Hillerby.

A CRUEL AND UNJUST LAW:- One morning in the month of August, some fourteen or fifteen years ago, I was sent for hurriedly to resume work, after a very short interval of rest. The messenger who came for me was the stationmaster's son, who, in reply to my objections as to want of rest (for I had been out the whole of the previous night) said I should oblige his father if I would come; and mentioning the train I was required to work. I suppose that as it should have started some 4 hours earlier, there was no guard to work it. Now the stationmaster was a kindly disposed man and much respected by the large staff he had under him, and it was impossible for me to refuse a request of his, especially when preferred in such a courteous manner. I therefore quickly dressed myself and repaired to the station, where the stationmaster informed me that the guard who had started with the train at its right time had met with an accident, and he wanted me to take the engine and van, which I should find standing near the engine shed, and go and complete the day's work allotted to this particular train. Going to the spot indicated, and getting into the van, I was shocked at the sight which met my gaze, for the floor was literally covered with blood,

A young Alfred William Hillerby. Courtesy Mrs Joan Hillerby .

and I shuddered involuntarily as I thought of what had happened to one of my most intimate friends. I soon obtained a few shovels-full of sand from the engine, with which to cover the sickening spectacle, and started on my journey. Arrived at the spot where the accident occurred, I soon learned the particulars. My friend, the guard, while shunting some wagons he had uncoupled from the engine, was required to hold a pair of points, the lever of which had to be pulled towards him at right angles with the rails. Having given the necessary signal for the driver to put them in motion, when the signal was given to stop, the wagons were only just separated from the buffers of the tender, and being anxious to save the engine from going in the same direction as the wagons, he forced the lever forward towards the rails; it came out of the socket and with it loose in his hand he fell headlong under the tender wheels. His injuries were terrible. The right arm was severed near the shoulder, one eye was knocked completely out of its socket and the jaws and some ribs were fractured. With such injuries and the shock to the system, I little thought that I should again see my friend alive, but after having finished the day's trip, I called at his lodgings, and found that he was still alive and perfectly conscious. The shattered arm lay beside him, a small portion of the integuments keeping it in its place. He was pleased to see me, and as well as he could articulate with his broken jaws he conversed with me calmly. Nearly 12 hours had elapsed and the Company's surgeon, thinking the case a hopeless one, had taken no steps to amputate the arm and it was not until the afternoon of the following day that this was done. My friend possessed an extraordinary strong constitution, and bore the operation bravely, refusing to be put under the influence of chloroform, and the only explanation that escaped him was, as the bone was being sawn through, "Hang you Doctor, there's a tooth out of that saw.!" From that time he gradually recovered, and when able to walk about he became more fully aware of his own helplessness, not only arising from the loss of his arm, but from the injury done to the remaining eye by the ruthless way the other was wrenched from its socket by the accident. Being such a wreck his condition gave rise to gloomy thoughts, and the idea of suicide was for a long time uppermost in his mind. By the advice of his friends and fellow workmen, as the Company were not disposed to assist him in any way, an action for compensation was commenced against them. The case was tried at the County Assizes, and my friend, who is a fine tall fellow being then just sufficiently recovered to appear in the witness box, his shattered frame excited the commiseration of the jury, who returned a verdict of £520 damages and costs. In presenting this action, he was assisted by his mates, his own savings being insufficient to meet the legal charges. The Company were dissatisfied with the verdict, and removed the case to a superior court, where the decision of the jury was squashed; the judges ruling "that an employer or employers are not liable for any accident arising to one servant through negligence of another". To employ counsel to argue the case on the appeal of the Company, another subscription had to be raised, and was, on the whole, cheerfully contributed to; but the result was a serious disappointment, and my friend then saw no

other prospect than the workhouse. But a final effort was resolved on to endeavour to raise a few pounds to start him in a little business of some kind. The secretary of the railway company was interceded with, and a donation of £20 on behalf of the Director was the result. A subscription list thus headed soon brought further subscribers, and with the money so subscribed, he commenced business as a tobacconist. Things have prospered with him since that time, so much so that he has acquired property of considerable value, and he is today honoured among his fellow townsmen with a seat on the Local Board of the town where he resides. It is not to be wondered at that my friend rendered valuable assistance in promoting the Employer's Liability Act, which came into

Alfred William Hillerby's shop in High Street, Mexborough, Circa 1882. The noticeboard above his shop shows that he didn't sever relations with his past employer altogether. Courtesy Mrs Joan Hillerby

operation last January. That measure, though a useful one, is deprived of much of its value by the limitation of the sum to be awarded as compensation to an amount not exceeding three years wages.

Mr Hillerby founded the wholesale and retail tobacconist business in High Street Mexborough, his shop was at the Montagu end of High Street in a property next to Harry Dews the chemist. He prospered well. In politics, he was a strong Radical of the old type, and he also took a deep interest in a long controversy which was carried on in Mexborough between exponents of Christianity on the one side and "Free Thought" on the other. The meetings were generally held in what were then known as Hewitt's rooms on Garden Street, afterwards used as a Salvation Army barracks. He was in sympathy with the teachings of prominent Free Thinkers of that day. Alfred William Hillerby died on November 24th 1901, aged 58 years, leaving a widow, five sons and two daughters. He was interred at Mexborough cemetery. The Business remained in the Hillerby family for 97 years, first being run by his son and then the grandson, also called Alfred William.

"THE EDWARD ROSS MEMORIAL FUND". Knowledge of this was taken from a letter sent by Mr Cyril Bradshaw of Swinton, former foreman at Mexboro Loco in the post grouping days.

"It is a very old fund with a rather interesting history. The story, as I have heard it, mostly all dead by now, is that Ross was the Secretary of the Manchester, Sheffield and Lincolnshire Railway, a very dedicated man both to men and management. Upon his retirement, to mark their appreciation, the staff decided to raise a subscription. The list of subscribers together with a considerable sum of money was presented to Mr Ross who intimated that he would like to see the money used to give temporary help to the Railways employees who fell upon hard times through unforeseen circumstances. Now, in referring to the Trust Fund Deed dated 1892, it states a fund in perpetuation of the Secretary, Mr Edward Ross, who died in that year, was established for the benefit of the Manchester, Sheffield and Lincolnshire employees who at that time liberally contributed thereto. A Trust Deed was executed on 15th June 1893, showing the sum of £1010 14s 0d had been received. The first Trustees of the fund were Richard Haig Brown and Oliver Stanbrook Holt representing the railway management (Holt was the Secretary and I think Brown was the Superintendent of the line). The Trust Deed states that the committee be made up of a Chairman, who shall be the General Manager for the time being of the M.S.&L.R., three members nominated from time to time by the Directors of the Company and three members nominated by the Committee of the Mutual Provident Society (now the G.C.R. Friendly Society). With the Chairman and two Trustees, the number of the committee is nine. I

have been a member of the committee since 1953. The Chairman at that time was Mr C.K.Bird, who was a very outstanding personality and who died very early in his career through cancer. He sent for me shortly before his death, in order that I could communicate his pending resignation to the committee. Had Mr C.K.Bird lived, it is my opinion that he would have become Chairman of B.R.

The fund now has an invested capital of £2,300 of 4% Consolidated Stock. Various sums of money were bequeathed and money from the sale of property, things left in trains etc., was handed to the fund. Since Nationalisation, this source has dried up. In 1924 there was a staff of about 26,000 G.C. men but at the last count only around 2,000 still remain, so the benefit is paid by the members of the Committee to widows; the sum being £6. A few years ago I went along with the Trustees to the Office of the County Commissioners to see if the Fund could be wound up, for we can only pay out the interest. We were told that the Fund must stay open until the last G.C. man or his wife remain.

The other union, and one that in modern times we all became familiar with was ASLEF. I only make mention of it here because one of its prominent leaders was associated with Mexborough. This is what I found on a biography web site:-

"Albert Fox (1857-1914), trade union leader and politician, was born at Farnborough, Hampshire, on 7ᵗʰ April 1857, the son of Charles Fox, a private in the 22ⁿᵈ regiment, and his wife Marcia. He attended the board school at Farnborough until he was 12, and in his early years was drawn towards railway life. In the early 1880s Fox got a job as an engine cleaner at the Mexborough railway depot. The Associated Society of Locomotive Engineers and Firemen (ASLEF) did not admit engine cleaners as members at that time, but in 1886 when he was promoted to fireman he immediately joined the union and played an active role, becoming secretary of the local branch. He noticed that every year some five new orphans resulted from accidental, or other, deaths of members, and in 1889, when he was a member of the national executive for Yorkshire, he carried a resolution establishing an orphan fund. When Thomas G Sunter, the union's general secretary, died on 20ᵗʰ September 1901, a ballot was held to determine his successor and on 8ᵗʰ December, Fox was elected.

With new leadership there were important changes in policy. At the union's triennial conference held in Swansea in 1903 it was resolved that membership should be open to engine cleaners and electric motormen. Funds were to be centralized, and an organizing secretary was to be appointed. It was also agreed that the society should affiliate to the Labour Representation Committee and contest a parliamentary constituency. In accordance with the new forward looking policy, Fox stood for the South

14

Leeds constituency, where the ASLEF head office was located. In the light of his late adoption he did well to poll 4030 votes to the victorious Liberal's 6200. In a by election in the same constituency in 1908 he did less well, being beaten into 3rd place by the Tory candidate.

Throughout his years as general secretary Fox claimed that it was essential for locomotive men to be organized separately from other railway workers. He expressed this view in evidence to the Royal Commission on the railway conciliation scheme of 1907. At a conference with the Amalgamated Society of Railway servants (ASRS) in 1903 to discuss closer co-operation, he said "It was not merely a question of hours and wages with enginemen. There are 101 ways in which they need protection in their calling which are not known to other workers, and which can only be taken in hand by themselves. Fox's policy was summed up in the words 'organise your craft, federate your union.' At about this time, J H Thomas of the ASRS pointed out that his union had more locomotive grade members than ASLEF. Not surprisingly the ASRS favoured amalgamation rather than federation and the negotiations broke down. Nevertheless during Albert Fox's time as general secretary, ASLEF membership rose steadily (from 10,502 in 1901 to 32,200 in 1913), thus strengthening the society's claim to speak for a majority of the 62,000 members of the locomotive grades.

Of course, the fascinating question for me, is why did Albert Fox come to Mexborough having been brought up in the south? I havn't researched this; it may not be possible, we will all have to guess.

By 1899, the MS&L Railway had changed its name to the Great Central Railway to reflect it's new London extension. Hitherto the MS&L had been a northern company with routes radiating from Merseyside, across to Manchester, over the Pennines into Yorkshire, Nottinghamshire and Derbyshire with an extension to the east coast via Immingham, Grimsby and Cleethorpes. But for the ambition of Edward Watkin, who became Chairman in 1864, the MS&L might have progressed no further, but he had the foresight to want to link by rail the industrial centres of Manchester and Sheffield with new expanding markets in Europe. It was not impossible, for he also had in mind to construct a railway tunnel under the Channel. The route to London was to be faster, straighter and more direct than any that had gone before and there would not be a single level crossing between Sheffield and London. A new terminus was built at Marylebone so that facilities would not have to be shared with other railway companies.

The evolution of the MS&L is outside the scope of my book, however it had relevance to Mexborough, now served by the Great Central Railway, in that it became a much busier railway centre on a much larger railway network.

Some interesting newspaper aspects of the day on railway related matters:-

February 1st 1878 - Railway Servants Meeting at Mexborough
February 1st 1878 – The Collision at Mexborough Junction
June 12th 1885 - Public request for extra train to Barnsley
January 9th 1891 - The Railway Fatality At Mexborough
January 9th 1891 - Notice of Late Train running from Mexborough to Wath.
July 10th 1891 - Mexborough Railway Station
January 1st 1892 - Funeral of an Engine Driver
August 31st 1894 - Trespassing on the M.S.&L. Railway.

EXTRACTS FROM THE MEXBOROUGH & SWINTON TIMES
FEBRUARY 1ST 1878

RAILWAY SERVANTS MEETING AT MEXBOROUGH

A meeting was held in the large club room, connected with the Mason's Arms, Mexboro', on Sunday last, when Mr Hague, of Nottingham, district secretary of the Almagamated Society of Railway Servants attended to address the meeting. Mr Aston having taken the chair he at once called upon Mr Hague to deliver his address, which was listened to with gradually increasing interest to its close. In the course of his remarks he gave considerable prominence to the programme of the Amalgamated Society of Railway Servants showing that continuous platforms, subways and bridges at crossings and stations, and additional brake power were very much needed. He also pointed out the need of having sidings well lighted and spoke particularly of one place where after three men had been killed because no lamps were fixed on the sidings, and that it took no less than 300 lamps to light it properly after the verdict from the jury. The shunting was strong deprecated and it was shown that in this and other matters connected with shunting the rules of the Companies appeared to be made (as had been stated in a Royal Commission upon the subject) only to be read after accidents had happened in order to throw blame for carelessness upon the men. A man named Elston had been told to fly shunt by his foreman, and threatened with discharge if he disobeyed orders. In his endeavours to do it he fell through on to the rails and his head was cut clear off. This was put down to his wilful neglect of a rule which seemed only to be made in order to be broken. In conclusion he urged that all railway men should join the society and unitedly try for the great alterations proposed and especially for compensation to railway servants in case of accident or death. At the close of the address the chairman read a letter from Mr J Dillamore respecting the case of Mrs Hobson, widow of a railway servant whose son was candidate for election into the Orphanage at Derby, and it was unanimously resolved to make a collection for the widow, on the hat being taken round the sum of £1 9s 6d was collected. A resolution proposed by Mr Alvey, and seconded by Mr Harding, "That this meeting pledges itself to support the Amalgamated Society of Railway Servants in its endeavour to better the condition of railway servants" was carried with acclamation. With the customary votes of thanks a well attended and enthusiastic meeting was brought to a close and the benediction pronounced.

The Collision at Mexborough

Major Majendie has reported to the Board of Trade the result of his inquiry into the circumstances on the 17th November, at Mexborough Junction, on the Manchester, Sheffield, and Lincolnshire Railway:- "As the 1-40pm Midland passenger train from Sheffield to Doncaster consisting of engine, tender, brake van, six carriages, and composite brake carriage, was passing from the branch on to the main line at Mexborough Junction, it ran into a Manchester, Sheffield and Lincolnshire coal train from Barnsley to Doncaster. The engine, front brake van, and two carriages of the Midland train were thrown off the rails and slightly damaged; and three trucks of the coal train were turned over. The permanent way was also damaged, but not to any great extent. The Midland train was not fitted with continuous brakes. It appears that collision was due solely to the driver of the Manchester, Sheffield and Lincolnshire Company's coal train mistaking the junction up home signal for the branch at Mexboro' Junction for that for the main line. The driver admits that he is to blame, and can offer no excuse for the mistake, which is an almost unaccountable one in the case of a steady man, with 14 years experience, and well acquainted with the road. The only other remark which is called for by this collision is that it is one which would probably have been prevented if the Midland train had been fitted with a continuous brake, under the control of the driver, who seems to have nearly succeeded in stopping his train, even with the brake power available.

At the last monthly meeting of the Wath Local Board it was decided to ask the Manchester, Sheffield and Lincolnshire Railway Company to run a train by way of Wath and Wombwell to Barnsley in the middle of the forenoon. The service between the places named is very defective, only six trains making the journey between Mexboro' and Barnsley during the day. Those persons who miss the first train, which runs at an inconveniently early hour in the morning, have to wait three hours and a half before they are favoured with another opportunity of travelling from Mexboro', Wath or Wombwell to Barnsley. There is an interval of four hours between the time of departure of the second and third trains. It is to be hoped that the railway company will grant the request of the Wath and Wombwell Local Boards, in their own interest as well as in the interest of the inhabitants of a thickly populated district. In another direction an additional train would prove very beneficial. On Saturdays persons having business at Doncaster have to wait nearly two hours and a half if they are unable to catch the 11-44am train before they are able to return to Conisboro', Mexboro', and the places lying between the latter town and Rotherham. Were the railway company to start a train from Doncaster at one o' clock on market days much valuable time on the busiest day of the week would Be gained to many persons.

The Railway Fatality at Mexborough

At the Montagu Arms, Mexborough, last Friday an inquest was held on the body of Jas. Carroll, aged 29, a miner at the Manvers Main Colliery, and living at Roman Terrace, Swinton, who was knocked down and killed on the M S and L Railway at Mexborough, the week previous. Mr D Wightman was the coroner, and the following were the jury:- Messrs. Wm Allsom (foreman), W.T. Tiptaft, G Schonut,, A Raynor, F Elliott, J Hartley, G W Bayes, J Clayton, A Popple, H W Tyas, J Instone and W Batty.

Elizabeth Carroll, widow of the deceased, said when she last saw the deceased it would be about eleven o'clock on Friday morning, the 26th ult. He then said he was going to Mexborough. He was alone, and she did not again see him alive. He said he wanted to see a man in the street.

Wm. Hy. Law, locomotive fireman for the M S and L Railway deposed that on the night of the day named, about 8-35, he saw the deceased. Witness was on his shunting engine in the "yard" near Mexborough when he saw the deceased in the 6 foot between the low up-line and the wharfe sidings. He stopped the engine and went to the deceased who was dead. He seemed to have been injured on the skull. Something had run over him. From his forehead to the back of his head was all torn off. There would be 32 or 33 wagons and the train was advancing "backwards", the engine being at the opposite end of the train. It was a private place where the deceased was found. The deceased appeared to be going the nearest way from Mexborough to Swinton.

The Jury had no question to ask the witness. Miles Thornton, inspector on the M S and L Railway, stationed at Mexborough, said he knew the deceased by sight He came to catch the 7-55 train to Barnsley on the night of the 26th. He said he wanted to catch the train. The train had gone, and the man asked witness if he could tell him how to get to Barnsley. He told him there was one at 9-46pm to Cudworth from Swinton on the Midland Line. The witness said he must go through Mexborough to Swinton. The manwas not quite sober. The body was nearer Mexborough than Swinton when found. There is nodoubt the deceased was taking the shortest route.

A Juryman: Would it not have been nearer by canal?

Witness: There would be very little difference in it.

A Juryman: It would be nearer than going round Mexborough.

The Coroner: Was it foggy?

Witness: No sir.

A Juryman: It was moonlight?

The witness said, in answer to a juryman, that the deceased went onto the Mexborough platform through the passage where the ticket office was; the gate further on , where luggage often left the station, was not open.

The Coroner: Is there anything more in the case than we have already heard?

Police – constable Cade replied in the negative.

A Juryman said the deceased had evidently been going the nearest way. He had not noticed whether a "warning" board had been put up so as to warn people not to go where it was so dangerous.

The stationmaster, who was present at the inquiry, said he did not think a notice board was necessary. It was not as though the place was a public highway.

The juryman who had asked the question said he believed the officials on the line did their best to minimise accidents.

The coroner observed that in the present case it was not as to a "crossing". It was a case of a man walking along the line.

A juryman asked if the deceased had just escaped a train to Barnsley, and the witness remarked that the train had already gone. The stationmaster said it would have been surprising if the deceased had been able to go along the line where his body was found without getting knocked down seeing the amount of traffic there.

A verdict of "Accidental Death" was returned.

Notes from Wath-on-Dearne

A late train will be run from Mexborough to Wath in order to afford the inhabitants of the latter place an opportunity of seeing the Mexborough pantomime. Those who have not seen Cinderella should do so at once. Fun flows like a river, and all admit it is the best of the season.

Funeral of an Engine Driver:- On Sunday the mortal remains of Arthur Welham, late Engine driver in the M.S and L Railway Co's Employ at Mexboro', were interred at Balby Church.. The deceased it will be remembered was drowned in the canal at Swinton, on Monday the 21st inst; and much sympathy was aroused with the deceased's parents, who for a number of years have been highly respected by the whole fraternity of railway employees. Through the kindness of Mr Haig Brown, superintendent of the M. S .and L. Railway, a special train was run to Doncaster on Sunday afternoon, and a large number availed themselves of the opportunity to show their respect by attending the funeral. A procession was formed at the house of Mr Welham at Hexthorpe, in the following order, headed by the M.S.and L. Railway servants subscription band, under the able leadership of Mr J Dawson:- Band; cortege borne by 10 railway guards in uniform; carriages containing mourners: M .S. and L. engine drivers and firemn; G N R engine drivers and firemen; Guards, signalmen, and shunters; friends of deceased; some of whom had journeyed from Elsecar, Swinton and Barnsley. The number in the procession was 270, and the route was thronged with the general public. Mr C Briggs of Mexboro', was the undertaker. The coffin which was made of pitch pine, with brass mountings bore the following inscription:- Arthur Welham; born Dec 4th 1854, died Dec 22nd 1891. A beautiful wreath was sent by the Mexboro' branch A.S.L.E.F. of which the deceased was a member.

MEXBOROUGH RAILWAY STATION: On Wednesday a substantial footbridge was completed for passengers at the Mexborough railway station. This is the outcome of a communication from the will be insured for £5 against all kinds of Manchester, there being great risks to persons crossing the line because of the extensive traffic carried on. The next improvement will be to have better waiting room accommodation on the central platform, great inconvenience being often occasioned when crowds are waiting for the Sheffield and Barnsley trains.

TREPASSING ON THE M S & L RAILWAY
John Henry Laming, William Heath, Thomas Crookes, Thomas Peake and William Cotterill, of Parkgate, all pit boys employed at Thrybergh Colliery, were charged with committing a trespass on the M S & L Railway after having previously been warned not to do so. – Inspector Hall appeared to prosecute. He said that these boys made a habit of walking to work along the line, and in consequence of the many accidents that had taken place, the company were bound to prosecute them for trespass. Only recently a lad had been killed while trespassing near where these boys were caught.— Evidence was given by Arthur Guest, former platelayer , and Walter Parnham, a platelayer, and the defendants were fined 2s 6d and costs each and warned not to trespass in the future.

Before moving on from this era, it seems appropriate to insert some notes by Ron Fareham based on extracts from a Mexborough railwayman's diary starting in 1867.

The conditions of employment at the two early Mexborough sheds could be said to be normal for the period. However, viewed from a remove of 130 years, they appear to be near slavery. Fortunately for us, we can glean a pretty accurate view of the working arrangements at Mexborough Plant in the 1860s and 1870s as follows:-

By sheer good fortune, I knew a goods guard at Mexborough whose wife's great grandfather was a footplate man at the "Old Plant", commencing in 1860 and who retired during the early years of this century. The goods guard's name was Roland Rissbrook. His wife's great grandfather was one William Alvey who kept a meticulous record of his daily work in book form. The only one of these volumes to survive is the one covering the years January 1867 to January 1878 (11 years) and I was priviledged to read and record some of its contents more than 25 years ago.

Mr Alvey kept a record of time worked, journeys made, the engine numbers involved and the amount of wages paid to him. This was the practice of most footplatemen at depots which worked predominantly goods and coal trains; I did this for all of my own 20 years on the footplate. The main reason for this practice was that every day tended to give different time scales, caused by the goods and coal train delays at different places and for varying periods; each day's work being of a different length meant that daily pay was variable. To keep track of a full week's time, one had to record it in order to challenge any short pay situation. The miracle in this case is that the "Time Book" for that was it's title, has survived for 133 years. It ran for 11 years and so recorded part of the first half of Alvey's career on the railway. This makes one wonder what happened to all the other books of his.

The first page of the book (Jan 14th 1867) is headed 'Firing', which leads me to believe that prior to that date, Alvey was employed on work of a regular nature and so not requiring to be recorded – perhaps engine cleaning – or why would it need the title 'Firing'? Time is recorded and wages paid once a fortnight. This goes on until July 22nd 1872 when time and wages go onto a weekly basis. On the third fortnight in the book, Alvey is still recording 'Fireman'. However, this ceases on Monday 11th March 1867, telling me that he is now an established fireman so that the title need not be recorded further. Again, during his third fortnight he makes a bare 12 hours a day for the twelve turns, thus enabling us to calculate his rate of pay. He drew £2.2s.0d for the fortnight revealing a rate of 3s.6d per day (three and a half pence per hour).

On Thursday 23rd May 1867, he records working on Engine No 176; this is the old SYR locomotive No 25 and was Alvey's booked engine. Alvey's spell as fireman on 176 lasts from 23rd May 1867 to 29th November 1871, four years and five months. There is no mention of who his driver might be and I find this strange, as a steam locomotive fireman's most important item at work is his driver! During his time on 176, there are odd days when this engine is missing; this would indicate that the engine was in the shed having its boiler washed out. From 20th December 1867 to 27th February 1868, Alvey records '176 been in shed 35 days'. Another entry for November 18th 1868 states, '176 light to Gorton', heavy repairs are now obviously being done at the MS&LR main works at Gorton, Manchester. On 19th December, the entry is 'To Gorton for 176' (32 days in the works). Later, on 17th April 1869 – '176 light to Gorton, 108 back'. 176 is again missing for 25 days in Gorton shops in early 1870 and another 34 days there at the end of 1870. The obvious inference here is that engine 176, by then only 5 years old is not standing up to the work – or is not being handled properly! Another thought is that 176 was not robust enough for the work in the South Yorkshire Coalfield, which was always a heavy duty for small engines.

176 was a Beyer Peacock engine and that firm was always highly regarded in the engine building world; one wonders if there were any strong words passed across the main line at Gorton as the MS&L and BP works were opposite each other! The BP works were known as Gorton Foundry.

On 20th June 1871, Alvey records 'Driving' for the first time: this appears spasmodically for the next 6 months until he writes 'Last firing' on Tuesday January 2nd 1872. For the next three weeks, he shows a 'D' at the side of the train description but after that he doesn't bother, as from that time he has obviously become an established Driver and would remain one for the next 30 years or so, until retirement. The period from 20th June 1871 to 2nd January 1872, six months, would, in later times, be regarded as that of the 'Passed Fireman', i.e. a senior fireman who was examined and passed to do driving work when required. The six months of such duties in Alvey's case would be an unusually short period in a footplateman's career – a few years was the norm.

From 8th June 1874 and for the next eighteen days, Alvey is engaged

A bill poster for a "cheap" half day excursion to Conisborough Castle. The tour operator was Swan & Leach who hired the Great Northern Railway to run the trip on Whit Tuesday 11th June 1889. Courtesy of Trustees of Tony Peart's private collection.

21

in learning new roads. The reason for this is not stated, but it can be assumed that it is in preparation for the complete absorption into the MS&L Railway, which took place on 16th August. Most of the roads learned are in the Manchester areas and beyond. From the list shown below, it is obvious that Alvey was already familiar with the lines to Manchester and Northwich, also the ones in the Sheffield area. The complete list of the roads learned is as follows:-

Eckington (Midland Railway)	1 day
Leeds	5 days
Lincoln	3 days
Peak Forest	2 days
Liverpool	2 days
Stayley Bridge & Oldham	1 day
Ordsall Lane (LNW Ry)	1 day
Helsby	1 day
Oxford Road	1 day
Macclesfield	1 day

For Mexborough men to be learning some of the above routes, it is obvious that some complicated forward planning by the MS&L Co was taking place, at the time, regarding the working of traffic to the various exchange points with other companies. However, the reason for learning such out of the way places as Helsby, Peak Forest and Macclesfield, are now lost in the mists of time. One thing is certain, that up to the 17th January 1878, the end of Alvey's time book – he never went anywhere near these places.

One place that Alvey did go to frequently in 1874 and 1875 was Liverpool. This was reached only over the tracks of the Cheshire Lines Committee and was not a regular run for Mexborough men. During this period in the 19th century, there was an intermittent but substantial traffic of emigrants from Eastern Europe to America: these were mostly Jews fleeing from the pogroms of Tsarist Russia to freedom in the United States.

When examining the situation with these emigrant trains, one tends to ask why, when the people were on route from Russia to America, did they have to come across England by train? Was it to give them a break from an over-long sea voyage? I doubt it. Britain was, at that time, a maritime nation par excellence; they had a profusion of ships of all shapes and sizes and could tackle sea going jobs anywhere in the world. So, to Britain came the east European exiles to commence the last, and longest, stage of their journey westward.

The emigrants arrived at the east coast ports at either Hull or Grimsby and were put into the oldest passenger vehicles that could be found and they were locked in! This was, of course, because of the immigration procedure, they were not wanted in England, and their treatment here was somewhat akin to that of cattle, so they were not to be allowed to escape from the train and settle in England.

One of the more important items during the 140 mile journey from Grimsby to Liverpool was, of course, the calls of nature: as the coaching stock was non corridor and the emigrants were locked in, the problem became a serious one, especially for the children. On the total journey, there was one toilet stop, sometimes at Mexborough but more usually at Penistone: people were let out of the compartments a few at a time and the conditions in the compartments, according to an old driver, beggared description. It is said that at Liverpool, after the people had boarded ship, the compartments were cleaned out with hose pipes.

For anyone to submit to such treatment and then sail to North America – mostly on the open decks of the ships of the time – makes one wonder what the conditions were really like in Russia for Jewish people in the late nineteenth century.

Having looked at the conditions of the emigrants, it is illuminating to analyse the working conditions of the enginemen concerned. The trains from Hull had a number of routes to Liverpool available to them – via Leeds (LNWR), via Normanton (L&Y) and Mexborough (MS&LR). From Grimsby the route could be either main line via Retford and Sheffield, or Mexborough and Barnsley. When routed via Mexborough from either Hull or Grimsby, an additional engine was attached at Mexborough station and continued through to destination at Liverpool. Water would be taken at Penistone during the'comfort' stop and again at Teviot Dale station at Stockport. On arrival at Brunswick Goods Station at Liverpool, the engines would uncouple from the train and go on to Brunswick shed (CLC) for coaling, fire cleaning etc then return to the train and work empty stock back to Hull or Grimsby, with the pilot dropping off at Mexborough. Special paths and running time were always listed in the MS&LR timetables for both directions, for this traffic.

The conditions on the footplates of these engines were Spartan in the extreme, with only a bent weather board for a cab and no side protection whatever. The time taken with an emigrant train to Liverpool and back was usually in excess of 20 hours. Eight trips to Liverpool are listed in Alvey's time book after he was made a driver, as follows:-

DATE	ENG NO	CLASS	DATE BUILT	WHEEL SIZE	TIME WORKED
06-07-1874	195	23	1865	4'6"	27 hours
27-07-1874	195	23	1865	4'6"	31.5 hours
10-08-1874	195	23	1865	4'6"	29 hours
28-09-1874	201	23	1866	5'0"	31.5 hours
05-04-1875	52	18	1859	5'0"	21.5 hours
07-06-1875	201	23	1866	5'0"	26 hours
05-07-1875	177	23	1864	5'0"	22.5 hours
13-09-1875	195	23	1865	4'6"	25.5 hours

The speeds attained with such an engine as No 195, Alvey's own engine at the time, with a wheel size of only 4'6", can best be imagined; it couldn't have been very fast if comfort and safety were considerations. In fact, average speeds were laid down in the Working Timetable for these trains.

Doncaster – Mexborough	29mph
Mexborough – Barnsley Jcn	25mph
Barnsley Jcn – Dunford	24mph
Dunford – Godley	28mph
Godley – Stockport	22mph
Stockport – Warrington	35mph
Warrington – Liverpool	33mph

Working periods in excess of 30 hours are really inconceivable to present day minds. Excessive hours on emigrant trains were, of course, something of a 'flash in the pan' occurring only infrequently. Alvey records only ten emigrant trains in two years; but there were other occasions what could be described as timetable working when long shifts were worked. One such case happened in the week commencing 16th February 1874. The train was to Northwich in Cheshire, with Alvey's own engine No 195. The week's work was as follows:-

DATE	TIME ON DUTY	TIME OFF DUTY	TOTAL TIME
Mon 16-02-1874	3-15am	Tues 2-15pm	35 hours
Tues 17-02-1874	OFF		
Wed 18-02-1874	NOT REQUIRED		
Thur 19-02-1874	3-15am	Fri 2-15am	23 hours
Fri 20-02-1874	NOT REQUIRED		
Sat 21-02-1874	1-30am	Sat 11-00pm	21.5 hours
Week's total (for 3 shifts)			79.5 hours

As can be seen in this case, Alvey makes seven and a half hours more than his booked times for the week – and signed on duty only three times! One factor that could have influenced such working was the time of year. February was a month when heavy snow was likely – remember February 1947?

Regarding the 35 hours worked on Monday 16-02-1874, Alvey records 'Axle broke on salt wagon at Mobberley'. Whilst on the question of long hours, the longest I have seen recorded on the MS&LR was that worked by Gorton Driver Isherwood, who clocked up 85 hours whilst working a train from Godley to Doncaster. The cause was a very heavy snowfall and Isherwood's train was at a standstill at Wentworth Junction for 43 hours. Driver Isherwood spent the early part of his career at Mexborough shed. (Extracted from GCR Journal) (Staff Magazine) (7/1911).

As coal traffic requirements varied considerably during the year – some means of providing for the varying demands for train crews has always been a factor of railway operation. In my time on the footplate and for many years before, the system of "splitting" an engine crew was used. This involved the senior fireman being qualified to act as Driver and for the engine cleaners to be capable of being firemen. When an extra set of men was required, the senior fireman was made up to Driver and two cleaners were called out of the shed – one to mate the newly made up driver and the other to mate the original driver; thus two sets of men were made out of one set and two cleaners. The system worked very well but was obviously not in use in William Alvey's time.

By studying Alvey's time book, it soon became apparent that the system in use in the 1860s and 70s to bring flexibility into the provision and use of engine crews was completely unlike that of "splitting" as previously described. The system used in Alvey's early days as a young driver was this: that the establishment of footplate crews was set at the maximum that could be needed; that being so, there would be many days through the year when this maximum number would not be wanted and the SYR answer to this was – tell them they were not required on that day – send them home and don't pay them! That way you do not need any floating staff – everybody is floating.

Having said that there is a 100% float, there is ample evidence that it was not applied equally. When Alvey was a senior fireman in the four years 1868 to 1872 he was 'Not Required' on 46 occasions; i.e. 3.6% In the first four years as a young driver, he is shown 'Not Required' on no less than 225 occasions; i.e. 12%, something less than equality and at the convenience of the Company. Nothing is ever mentioned about spoilt food on the days off, as it must be assumed that the men turned up for work fully equipped before being told 'Not Required'.

One of the reasons for being 'Not Required' was when, owing to excessive overtime it was not possible to book in on the day in question, so a day's work and pay was lost.

I have a full list of the Drivers, Firemen and engines at Mexborough for the year 1886, when the new locomotive superintendent Mr Thomas Parker, had a survey made throughout the MS&LR Co's locomotive depots. In this survey, Thomas Alvey is listed with engine 487 and fireman R Adamson, and given the title 'Spare driver'. It is obvious that Alvey is a man who habitually makes, or even seeks, overtime, as even in 1893 the two following letters appeared in the 'Railway Review'. This was the weekly organ of the Amalgamated Society of Railway Servants which was later re-named 'National Union of Railwaymen', who still publish the Railway Review.

A deputation of 'long hours' railwaymen to the President of the Board of Trade, Mr Mundella, on Saturday 22nd April, all drivers from various companies, and included Alvey.

May 12th 1893
Letter, 'Long Hours Brigade'
Sir
Through the medium of your paper, I should like to ask Mr Alvey of Mexborough a few questions.
1 *Is it consistent that after seeing the doctor and being told by him he required a fortnight's rest and was not even fit to use his right arm to raise a cup of tea to his mouth, that he arranged to be booked on leave instead of off ill so that he could go to London to meet Mr Mundella?*
2 *Is it consistent that on the following Sunday he could attend two meetings, one in the morning with a view to being elected delegate to the annual meeting of the Mutual Provident Society, and one at night to give his report re attendance at London, preparatory to declaring on the clubs?* [sick].
3 *Is it true that during the following week he was booked on leave instead of off ill although he had declared on the sick clubs and was this an oversight of the officials in not having it altered in time?*
4 *Is it true that the bulk of the men knew nothing about his going to London until the following Friday, when they saw it in the Review and yet he pretended to represent the men, and had the nerve to want them to go and hear his report?*
5 *Is it true that he is one of the biggest grumblers there is at Mexborough about long hours, and states that it is the chief reason why he is so often on the sick societies' funds and yet can oppose a reduction in working hours?*
6 *Is he sincere in his opposition to the shortening of hours, or is it with a view to obtain favours with his masters, and does he not think they are cute enough to see through his transparent hypocrisy?*
7 *Does he think it would be most honourable to leave the ASRS, or to be expelled for constantly fighting against the society of which he is a member?*

'Inquirer'

Same date
Letter
Sir,

I fully expected on getting my last week's Railway Review, seeing that someone had taken up the case of W Alvey, engine driver, Mexboro', MS&L being on the long hours brigade deputation to Mr Mundella. How men have the audacity to attend such deputations without being elected I cannot understand, as there had not been any meeting called to elect anyone, as the greater portion of the staff at Mexboro' are in favour of the National Programme (not 15 hours per day). Mr Alvey is a member of both the 'Associated' and the ASRS. Therefore, as this long hours brigade are working against the best interests of the ASRS, I suggest that the General Secretary take proper steps to have this member expelled from the ASRS, as he is a disgrace. He was off ill at the time and on club pay, but he could go down to the shed and get permission to be on leave to go to London and when he came back he declared off ill again. I cannot say whether he advised the clubs or not. If I had been a member of the Mexboro' No 2 Branch, I should have proposed that he had been expelled the society. Hoping the members of that Branch will take it up.
'Foxey'

There was another item of particular interest in the 'Time book'. This involved none other than the 6th Earl Fitzwilliam who lived 6 miles from Mexborough. This man was a power in Yorkshire and owned many acres in the West Riding: he was also a landowner in North Yorkshire, Northamptonshire and in Ireland. For the first seven years of the South Yorkshire Railway, he had been the Chairman of the Company. His country seat at Wentworth Woodhouse is said to be the largest private residence in Europe, with more windows than there are days in the year.

Fitzwilliam had extensive colliery interests in the nearby village of Elsecar and substantial workshops to service the other pits. Within these works was a private railway station which merits a short description. The station was a two storey building of noble proportions with interior fittings of stately quality. The ground floor enclosed a railway platform, the entrance to which was gained by way of a long sweeping staircase from the upper floor. The latter was mainly occupied by a large handsome reception room where guests would be entertained prior to entraining. There were two further guest rooms with a butler's pantry and a caretaker's cottage completing the ensemble of rooms. Special trains were run for the Doncaster Leger week races and large house parties were held for the event. Royalty were often included in the party, and Edward, Prince of Wales, was a regular visitor, which continued after he became King Edward V11 in 1901. To grace the presence of the future king, the Railway Company provided a Royal Standard, which is now in a private collection near Wentworth.

William Alvey was involved, as a fireman, in the running of these trains, which he listed as 'EFW' Specials. Together with his driver (unnamed) he worked the 'EFW' Specials on Wednesday, Thursday and Friday September 15th to 17th 1869 and again on three days in September 1871. On the latter occasion, Alvey was a spare driver, but would be given the job because of his experience as a fireman.

These specials would be the equivalent of Royal Trains, with one exception: the locomotive used during both years, was the diminutive 2-4-0 well tank engine No 210 built by Charles Rebaul Sacre in 1866 for the MS&LR Co. Because of the short distance from Elsecar to Doncaster and the very light train, the authorities obviously considered a 2-4-0 well tank engine adequate for the job. These small engines normally worked the passenger services between Manchester London Road station and Altrincham for many years but 210 was, in 1886 stationed at Widnes for working the short distance local trains to Liverpool Central and Warrington (CLC). No 210 was the only passenger engine on the books at Widnes at that time and was the property of Driver J Baldwin and Fireman F Davies.

The 7th of July 1874 was the date that William Alvey, and all the other staff at the 1855 shed, had been looking forward to for many years. It was the opening date of the new Mexborough Engine Shed half a mile to the east, adjacent to the new station. This was for the period a very large shed, with a long, two road wagon repair shop, a three road engine repair shop and fifteen shed roads with standing room for over 90 of the small engines of 1874. To move from the cramped conditions of the 'Old Plant' to the spacious premises of the new shed must have been heaven indeed for the staff concerned. The actual opening date has not been discovered, but as Alvey worked the 'Old Plant pilot' on 8th July 1874, it is safe to assume that the move was on the previous day, and Alvey was working on the pilot involved in the clearance of material.

CHAPTER 3

GCR DAYS PRE GROUPING 1923

Whilst this period was too early for me to interview railwaymen, there are nevertheless many archival notes left from former local railwaymen which give good accounts of this era at Mexborough Loco Depot. I have selected those which give insights into the workings and the engine types of that period. These notes, prepared by railwaymen at Mexborough, have been handed down to later generations. We start with "Some notes on GC Section Traffic Working that fell within my experience", written by D L Franks.

CONISBOROUGH PILOT – The working of this pilot did vary over the years but for long enough, it did two trips between Mexborough, Conisborough and Hexthorpe. The first trip was around 8-00am from Mexborough where it would shunt Conisborough Goods Yard and set in place wagons brought from Mexborough. Kilners Glass Works were then shunted before a run was made to Hexthorpe via Warmsworth Sidings on route. The return from Hexthorpe brought empty wagons for the lime sidings at Warmsworth together with empty wagons for Conisborough Cliffe Siding. After shunting anything that may have been required, the pilot proceeded to Mexborough No 4 signal box (near Whitelea Road) with any wagons required for the Mexborough Area. A fresh set of men would then take over the engine in the early afternoon and perform exactly the same duties as the morning

Kilners Glass Works, 1913 painting. A signed watercolour by W. H.E.Wilde

men did. This second turn was also responsible for bringing coal wagons from Denaby Colliery to Mexborough. One driver recorded that in the early part of the century, the pilot would wait at Mexborough No 4 Signal box after completing its normal duties and connect with the pea traffic from Thorne and Crowle (seasonal) then work the trains of peas through to London Marylebone Goods Yard.

(My own research on Kilners Glass Works confirmed its location in Denaby, on the side of the railway, in an area facing the Public House, which used to be called Denaby Main Hotel, locally known as the Drum. The works were established in the 1860s; in 1878 they employed upwards of two hundred workpeople. At their peak, they employed around 500, and production ceased just prior to the 2nd world war. The firm was well known for it's Kilner Jar used for preserving fruit but unfortunately went out of business, the victim of economic recession and changes in glass bottle making technology. The works have long since been demolished but the house in which the manager lived, still stands).

Liverpool Sea Traffic – Until the White Star and Cunard Lines were amalgamated, (in 1936) and all passenger traffic was moved from Liverpool to Southampton and the liners were coal fired, double headed 2-8-0s would take liner coal from the new Doncaster pits to Liverpool. These trains also ran via Barnsley; they were classed as specials, being given a special path.

Kilners Glass Works. The manager's house situated at the side of the main line. This house still stands today, albeit the surrounding properties have long been demolished. A watercolour by W.H.E. Wilde.

COLLIERY TRAFFIC – The clearing of collieries east of Wath Yard was done by individual colliery trips, irrespective of load. The Brodsworth trip used to leave Wath Yard with 80 empties, 40 for Denaby Colliery which were detached at Lowfield Junction and 40 for Brodsworth. The odd thing about this working was that it often increased delays at Lowfield Junction, this included passenger trains. This method of working carried on for 20 years or so after the Grouping. Mr Franks blames the conservative attitude of the railway, stuck in their ways. He goes on to say that eventually, the train of empties, instead of being detached at Lowfield Junction for Denaby, a move which occupied the main Doncaster to Sheffield line, the wagons were detached for Denaby at the former Hull and Barnsley signal box, off the main line, thus keeping the G.C. line clear for traffic. The Bullcroft Colliery trip used to take traffic to the former Hull & Barnsley station at Doncaster, York Road; then having been turned into a goods station. This train was left at the triangle at Doncaster Junction and the loco took the wagons into York Road, a terminus by the way; without a brake van attached. From Mexborough No 4, the first Elsecar Colliery train used to take goods traffic for Wath station and the Elsecar Branch and then spend the rest of the day as a Wath Pilot.

GOODS YARD TRAFFIC – Most of the station goods yard traffic between Mexborough and Sheffield was arranged from Broughton Lane and Sheffield. Between Mexborough and Doncaster in the other direction, there used to work a Hexthorpe to Sheffield train to clear traffic in all the goods yards between these points. The 6pm Mexborough to Sheffield train used to be a "maid of all work" on that line. The return was from Broughton Lane and went under the name of the "Chips and Fish", possibly because of the late hour it arrived back. Strangely, it was never called the "Fish & Chips". I wonder why. Its day would end between 10 & 11pm.

LETTERED TRAINS – On this section there ran "lettered trains" from Hexthorpe Yard to G.C. line collieries; each train had an identifying letter for its rake of empties; for example, "K" meant to Tankersley Colliery, "P" was for Pinder Oaks etc, and it covered the return trips with full wagons. There were about 20 of these trains operating. This working was simply empties from Hexthorpe to the collieries and back, with very little stopping for attaching or detaching en route. Between 1900 and 1910 these trains were worked by both GC and GN engines.

TINIES – The first ever Tiny working was the 1-15am Wath to Frodingham; this train was then known for the next forty or fifty years as "the first Tiny".

FISH TRAINS – Generally there were two Grimsby to Manchester District fish trains around 5-00pm. The amusing thing about them was that after they had passed, the following heavy coal trains would often slip badly on the greasy rail; left greasy by the drippings from the fish vans. This traffic was routed via Barnsley. There used to be a rather dishonest practice at some stations of removing labels from fishboxes. Most fish arrived at the different stations when the stationmaster was off duty. The unlabelled box of selected fish would be mixed amongst all the labelled boxes which had not been interfered with. The next morning when the fish merchants collected their fish, any unlabelled box was impounded by the station master, as he was expected to salvage all perishable goods. The box would be opened and the contents sold, at remarkably low prices, to the station staff.

MEXBOROUGH TO WORKSOP – This was an interesting diagram. The engine would leave Mexborough Loco about 1-00pm and run light to Doncaster. It then returned with the 1-50pm Doncaster to Sheffield slow passenger; fresh men taking over at Mexborough. After putting the coaches away at Sheffield, the engine ran light to Worksop to work a 3-15pm (approx) passenger train over the South Yorkshire Joint to Doncaster. The engine then ran light, back to Mexborough.

Mr C Bradshaw was a Driver and Shed Foreman at Mexborough Locomotive Depot in the G.C. days. In retirement, he wrote a brief in 1972 to a Mr Jackson; an enthusiastic delver into railway history, who had asked numerous questions. The following are extracts from the papers of the late Mr Jackson containing information provided by Mr C Bradshaw.

MEXBOROUGH AND THE FISH TRAFFIC – He confirmed that *all* fish trains from Hull were worked by Mexborough engines and men prior to 1923. This traffic was worked to the Manchester area and Banbury for the West of England. The "Fish engines, allocated to Mexborough in Great Central days, the B4s and B5s, were employed on these trains and are worth a mention because the names of the drivers associated with the individual engines are given with comments on the fine work done by them.

ENGINE

No 1094	E Hague – previously had 1071.
No 1095	J J Gordon
No 1098	G F Sadler – top driver at Mexborough. It was said that to be booked as a fireman with GF Sadler was like receiving an invitation from Buckingham Palace.
No 1099	J Ford, one of three top link drivers/brothers.
No 1104	W Towers
No 1068	This was a Class B5 and was Tower's engine before the Fish engine.

After the Grouping Doncaster took over the Hull Fish trains from

Mexborough, and the men transferred too. These engines were regarded as being most important at Mexborough, especially during the First World War when they worked many troop and ambulance trains. Shortly after the war, there were a great number of refugees from Europe who flooded into Hull and were moved across the country to Liverpool, for the USA, and the Fish engines covered much of this type of work.

PASSENGER WORK – Prior to the 1923 Grouping, the D7 4-4-0s were the most numerous passenger class at Mexborough depot and 4 engines allocated to the shed were fitted with the Westinghouse brake to enable them to work G.E. stock between Doncaster and Sheffield. The engines involved were nos 700,705, 857 and 859. Nos 869 and 870 also appeared at Mexborough but they were not allocated there. The two Mexborough drivers who regularly worked this traffic were S Holmes and W Wright. The first mentioned was described as a picture book driver with long flowing white hair around his chin. These two men worked the trains until 1923 when Holmes retired and Wright moved on to the passenger link. The work was transferred to Hull after Grouping and two Mexborough drivers, W.J. Ford and P. Fairer transferred to Hull themselves in order to continue working the trains.

ELECTRIC TURNTABLE – There was an electric turntable at Mexborough as early as 1917. It was worked by DC current and was very efficient. apart from when it had to turn Green Arrows which were just 3 inches short of being too big for the turntable. Being so much heavier, they often blew the fuse. When men transferred to Doncaster in 1924, they were amazed to find the shed lit by gas and the turntable had to be man handled. This seemed to confirm a feeling in railway circles that the Great Central was often in front for best working practice, the Great Northern at Doncaster was rather a poor show.

Here are some interesting accounts of Mexborough which I extract from a letter written by Mr G White to Mr Jackson.

"You ask for a picture of the traffic at Mexborough and Doncaster involving G.C. section engines. Until the merging of the two depots in 1923, Mexborough could be said to be almost solely engaged in the coal trade supplying pilot engines to each colliery for working the traffic from their sidings to Wath Yard (opened about 1907) and from where engines and men from Mexborough worked trains to Manchester District, (Guide Bridge, Ashton Moss, Ardwick, Heaton Mersey etc until Mottram Yard was opened, when all trains terminated there), and to Woodford, Annesley, Frodingham, Grimsby and Immingham. All these turns were lodging turns. There were a good few turns, one from Stairfoot to Banbury with glass traffic ex Stairfoot, picking up at Mexborough traffic from Barnby Dun (again chiefly

glass) together with traffic worked into Mexborough from the N.E. We had no express goods trains and the only one we ever saw was the 5-10pm Grimsby Manchester fish worked by Grimsby men with No 4 "Glenalmond", which was a rare sight. The fish still goes through Doncaster but in a motor truck labelled "Grimsby Fish". In addition to Wath Yard services, we also served Hexthorpe Yard which drew on pits in the Doncaster District to which the G.C. had access. We had trains to most of the places stated above for Wath Yard. We also supplied a large number of shunting engines for these yards, in the early days being saddle tanks and later Sacre 0-6-2T tanks, or if water was a problem, 0-6-0 tender engines. Wath Yard of course, had the tanks specially designed for that yard."

The following is an extract taken from a letter sent by Tom Willers of Doncaster, a retired driver.

"I started work as a Cleaner in 1919 (December) and was made a fireman in 1920. The District Superintendent was Mr C. Hugill. There were several links at Mexborough at that time, the Woodford link being only one of them. It was a link of chiefly fish trains, these worked between Marshgate Goods, Doncaster and Banbury via Sheffield (Darnall) and the Great Central route to Woodford and Banbury. Before that time, it had been worked to Marylebone and after the 1919 railway strike, when the 8 hour day was introduced, it was decided that this would not go beyond Banbury with Mexborough men. After the Grouping of 1923, this link was transferred to Doncaster and the men transferred with it. Some years later, the Banbury link was re-routed via Tuxford and Annesley to Woodford. One of the trains worked back was the Penzance to Aberdeen express from Banbury to Sheffield Victoria.

The Immingham link (coal trains) was also a lodge link and the drivers were Padgett, Perriam, Porter, Noble and Seed. I retired on my 65th birthday, 12th October 1964 having completed 44 years 10 months and 1 day. The last train I worked was the 1-45pm Kings Cross back to Doncaster. I received a letter from the District Superintendent at Gresley House, thanking me for services rendered, but no gold watch".

Cyril Bradshaw, who I have referred to previously, commenced work at Mexborough on August 8th 1917 passed for fireman in February 1919. Of his recollections he wrote about joining Driver J Wilde in January 1922 and shared with him a regular engine, 2-8-0 No 1184. With this engine they worked on all types of lodge work visiting Manchester, Grimsby, Immingham and Annesley. Driver H Hutchinson was Mr Bradshaw's next regular driver but he did not see much of him owing to the General Strike and the three day week imposed upon railwaymen. At the time it was possible for a man to appear on the weekly list without a regular mate for some time and this was the case with Mr Bradshaw until 1928 when he was regularly booked with one of the characters of the shed; public enemy number one of the firemen! Many men had refused to work with him but in the end Mr Bradshaw managed to work with this man, Driver Woosey for eight years and eight months, due no doubt to Mr Bradshaw's temperament, which, I gather, was liable to boil over if crossed. After he left Driver Woosey, he passed for firing and saw that his one time mate got through four firemen in three months. The engine they had shared together for those eight years and eight months was 2-8-0 G.C.R. No 1252, later L.N.E.R. No 6252, later BR No 63599. The rest of his career spanned LNER and BR days but I will mention it here to complete the picture. Having passed for driving in 1936, and being a young hand, he had to start at the bottom but thanks to his good route knowledge and his friendliness with George White who made out the rostas, Mr Bradshaw got a fair amount of better class main line work, when available. Throughout the Second World War he worked many troop and ambulance trains and saw much of the Pacifics and Green Arrows. In 1954 he became foreman at Mexborough and in 1962 moved in a similar capacity to the new diesel depot at Wath.

The water supply at Mexborough was of poor quality for steam engines; it was 'hard' and just as we see in boiling a kettle, calcium deposits occurred which impaired good locomotive steaming. The G.C.R. installed a water softening plant at Mexborough and this was in use right up to the closure of the depot in 1965. It's tower like construction made it the tallest structure of the shed complex and its profile made Mexborough sheds so easily recognisable when seen on a photograph. I have produced below the tender for the plant which was done by "Kennicott Water Softener Company" of Wolverhampton and sent to O.S.Holt Esq, Secretary of the Great Central Railway on 5th February 1913. I happened to acquire it from Brian Longbone who, whilst researching for his own railway book on Scunthorpe, came across it and through his own interest in water softening; it was part of his job at the Redbourn Iron & Steel Works; he kept a copy. I do run the risk of boring readers but it is written in a quite convincing manner; in a way that says, buy our plant and we won't let you down. Today's tenders I can imagine would contain many caveats to avoid libellous litigation. It reads as follows:-

O.S. Holt Esq.,
Secretary
Great Central Railway Feb. 5th 1913

Dear Sir,
    With reference to your esteemed enquiry of the 27th ult., we have now pleasure in enclosing you herewith our Tender & Specification together with a drawing for the proposed Water Softening Plant at Mexboro' Engine

Sheds.

We have analyzed a sample of the water from the Mexboro' well, and beg to hand you our Laboratory Report on this, giving particulars of the cost of treatment, and a few remarks on the quality of the water.

With regard to the Softening Plant itself, there are a few points to which we would like specially to draw the attention of your Engineers:-

1 *The cost of a Water Softening Plant is greatly influenced by the size of the settling tank provided, and you will notice from the drawing that we have specified a settling tank 48 feet high and 12 feet diameter, and this will allow the water just over 1½ hours in its passage through the plant; but if you refer to the remarks on our Laboratory Report you will see that our expert recommends a settling capacity of THREE HOURS, and we should very strongly advise your Company to install a settling tank of THREE HOURS capacity.*

A settling tank of TWO HOURS capacity would be 48' high x 14' diam and a settling tank of THREE HOURS capacity would be 48' high x 16' 6" diam.

By installing a tank of THREE HOURS settling, a larger Filtering area is obtained and as the chemical action is quite completed before the water reaches the filter the greater part of the precipitate which is formed by the addition of the chemicals is allowed to settle on the bottom of the tank, and this very greatly increases the life of the filter.

This point is so marked that in many instances we have plants running for 12 months at full capacity without the filter being cleaned in any way. The average length of life in the "KENNICOTT" Plant is nine months.

2 *We think that your experience with Water Softening Plants will have proved to you that although many elaborate devices are in use for removing the sludge from the bottom of the tank, this is always a very serious problem, and in spite of elaborate precautions will cause considerable trouble.*

Now, the "KENNICOTT" Patent Revolving Sludge Pipes absolutely do away with any trouble whatever due to sludge accumulation and by their operation once daily, the whole of the precipitated matter is removed, much in the same way as the Vaccuum Cleaner does its work.

3. *The Proportioning Gear by which the correct quantity of chemicals are added to the hard water, is perhaps the most important point in a Water Softening Plant, and we wish specially to bring our system before you.*

The "KENNICOTT" Type "K" is the only plant of its kind on the market in which THE PARTS REGULATING THE SUPPLY OF CHEMICALS TO THE HARD WATER DO NOT COME INTO CONTACT WITH THE CHEMICALS. NO CHEMICALS ARE MEASURED AT ALL., the whole of the proportioning being done by the measurement of WATER. You will readily see that where a cup or valve will very soon become made up with milk of lime, or attacked by the chemical solution, but in the "KENNICOTT" Plant such a thing is entirely eliminated.

Morever, should the quality of the water change at any time the proportion of chemicals can be immediately increased or decreased without touching the chemicals at all.

4. *We construct the whole of the plant in our own Works and can therefore give the work our personal attention.*

5. *Our Tender includes for the supply of a vertical ladder, but we should like to draw your attention to the very fine spiral ladder which we have supplied in many instances, and which we show on the drawing, the extra price over and above the straight ladder for such a spiral ladder would be:- £20/-/- (Twenty pounds) NETT.*

6. *AUTOMATIC CHEMICAL HOIST. You will see from the drawing that we have a special arrangement for hoisting the chemicals automatically; this being done by a loose drum and clutch with a foot brake attached to the Water Wheel, and by this means a complete charge of chemicals can be hoisted in quite a short time on to the top of the Softener, where there is a small hand crane to lift the chemicals into the mixing tank. This automatic hoist also serves the purpose of hoisting the Wood Wool for the filter, etc.*

If you require it, we can fit an arrangement for hoisting the chemical solution after this has been prepared at ground level,

The water softening plant at Mexborough MPD. A towering edifice at the rear of the shed. The Directors must have opted for the "fine spiral ladder" up the tower, as this can clearly be seen.
Courtesy Brian Longbone

37

but we should like to point out that the ground space at Mexboro' is very limited, and also should anything go wrong with the solution hoisting gear, the Softener would have to be stopped on account of this, whereas our method of hoisting the dry chemicals and mixing these on top of the Softener is absolutely reliable, and can be carried out 12 hours before it is necessary to charge the solution tank.

We shall be very pleased to give you any further particulars regarding the working of our plant, and would refer you to page 24 of the enclosed Catalogue, where a photograph is shown of a plant we have erected for the Great Western Railway at Severn tunnel to deal with 30,000 gallons of water per hour; both this plant and the one on the opposite page are fitted with a housing completely enclosing the Upper Works, and fitted with automatic hoisting arrangements. Trusting we may be favoured with your esteemed order, and assuring you of our best and prompt attention at all times.

The water softening plant at Mexborough MPD. This must be a later photo as there is no spiral ladder and much more of the wooden piling has collapsed into the river. What looks like a house are the General Offices, the Time office was on the lower floor.
Photo: British Railways Illustrated Vol 10 No4 January 2001"

We are,
Yours faithfully
KENNICOT WATER SOFTENER Co.,
ENGINEER AND MANAGER

It was accompanied by the tender document

GREAT CENTRAL RAILWAY
WATER SOFTENING PLANT AT ENGINE SHED MEXBORO'
To,
The Directors of the Great Central Railway Company.

Gentlemen,
We hereby offer to execute and complete to the entire satisfaction of the Company's Engineer the whole of the works required for the above in strict accordance with the drawings and Specification, and the terms and conditions mentioned therein and exhibited to us and will provide all labour, material, (both temporary and permanent) and everything requisite to complete the same for the sum of :- £975/-/- (Nine hundred and seventy five pounds) NETT
The provisional sum mentioned in Clause 35 of Specification and provisional quantities, and all P.C. amounts, being included.
And we beg to hand you the Schedule of Prices annexed hereto to be used as the basis for any addition and deductions.
And we hereby undertake to complete the whole of the several Works to the entire satisfaction of the Company's Engineer and hand over the same ready for use on or before the 31ˢᵗ May 1913 and in the event of our failing to complete in the time stated we shall pay to the Company by way of liquidated damages, and not as a penalty, the sum of £1 (One Pound) per day, for each and every day the Works remain incomplete after that date. And we further agree to uphold and maintain in perfect repair, and at our expense the whole of the works for six months after receiving the final Certificate of Completion.

As witness our hand this 5ᵗʰ day of February 1913.
FOR KENNICOTT WATER SOFTENER CO
WOLVERHAMPTON
ENGINEER AND MANAGER

The lab report of an analysis of a sample of water taken from the well at Mexboro' Engine Sheds showed:-

INCRUSTING SOLIDS (Grains per Gallon)		NON-INCRUSTING SOLIDS (Grains per Gallon)	
Calcium Carbonate	16.20	Sodium Chloride	1.60
Calcium Sulphate	2.40	Total	1.60
Magnesium Sulphate	7.80		
Magnesium Chloride	5.00		
Iron & Alumina	0.90	Alkalinity	16.20

| Silica | 0.20 | Hardness | 30.39 |
| Total | 32.50 | | |

Incrusting solids in one thousand gallons – 4.64lbs.

The above analysis shows this water to be of an exceedingly hard and corrosive nature, and one which should on no account be used for Locomotive purposes without previous treatment.

In order to satisfactorily treat this water, the Softening Plant should have a settling capacity of at least three hours, and owing to the large amount of Magnesium Salts present, mechanical agitation should be provided.

Moreover, as there will be approximately 1½ tons of precipitated matter produced in 24 hours, it is essential that a most efficient sludging device should be provided.

On the basis of the above analysis, taking the cost of soda ash (58% Na_2O) as being £3/10/0 per ton, and Buxton Lime (90% CaO) 15/- per ton, the cost of softening will be 1.07 pence per 1,000 gallons and the hardness will be reduced to 5 degs. Clark.
CHIEF CHEMIST

Needless to say, the Directors of the G.C.R. opted for a settling tank of 14′ diameter at an adjusted tender price of £1150. The contract was placed with this Company.

CHAPTER 4

L.N.E.R. DAYS AFTER GROUPING

Almost immediately after the grouping, in 1924, the movement of men to Doncaster started. It wasn't compulsory, men were transferred by application, but so much work was transferred to Doncaster that it started a chain reaction as engines were moved and with them went fitters, boilersmiths and handymen.

Further detail was given in a letter from Mr C Bradshaw to Mr D Jackson:-

"In 1923, when the merger with the G.N. took place, Doncaster Depot became the parent depot for the district and Doncaster depot took over most of the G.C. workings originating in that district, ie Hexthorpe, Marshgate, Stainforth, besides supplying pilot power for the local collieries. This entailed a transfer of engines and men from Mexborough to Doncaster. In it's heyday, I have known Mexboro to have about 140 engines and upto 700 footplate staff, but by this reorganisation the total staff at Mexborough was reduced by almost a third. I might have mentioned one of our Mexboro workings was the 3-20pm Marshgate to Banbury fish (ex Hull and Grimsby) which ran via Mexboro, Killamarsh Junction, Langwith Junction and Nottingham. Doncaster took this over and worked it via Tuxford and Langwith. As a result of the merger, trains from Wath were extended to places on the G.N. and G.E. such as New England and Whitemoor but while the engines worked through, the Mexboro men were only allowed to work to Doncaster. Doncaster depot, being on the main G.N. line always had a large number of express goods trains but of the G.C. Secction trains they worked these were confined to those as stated above

You ask for Doncaster and Mexboro passenger turns. [A turn is a timetabled passenger service for which Mexborough had to provide the locomotive.] *Mexboro turns were limited to those operating between Penistone and Cleethorpes and New Holland and Doncaster and Sheffield with an occasional one to Hull. We had about 8 sets of enginemen engaged on this work. Our engines at Mexboro in the early days were D class 4-4-0s Nos 688, 689, 690, 691. These continued to work I think until the 1930s when, as they wore out, they were superseded by the odd G.N. Atlantic 4-4-2, which were no longer required for the London jobs as the Pacifics had taken over. The brunt of the passenger work however, was taken over by Gresley K2s 2-6-0, known in Mexborough as the G.N. Ragtimers. These locomotives monopolised the passenger work until they were replaced by the Thompson B1s. We had at Mexboro a number of "Fish" engines of the B Class, ie 4-6-0s being Nos 1068, 1095, 1097, 1098,1099 and1104. All these had regular drivers and were used throughout the first war on troop trains between Mexboro West (with trains ex the N.E.) and Banbury. After these engines had departed (to Copley Hill), Mexboro had always to loan K3s etc from Doncaster for any important specials. I should also mention the amount of running made by the "fish" engines and men to London for the Wembley exhibition and later to the Cup Finals. The passenger work at Mexboro also included excursions to Scarboro, Bridlington, Cleethorpes, Skegness, Southport, Liverpool and Aintree"*

Bradshaw also noted that there were several Class L1 2-6-4 locomotives at Mexborough. These were known locally as "Crabs". There was a shortage of motive power at some depots and these locomotives were reallocated out, being replaced at Mexborough by a G.N. type of tank engine the N2, which had become surplus to requirements at Kings Cross. They were locally named "Dive Bombers", or "Beaufighters", after a plane used in the war which fixes the date. The "Crabs" however, proved unsuitable at the depots to which they were allocated, because of the old trouble of slipping and were inclined to "pick up their wheels" when braking. They were returned to Mexborough and assisted trains to Dunford, a job they continued to work until replaced by electric locomotives. Whilst the N2 Class were strong engines, they also proved unsuitable to the jobs they were given at Mexborough. Their work was also the banking and assisting of trains to Dunford, from Wath Yard and other starting points. These engines were not at all popular at Mexborough for various reasons. First of all, they were tank engines and it was necessary to fill the tanks at least three times each turn and the old G.N. water cranes were not so suitably designed. Also, by having to fill the tank so often, the water would become "mixed", which caused priming. (Explained on page 86). The engines had been designed for local passenger work in the London area. They had a bigger wheel (5'8" as opposed to 5'2"), smaller firebox and the G.C. engines, working as they did, largely on bad water with a high lime content, had the steampipe in the dome with the regulator valve in the highest part. The N2 didn't have such a high opening point (for steam) and as their regulator design was different and they worked on London water all the time, they would not have much trouble with priming. The idea behind sending these trains to Mexborough was that they should bank light goods trains. That was the theory, but in practice, especially in war time conditions, there were no light trains. It was commonplace to see 30 tons of chemicals loaded into 12 ton wagons. The wagon springs would be resting on the axle boxes. To move this type of train, an engine had to be worked to capacity, but with the priming that followed with the N2s, there was a tendency for steam pipe joints to blow in the smoke box, thus preventing the engine from steaming. Another factor was that good class coal, which was always reserved for passenger work, was not available for these engines and the low grade coal was no use at all. Nevertheless a

Class N5 at Mexborough circa 1930. The view of the turntable is obstructed by the tender; but in the background can be seen the lifting tackle known locally as the "sheerlegs". They were manually operated without steam or electricity. Courtesy Great·Central Railway Society

good crew could handle them and make them work. At the first stop for water, the fireman would be filling the tank whilst the driver would clean the firebox, and this went on from point to point. With so much priming and the resultant blowing of steam chest covers, it was decided to wash out the engines after every trip; which meant that half the allocation was out of commission at any one time. These engines were meant for short, fast work on suburban services with good coal and water, plus light loads. This was not the set up at Mexborough. They replaced the G.C.L1 tanks which were more suitable. The only other work they did was the Conisborough Pilot and Loco Pilot (shunting on the depot).

Mexborough also had a small allocation of Class Q1 engines. These were Thompson rebuilds of the Robinson Q4 0-8-0 introduced in 1902. In the opinion of Mr Bradshaw, a Driver and Foreman at Mexborough, he said, "these engines were a good locomotive spoilt by replacing the tender with side tanks which only held 750 gallons. The result of this was that water was required at almost every water crane en route and more often than not, they were unable to manage from one crane to the next. The coal bunker was also inadequate; the total held by the bunker being only about 40cwts. The limitations imposed by the coal and water capacity meant that the scope of the engines was severely limited". Again I quote, "I can only imagine that they were the result of a bad dream on someone's part" Another Driver C Goldsborough, said "The engines could do their work except for priming and failures everyday; a good engine spoilt, a tender taken off and side tanks put on. These engines worked between Wath Yard and Rotherwood.

Mexborough drivers thought the engines a failure and a disgrace to the designer". They were eventually re-allocated to depots in the North East. 750 gallons of water and 40 cwt of coal did not go far on the main line. It is on record that the late Driver J H Fisher stopped at Warmsworth signal box and took all the signalman's supply of coal, used normally for his stove in the box, to get the Q1 into the Hexthorpe yard and off the main line.

Around 1924, a few Class D9 locomotives came from Immingham and were provided for passenger work but they had to be moved away when it was discovered that a railway overbridge at Barnsley Courthouse Station would not take the weight of the larger 4-4-0s. As a result, some passenger work was actually transferred from Mexborough to Barnsley; although no turns were lost at Mexborough through it. It was mainly seasonal and it used Barnsley men on the Penistone to Cleethorpes summer service and other Sunday excursions. Barnsley had a number of small engines capable of taking a ten coach train to Cleethorpes

During this period, there was one quite famous G.N. Atlantic shedded at Mexborough which was bore the name "Henry Oakley", after the Company's General Manager. It was a popular engine despite being of G.N. origin, always kept clean; had regular drivers and operated on passenger work. Some notes of Mr C W Hepworth described a typical days work for a Mexborough crew on "Henry Oakley".

"The driver and fireman would sign on at the shed and walk to Mexborough station, where they would take over the engine. A relief link set of men would have already prepared the engine and brought the

Class D9 "Passenger Pom Pom" No 6021 named "Queen Mary" is standing at Mexborough. There is no date on this photograph but it would probably be early 1930s. These engines undertook passenger work from Sheffield Victoria to Cleethorpes, New Holland and Hull. After nationalisation, this engine was renumbered to 62307. Courtesy Great Central Railway Society.

locomotive to the station. The usual handing over point was the cattle dock, Mexborough station. The Sheffield to Hull passenger train changed engines at Mexborough, so with Henry Oakley at the head of the train, the Mexborough men would work to Hull returning with a stopping passenger train, leaving Hull around 12-15pm. This train ran through to Sheffield, the Mexborough Driver and Fireman working right through to this place and then working back, finally completing their day's work at Mexborough. In some earlier correspondence, Mr Hepworth had remarked that the engine rode like a passenger coach.

It is worth mentioning the excursions which took place to the Wembley Exhibition in 1924. Being on the G.C. main line all trains originating in Scotland, N.E. Region, Hull and Leeds passed through Mexborough and were invariably worked from Mexborough by Mexborough engines and crews or by the original crew with Mexborough conductors. The engines used were the 'Fish' engines with a few loans from Doncaster, of probably K3s. A typical diagram of such a train would be:-

ARR		DEP	
	Mexboro Loco	06-10am	Light Engine
	Mexboro West	06-30am	41 Special ex N.E.
10-00am	Wembley	10-30am	E.T.
10-50am	Neasden	11-00am	Light Engine
	Neasden Loco		
	LODGE		
	Resume Duty	08-30pm	
	Neasden Loco	09-30pm	Light Engine
	Neasden	09-50pm	E.T.
10-10pm	Wembley	10-30pm	41 Special ex N.E.
02-00am	Mexborough West	02-10am	Light Engine
02-30am	Mexborough Shed		

Wembley continued to be used for such events as Cup Finals, Rugby Finals, Schools Hockey finals etc and these events always entailed Saturday excursions worked on diagrams similar to or the same as above.

Lodgings or "Barracks" as they were termed were provided by the Company at most crew relieving points such as Woodford, Neasden, Gorton etc, but curiously enough, none were ever built at Mexborough where foreign crews from Woodford, Annesley, Immingham and Gorton lodged in large numbers. There was a list of private houses who took in these men and of course, the men always had their preferences which they always used.

The following information was sent to Mr Jackson by Cyril Bradshaw in a letter dated 3rd May 74 on the Gresley Green Arrows which were allocated to Mexborough:-

"With regard to your queries about 4812 and 4877, I remember them being allocated to Mexborough at the time of the Dunkirk evacuation. It was a time of intense activity and the old G.C. line was the main centre. These two engines were used to re-engine trains which came from the south coast ports or from Scotland and for general WD arrangements."

"At times there would be as many as a dozen trains requiring to be re-engined at Mexborough West Junction and of course our two Green Arrows took the first two trains, while the others were being reconditioned. These engines had a very mixed reception at Mexborough. The fitting staff had a saying which went like this, "Gresley must have a grudge against the maintenance staff because everything is so inaccessible". I think this was a fair comment. With all G.C. loco types it was possible to oil all bearings without having to use a pit, awkward in some cases, but possible. But with the Gresley engines, the Green Arrows, it was necessary to use a pit and there to oil the big middle end, it was quite easy to get a hot cinder down your neck while oiling beneath the engine. Now this meant that if the middle bearing ran warm during a trip, a driver would not be able to do anything about it. A small phial was built into the bearing which had a strong odiferous chemical and when the bearing ran hot, this phial burst and gave off a rotten smell. They were known as stink bombs. I never had one go myself, but I went out to assist a Green Arrow home once and the stink on my overalls lasted for weeks. The windows in the cab were so placed that it was impossible to see anything and the vacuum brake prevented that in any case. These windows could not be cleaned on the outside without the aid of a ladder.

They were powerful machines and could cope with wartime requirements without much trouble. They were very prone to wheel slip and the fact that Gresley always fitted steam sanders which never worked after the first blast, caused a lot of trouble. Left hand drive caused the fireman trouble unless he happened to be left handed. I was lucky for my fireman could fire equally well with either hand.

After some incident, they were not allowed to work Penistone to Manchester. I believe this was because of the curve at the old Dinting station on the down line and the hammer blow over the arches".

RUNAWAY GOODS TRAIN.

THREE MEN KILLED NEAR DONCASTER.

(FROM OUR CORRESPONDENT.)

DONCASTER, APRIL 16.

Three men were killed in an accident on the old Great Central avoiding line of the London and North-Eastern Railway near Sprotbrough Junction, two miles east of Doncaster, at 3 o'clock this morning. A mixed goods train from Barnetby had reached this spot when, owing to the breaking of a drawbar, 32 wagons broke loose and ran backwards on a decline of one in a hundred, eventually crashing into a standing train of empty mineral wagons, which had come from Immingham for coal at the Denaby Colliery, Doncaster.

Five of the rear wagons of the runaway portion were derailed and smashed into matchwood, and of the four men who were riding in the rearmost van, three were killed and one seriously injured. No one on the standing train was injured, the driver and fireman having jumped clear as they saw the runaway wagons approaching. The dead men are :—

Goods Guard Quickfall, of Barnetby.

Fireman R. Scorah, of 5, Northgate, Mexborough, and

Goods Guard J. Brown, of 31, Albert-road, Mexborough.

The injured man is Driver C. Brown, of 44, Hampden-road, Mexborough.

These four men were riding in the brake van at the rear of the runaway wagons, Quickfall being in charge of the train. The other men had finished duty and were riding back to their homes in Mexborough. Quickfall, Scorah, and Brown were killed almost immediately and their bodies have been removed to a Doncaster inn. Driver Brown was conveyed to the Montagu Hospital, Mexborough, where he is being treated for injured ribs and cuts. He was reported this afternoon to be comfortable.

A breakdown gang from Doncaster and Mexborough soon had the line clear, Mr. F. J. Trotter, Great Central Divisional Superintendent, supervising the work. The wreckage was piled high on either side of the line, which at that point is near a large quarry. One smashed and overturned wagon contained straw, and others had contained potatoes, which were strewn about the line. No dislocation of passenger traffic occurred, as the line is used for goods trains only, to avoid the congestion at Doncaster station. It is largely used for coal traffic, which was resumed soon after the accident.

This article appeared in The Times *on April 17th 1925 concerning a rail accident on the Doncaster avoiding line. Unfortunately three Mexborough men were fatally injured.*

Chapter 5

Mexborough Locomotive Depot – Shed Code 36b

It was situated about 300 yards WSW of Mexborough station adjacent to the River Don, it had no vehicular access, pedestrian access was via a tunnel under the line at the eastern end of Mexborough station and along the river bank. Oddly enough, Mexborough Depot was actually in the parish of Swinton; a fact little realized.

Mexborough Depot had a large stud of heavy freight locomotives which were employed mainly on coal trains from the Yorkshire Coalfield. The function of the depot was to keep these locomotives in running order, the most basic duty would be to provide each engine with coal and water. At weekly, or so, intervals, a steam loco would then be taken out of service for a thorough inspection. From first arrival onto the shed, this would involve:-

Aerial view of Mexborough in the early 60s. The Motive Power Depot is at the top of the photograph. The Cripple and Carriage sidings can clearly be seen. The cross marks the building that is now Constant Security Services Ltd on Cliffe Street at the side of the relief road. Studying this photo makes it become apparent just how many properties had to be demolished to make way for the new road. Courtesy Giles Brearley.

1.	Removing the fire by standing the loco over an ash pit, dropping the fire and raking the firebox and ashpan clean.
2.	Opening the front boiler door and removing soot and ash from the smokebox.
3.	Shunting the loco onto the shed to let it cool down.
4.	Draining the boiler and washing it out.
5.	Cleaning all the tubes of soot running through the boiler using flu brushes.
6.	Simultaneous to the above tasks, a thorough mechanical examination of the loco would be carried out and repairs undertaken. Mexborough was equipped to take on most heavy repairs.

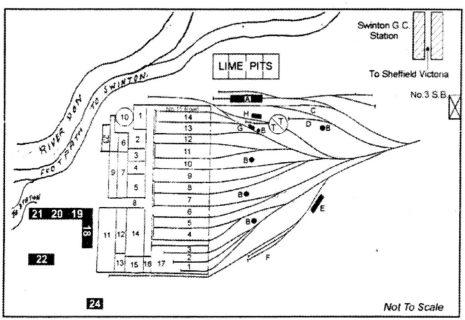

(Fig.3) Sketch plan of Mexborough Shed L.N.E.R.

1. Cabin For Washers-Out	13. Steam Boilers	23. List Clerks Office
2. Toilet	14. Machine Shop	24. No.2 Jct. Shunters
3. Rag Store	15. Blacksmith's Shop	Cabin
4. Lamp Room	16. Tool Stores	
5. Oil Stores	17. Repair Shop	A. Coal Storage
6. Foreman's Office	18. Locker Room	B. Water Columns
7. Enginemen's Room	19. Joinery & Paint Shop	C. New Pit
8. Passageway	20. Mutual Improvement	D. Old Pit
9. Offices (on second floor)	& Ambulance Room	E. Top Pit Cabin
10. Water Softening Plant	21. Canteen	F. Cripple Sidings
11. Pump House	22. Tin & Coppersmith's	G. Sand
12. Stores Compound	Shop	H. Shed Shunters Cabin

Sketch Plan of Mexborough Shed. Courtesy J Raybould.

All these tasks had to be performed within strict timetables. Steam would then be raised and the loco would be made ready for its next duty.

Understandably, such intense synchronised activity spanning a 24 hour day required a huge staff force and at its peak there were well over 700 males and some females employed here. Their occupations could be broken down into 3 hierarchies.

CLERICAL AND SUPERVISORY OPERATIONS COMPRISED OF:-

1 Chief Clerk, 1 Shedmaster, 1 Foreman Boilersmith, 2 Foremen Fitters, 3 Foremen Cleaners, 3 Train Crew Supervisors, 3 Outside Running Foremen, 1 Stores Clerk, 1 Messenger, 3 Clerks, 1 List Clerk & Assistant, 3 Signing on Clerks, 3 Telephonists and 2 Typists.

FOOTPLATE OCCUPATIONS COMPRISED OF:-

Approximately 100 Cleaners, 300 Firemen and 300 Drivers.

Maintenance and Shed Staff comprised of a mixed variety of grades. There could be as many as 30 different types of jobs, some required tradesmen's skills, some were semi skilled and others were labourers who, as experience was gained could be rotated through different roles depending on the demands of the work. These grades were known as:- Washer Out men, Firelighters, Coalstage men, Tube cleaners, Fitters & Turners, Blacksmiths, Carpenters, Tin & Coppersmiths, Painter, Electricians, Labourers, Toolmen, Storesmen, Oilmen, Fire droppers, Ashpit men,Cranemen, Knocker-up men, Lampmen and Boiler Attendant.

There were also men, controlled from Mexborough, but who were outstationed at Wath Hump, Aldham Junction or Rotherham Road Yard. These were all volunteers who would remain on outstation duty until as such times as they applied for a transfer back to the main depot. Any temporary vacancy at an outstation would be filled by men travelling out on a daily basis from Mexborough.

AN ENGINE CLEANER'S DUTY

This comprised the cleaning of a locomotive, eg wheels, motions, exterior of boiler, smokebox and tender. Additionally, and when required, he would also work as a coalman, barlayer, toolman, fitter's labourer and any other miscellaneous duty which became vacant. After a short period, the Cleaner was examined by the Running Foreman on all aspects of his duties, including rules and regulations. If he passed, he would be designated a PASSED CLEANER and as such, would be eligible to be used as a fireman when required. No training was given for the firing duty and the Passed Cleaner would learn how to do the fireman's job through conversations with other cleaners and firemen, and by the myriad jobs he did, eg firelighting, steamraising, ash clearing etc and by instruction from the driver he was working with.

Much later, from around 1956 onwards, cleaners were sent on a short training course to learn firing duties. Eventually, when regular firing vacancies arose, Passed Cleaners were promoted to Fireman in strict seniority order and allocated to a regular driver who he stayed and worked with regularly for a period of six months or longer; sometimes even years.

A FIREMAN'S DUTY
His job was to fire the locomotive and maintain a head of steam by also regulating the amount of water in the boiler, keep the footplate tidy, and give assistance to the driver by working to his orders, keeping a sharp lookout and being vigilant at all times, especially when shunting or passing signal boxes. He would also pass on any messages or instructions he receives, to the driver. In addition, in his spare time, and when off duty, he was expected to familiarize himself with all the rules and regulations appertaining to his job, and acquaint himself with all the parts and functions of a locomotive. This was done by attending classes run by volunteer drivers and firemen when off duty. These were known as "Mutual Improvement Classes". (More on this in Chapter 18). A Passed Cleaner would have to pass a practical and a theoretical exam carried out by a Locomotive Inspector, before being promoted to fireman. This exam consisted of firing a locomotive on a local passenger service. If successful, the Inspector would then test on theory; ie Rules and Regulations and mechanical knowledge of a locomotive. If he passed, the final requirement would be to take an eyesight and medical examination by the Company's Doctor. If he passed these, he was promoted to Regular Fireman.

The next footplate progression would be to Driver but with such a huge complement of permanent Drivers, there was need for a "reserve pool" and these men were known as PASSED FIREMEN or SPARE DRIVERS.

A PASSED FIREMAN'S DUTY
To become a Passed Fireman, a man had to serve a period of time as a fireman. This varied according to the operational need or lack of vacancies for drivers and could vary from a few years to a lot. In Joe Raybould's case, he started on the railway in November 1943 and was passed as a spare driver in May 1961. Cedric Lockwood was similar, starting in 1942, became fireman in 1944 and was registered a driver in 1963. The exams for driving consisted of a practical exam in driving a passenger train and an exam on Rules and Regulations, locomotive management and mechanical knowledge. These were conducted by a local Locomotive Inspector. This was the half way stage, and if he passed, he would then, at a later stage, have to take a further theory exam conducted by a Chief Locomotive Inspector who came up from London Headquarters. This exam lasted from three to four hours, and was quite stiff. If one failed, one had two more attempts but failing those meant "curtains" for the footplate grade and the candidate would have to revert to a labouring duty. Of course, having passed, there was still the eye and medical

tests to undergo. Having passed them all, one would be graded a Passed Fireman and as such, would then be utilized for driving duties as and when required. If not required, then he would carry on as fireman. This state of affairs carried on until your seniority came up for a regular driving position at the home depot or one applied for a driver's position at another depot; these were all advertised on internal notices. Kings Cross was a depot with vacancies often cropping up. This was because it was a busy depot , but it was also situated in London where there were many competing industries with more attractive wage levels and shortfalls in manpower did occur. An ambitious passed fireman, prepared to work and lodge in London, would apply for a driver post and readily transfer from Mexborough. He would then be in a position to apply for driving posts in other Motive Power Depots. A Mexborough man could therefore apply for a driving vacancy in Doncaster, if advertised, and he would be given seniority preference over other passed firemen in Mexborough who also applied; because he was already on driver grade. Indeed, this man may ultimately apply for a driver vacancy at Mexborough and the system therefore created anomalous situations whereby much older drivers had less seniority than younger drivers. It created ill feelings but at least if there was justice, the driver who was prepared to bear a little hardship working in London was rewarded over his counterpart who only wanted to stay at Mexborough.

The railway was an industry that many Mexborough people were proud to serve in. The work was physically demanding, the daily working hours were unpredictably irregular, rank prevailed, promotions were fiercely guarded by seniority, but there were long term job prospects and conditions were construed by many as no worse than working in the coalmines or steelworks. Not surprisingly, many local families had several generations in employment there; often father and son, but also uncles, nephews and brothers. Such well known family names at the Mexborough depot were, for example,

POTTS	Charles, Jack, George, Louis and young Charles
CHAPPELLS	Jack, Charles, Leslie, Maurice, and Wilfred
LIVERSIDGE	Ernest, Sidney and George

So many men, with so many characteristics; inevitably nicknames & pseudonyms abounded. They were personal, not always flattering and how they came to be derived is best left to the imagination; some would perhaps reflect how that person approached a job or drove his engine.Some of them that stuck were:-

CLOGGY	CRASHER	BANGER	MUDEYE
COLONEL	TUGBOAT	TOMMYGOB	BUDGIE
SUTDOWN	CUSH	WHACKER	PANSHINE
BOXER PIGGY	GRANDFATHER CLOCK.		

There were also identity problems. There were so many F SMITHS that they were numbered, F SMITH (1), F SMITH (2) and so on, possibly upto 6. If a man had two christian names they were both invariably used; GEORGE FRED, MARTIN CLARENCE, JACK HARRY, WILLIAM HENRY and GEORGE HENRY are just a few that spring to mind.

Being an important railway junction, Mexborough also saw footplate crew from other regions. Apart from the one thing in common; they drove an engine; everything else about them was alien to Mexborough. They drove locomotives different to the types kept at Mexborough, driving and firing practices were different, their routes were different and so even they, received nicknames in true railway parlance. So we had:-

G.C.R.	POGGY MEN
L.M.S.R.	DARBY MEN
G.N.R.	G.N. MEN
N.E.R.	GEORDIEMEN
G.E.R.	SWEEDIE MEN
L.&Y.	LANKY MEN
D.V.R.	PUSHERMEN

The area covered by Mexborough Depot staff insofar as train working was concerned was quite extensive. Freight trains were worked daily to Woodford or Banbury in Oxfordshire. Many of these had originated in the North East or Scotland carrying just about everything which, in those days went by rail freight, including fish and imported fruit from Hull & Grimsby docks. This was the extent of the Mexborough men's route knowledge and the crews would be relieved (lodging overnight) and the relief crew would continue with the train to South Coast or South West destinations.

Similar freights would be worked to Annesley near Nottingham for trains bound for the London areas. Freights and coal trains were worked to Guide Bridge and Manchester, there could be 20 or so trains a day. The return traffic would also require moving freight to York, for Scottish and North East destinations, to Hull with exports and to Scunthorpe and Frodingham with raw materials for the steelworks.

Mexborough worked a few passenger trains daily, to Sheffield, Penistone and Barnsley, Hull, Cleethorpes and surrounding stations. In the summertime, this would extend to running excursions to Blackpool, Southport, Belle Vue, Whitby, Scarborough, Bridlington and Skegness. Many excursions would be organised by the local workingmen's clubs and local collieries; they would charter a whole train for their children's outings to the seaside. These trips were very often the only time the children saw the sea, before the war. Occasional specials were also run to Wembley for large sporting events. In 1951, 1952 and 1955, Newcastle United made three appearances at Wembley for the FA Cup. All the supporters came on trains

A stirring view in July 1958 from the back of a tender looking outwards down the yard from the shed front, - that is south westwards. The clutter of cabins housed the senior running foreman, platelayers and so on. The coaching stock is standing in the Small Junction Yard. Further out on the right hand side is Queen's Foundry, and more or less middle, is the top of the gasometer of Mexborough & Swinton gas works. The box out where the shed lines join the main line is Mexborough No 3. There are two engines on the ash pit and an O4 entering the shed.
Courtesy Mexborough Heritage Group.

via York to Mexborough where Mexborough men took over, for the run down to Wembley or, in some cases Marylebone.

Local steelworks, glassworks and other industries were also served from the Mexborough depot. This was in addition to all the collieries on the South Yorkshire Coalfield. Over 120 or so years of operation; collieries opened and closed, new ones opened but at its full extent Mexborough was servicing; ie transporting full coal wagons to their destination and returning the empties to approximately 30 collieries. These were:-

Aldwarke Main, Barnsley Main, Barnburgh, Barrow, Bentley, Blacker, Brodsworth, Bullcroft, Cadeby, Darfield Main, Denaby Main, Dodworth, Dovecliffe, Ecclesfield, Frickley, Gawber, Goldthorpe, Hickleton, Houghton, Kilnhurst, Manver's Main, Mitchell's Main, Pilley, Rockingham, Rotherham Main, Silverwood, South Kirby, Wentworth, Wombwell Main, Woodmoor, Woolley, Yorkshire Main.

SILVERWOOD COLLIERY was reached by means of a branch line which branched off to the left at Thybergh junction signal box. It was a very steep and winding route for approximately two miles before reaching Silverwood Colliery Junction Signal box where a single line branched off to the empty wagon sidings. The main branch line continued on to Brantcliffe Junction on the Sheffield – Worksop line. This branch was operated by a joint agreement of the G.C.R. and M.R.

Access to this line, for the Midland, was from Roundwood Yard on the Midland line. This line joined the branch at Don Bridge signal box. One of the unique features of this branch was that the colliery had some large colliery tank engines and the colliery engine drivers had to pass an examination by a Railway Locomotive Inspector. This examination, if passed, allowed the drivers to work small numbers of wagons with their own locos down the branch to the coal staithes on the S. and S.Y. navigation at Roundwood.

The gradients on the branch were very steep (1 in 40) and when working loose – coupled trains (ie: trains which had only the brakes on the locomotive and the handbrake in the guard's van to slow down or stop the train), it was necessary for the guard and shunter to apply brakes to the first six wagons and then every other wagon before the train started down the branch. The brakes had all then to be released when the train arrived at the bottom of the branch. Every driver you spoke to seemed to have had their "little tipples" (incidents); and one can be recalled here. On leaving Silverwood (in steam days), the engine would not exceed 10mph; it was usually 5/6 mph and on this night the driver was allowing the fireman to set off; all part of learning how to be a driver for there were no training courses then. It wasn't long before the driver said "you're going too fast" to which the Fireman said "I'm not". When passing Silverwood signal box, the driver could see that the train was going too fast for the guard to get back on. He jumped off the engine and started to drop every wagon brake as fast as he could. Eventually the train did stop but it certainly made his heart flutter at the time.

One train did unfortunately come to grief in the late fifties. A Midland train had left Roundwood L M Sidings to take empty wagons upto Silverwood Pit. It then coupled onto a train of approximately 35 wagons of loaded coal in the Colliery Sidings. On this morning, the driver failed to stop, with the result that the guard didn't get sufficient brakes "pinned" down before the train commenced running away towards Don Bridge. The fireman jumped off the engine as soon as he realized the train was running away, but the driver stayed on the footplate continually blowing the engine whistle. Relief Signalman Fred Griffin, on duty at Don Bridge Signal Box estimated that the train passed his box at 60mph and the signalman Mr O Vickers at Parkgate siding, set the route towards the disused Roundwood Pit. On realising how the route was set, the driver jumped off the engine, only suffering minor bruising, but the engine finished up with its front end hanging over the pit shaft, with many wagons derailed, piled up at the side of the engine and coal spilled everywhere. The signalmen at Silverwood Junction, Don Bridge and Roundwood had all carried out the correct rules and regulations in the emergency..

Silverwood branch was not a popular line to work on, owing to the large amount of vandalism on the branch. Large stones were often dropped on the trains from overhead bridges and the lines often blocked with debris either placed or thrown onto the line. In the cutting at Dalton, a long fence constructed of railway sleepers had been erected where the houses were. Over the years, the wooden sleepers rotted and trespassers found it very easy to squeeze through them to get onto the line. A replacement chain link fence was erected, but within a couple of weeks, it was beginning to prove unsuccessful. A concrete panel replacement fence was then erected but this also had a short life and was soon pulled down and dismantled. In a period of ten years, Silverwood loaded sidings, Silverwood Junction and Don Bridge Junction signal boxes, a shunter's and platelayer's cabins had all been vandalized or burnt down. It is not to be wondered at that this branch was known as "Bomb Alley". In later years, it became the practice to send a light locomotive up the branch before any trains, to clear the track of debris which had been placed there overnight.

Extraordinarily, there was about a five year period starting in 1958 when the Silverwood Branch was used on one day in the year to run two passenger excursions to Bridlington.. Hitherto, the Silverwood Working Men's Club had hired fleets of buses for the annual children's outing but the Sheffield BR District Commercial Rep had presumably offered this attractive alternative. For the first year, the children and parents alighted the 12 coach train (there was a special van in the centre carrying the children's pop, sweets and fruit and not forgetting the cases of beer for the parents) from two sets of steps provided in the colliery sidings. This was a big success and so for the following years, the BR management built a wooden platform, of one coach in length on a section of the branch line which had an easy access from a side street. It was called "Thrybergh Tins Platform". The train would then stop with the third coach in the platform for passengers to alight, and then it would draw on until the 9th coach was in place.

I now refer to 8 daily local freight trains which Mexborough men always referred to by nicknames. These were the:-

FLYING FLEA – This transported coal from the Wath marshalling yard to Mexborough for supplying the locomotives. One or two wagons of coal would also be taken to Dale Brown's; the local glassworks.

WATH ANNA - This served Wath Main Colliery taking the coal from the pit to Wath Marshalling yard.

E.C.1+2 - Similar to the Anna, this serviced Elsecar Main and Cortonwood plus the NCB workshops at Elsecar.

SCUFTER - This worked between Doncaster Shakespeare Dock sidings,

Hexthorpe Yards and Mexborough Top Yard.

SANITARY - Worked trains of sewage from Sheffield City Sewage works at Blackburn Meadows to Thrybergh sewage tip. It was a train of long standing. D.L.Franks made some notes on this. The train ran engine and brake to Tinsley West Junction leaving Mexborough shed between 6-30 and 7-00am. Then onto Sheffield Sewerage works to pick up the previous day's wagons to take to Thrybergh. It would then return from Thrybergh with the previous day's empty wagons. In between times when at the Thrybergh end, it would receive other orders from Control, mainly to shunt Baker & Bessemer's steelworks or the Yorkshire Tar Distillery at Kilnhurst.

The train is said to have worked daily with ordinary open wagons containing sewerage, there being insufficient room to dispose of the accumulated sewerage at the works. Each wagon is said to have a wooden board fitted across each end to prevent the contents spilling while the train was in motion. The progress of the train was followed with a wary eye by lineside workers and the cry of "Here's Sanitary" ensured everybody stood well back and clear of the passing train. (I don't think it would be said with such politeness, these days). The train was barred from taking water at Rotherham Central station in case passengers were offended or splashed with the contents of the train. On arrival at its destination, the sewerage was emptied via the wagon's side doors. These were dropped and the contents spilled out and away into a large settling area. These were located as follows:-

1 North of G.C. line at Thrybergh, south of the Midland mainline and between the colliery tip and the old G.C. and Midland Joint sidings at Roundwood

2 The original site was eventually filled and another area had to be found. This was on the Silverwood side of Don Bridge East Box. Here the hillside provided natural scope for the sewerage to drain away, flowing from the point of tipping to the settling area.

MUCKY DUCK – This serviced Mitchell's Main, Darfield Main Colliery and shunted Wombwell Goods Yard.

ROCKY. – Serviced the collieries on the Rockingham branch; ie Rockingham Colliery,Birdwell & Pilley Colliery, Ecclesfield Colliery & Coking Plant, and the Barrow Colliery & Coking Plant via Dovecliffe Sidings.

DIDO - This was the name of the staff train, which operated six days a week Monday to Saturday at 12 noon. It ran from Mexborough Station to New Oaks Junction signal box near Stairfoot, then across the branch to

Wombwell Main Junction signal box, then down to Aldham Junction and back to Mexborough Station. Its main purpose was to transport relief train crews out to various trains etc. which were working the local collieries, and so it stopped anywhere on route, not only at stations; for the purpose of dropping off and picking up these crews

Another train used solely for transporting staff on its outward journey was the 12-30am from Mexborough Station to Penistone; it then worked the Manchester to Cleethorpes newspaper train through to Cleethorpes.

In January 1958, a new division of British Railways was formed at Sheffield. It included some ex LNER sheds and also a number from the erstwhile LMS. This was a radical change for the Mexborough and Barnsley Sheds, as they had been for the previous 35 years part of the Doncaster District. Prior to the Grouping in 1923, Mexborough had been a District Headquarters in its own right with Barnsley, Wakefield, Barnsley Junction and Keadby as outstations. The new Sheffield Division was big as far as footplate staff were concerned, there were now nearly 1300 enginemen spread over the following ten depots:-

		New Shed Code	Previous District & Shed Code	
Ex LNER	Darnall	41A	Manchester	39B
Ex LMS	Grimesthorpe	41B	Sheffield (LM)	19A
Ex LMS	Millhouses	41C	Sheffield (LM)	19B
Ex LMS	Canklow	41D	Sheffield (LM)	19C
Ex LMS	Barrow Hill	41E	Toton	18D
Ex LNER	Mexborough	41F	Doncaster	36B
Ex LNER	Barnsley	41G	Doncaster	36D
Ex LNER	Staveley	41H	Colwick	38D
Ex LNER	Langwith	41J	Lincoln	40E
Ex LNER	Tuxford	41K	Lincoln	40D

My focus so far, has been on railwaymen who manned or maintained the engines and signed on at Mexborough Depot. Essential other duties however were required to make a railway operational and I make brief mention of them here in so far as the Mexborough based staff were concerned between the late fifties and closure.

STATIONMASTER – Was also known as the Yard Master. In September 1964, Mr F Adams transferred to Mexborough from Kilnhurst Central Station. He had been Station Master there since 1956, and in 1960, he was in charge of both stations, Kilnhurst Central and Kilnhurst West, and lived in Kilnhurst West Station House. This was a promotional move following the sudden death of his predecessor Mr Gregory. Other staff under the Station Master's control were:-

Goods Clerk – located in the Goods Yard – Mr Gibson
Chief Booking Clerk - Mr Stubbs
Station Foremen Mr B Huck & Mr S Tongue
Porters on Mr B Huck's shift Mr S Straw, Mrs A Salmons
Porters on Mr S Tongue's shift Mr I Huck, Mrs Greenwood

Additionally, there were two shunters who covered the carriage sidings and goods yard. There were also two parcel vans for delivering parcels and produce to local shops and houses in Mexborough and the surrounding district. One particular product, common to Mexborough, but maybe unusual elsewhere, were tins of maggots from the maggot farms at Harlington, Conisborough and, probably the largest railway user of all, Farley's Maggot farm situated between Mexborough sheds and Swinton Central station. These were dispatched to shops and other retail outlets anywhere on the railway system; but particularly on the Boston to Lincoln line for Angling Matches. Tins of maggots were at one time, sent weekly to Chartwell for Winston Churchill's fish.

CARRIAGE SIDINGS – 1 Male foreman and 6 female carriage cleaners. The task here was to clean both local passenger coaches and other sets of coaches which would come from all parts of the Eastern Region. The cleaning was quite thorough including all the interior and exterior, the seating and upholstery had to be cleaned with a special solvent, paying particular attention to the 1st class carpets. Mexborough carriage cleaners were well

A good view of Mexboro No2 Junction in July 1958. At the left is the rear of the engine shed. An N5 is preparing a passenger special in the junction yard and it being a Sunday morning, the special will be for the coast. The triple signal bracket reads (left hand) the line to Rotherham & Sheffield, (centre) main line to Barnsley, (right hand) goods line to Barnsley.
Photo: British Railways Illustrated Vol 10 No4 January 2001.

known for their work. On Saturdays and Sundays during the summer there could be as many as 12 sets of coaches to leave the sidings for excursions from various stations to seaside resorts. Some of these sets of coaches wouldn't arrive until after Saturday midnight, yet they had to be cleaned and equipped with toilet paper, soap and towels before they could be formed into sets by the shunters for an early departure excursion train.

GUARDS - The Guards depot was situated in the western side of the triangle. The Station Master also had an office there as well as on the station platform. The chief staff clerk was a Mrs Pearl Johnson and an assistant Mr G Tanser who compiled all paybills, paid out wages and rostered the staff. Additionally, there were three traffic inspectors who worked round the clock shifts, to sign on and off and roster approximately 48 guards. It was the Station Master's responsibility to examine all new guards in their knowledge of rules, regulations and knowledge of train working and re-examine them every two years.

SIGNALMEN – There were 6 signal boxes in the immediate area of Mexborough. These were:-

The young man on the left is training to be a Train Register Lad, on the first step to becoming a signalman. This is Mexborough No 2 signalbox in the 1960s. The lad was Tony Capstick who became more well known for his radio and light entertainment career.
Courtesy Swinton Heritage.

Mexborough No 1 – located above the LNER Athletic Club ground on the Swinton side. This controlled trains from Mexborough Nos 2 &3, the entrance to the goods sidings and trains to and from the Swinton Midland line.

Mexborough No 2 – located at the end of the platform on Mexborough station. Controlled trains to Doncaster or from Doncaster to go either Kilnhurst Central via No 3 or York, Barnsley or the Midland line via No 1.

Mexborough No 3 – located near the entrance to Mexborough Sheds. Controlled trains from Kilnhurst Central to either No 1 or No 2 boxes, the entrance and exit of all engines & wagons onto Mexborough Shed and it had control of the crossing gates to the GEC factory which were opened to road traffic by GEC men. This was, incidentally, the last surviving box. With modernisation, it became a part manual and part power box , operating power signals and controlling the west and east junctions and right through to Denaby Main. It is long gone now.

Mexborough No 4 – Located on the Barnsley line near to Whitelea Road. This controlled the goods line only.

Mexborough No 5 – Located between Mexborough No 1 and Swinton Junction near Whitelea Road. It controlled trains from Nos 1,2 or 3 boxes onto the Midland Line.

Mexborough West Junction. Located on the Barnsley line near Wragby Row. It controlled trains from Mexborough Nos 1&3 to Barnsley, Leeds or York

Examining the track. Dearne Junction 1955. I believe this gentleman is Fred Wroe. Courtesy Danny Canning.

Numbers 1, 2 and 3 boxes were "continuous" in that they were manned 24 hours per day and each had a train register boy on the weekday shifts. There were certain controls exercised by the Station Master in respect of staffing and discipline. So much then for the highest class Station Master just looking after his station!

While Fred Adams was the Mexborough Station Master, he recalled, the newspaper train leaving Manchester Victoria at approximately midnight and calling at Sheffield Victoria, Rotherham, Mexborough, Doncaster, Grimsby and Cleethorpes. The train was pulling parcel vans for each of these stations. It would arrive at Mexborough approximately 2am on Sunday morning and Mr Briggs, the Sunday newspaper wholesaler would be waiting for it. The newspapers were for Mexborough and the surrounding districts of Conisborough, Swinton, Kilnhurst, Parkgate, Wath, Goldthorpe, Thurnscoe and all intermediate places in between. Unloading was a hectic little period, the train could not be delayed, and six or seven four wheeled wheelbarrows would be used; all piled very high with newsprint. They were then wheeled into a waiting room on the UP platform (to Doncaster) where they would be sorted into the various bundles of different quantities and types of newspaper for each newsagent; and these were numerous. At one time, there were as many as four newsagents on Highwoods Terrace alone. They were all delivered by van. Frank Briggs had a shop, at 39-41 Swinton Road, Mexborough which he used as a wholesaling warehouse. After sorting

39-41 Swinton Road, Mexborough circa 1965. From left to right is Freda Bickerstaffe, her father Frank Briggs and an employee. No 41 adjoined this property which was also owned by Frank Briggs. It was let out to become the first Sheila's Florist shop. Sheila moved to the High Street premises before this property was compulsorily purchased. The actual property location would have been on a line drawn between the South Yorkshire Hotel and the large roundabout opposite. Courtesy Freda Bickerstaffe.

on the station, the surplus newspapers would be taken down to Swinton Road where any Newsagent in the District could come and purchase more papers if they ran out. I am digressing now, but this continued until the Swinton Road property was compulsorily purchased and demolished around 1968 to make way for the new relief road. The use of the waiting room for sorting the Sunday Newspapers was sanctioned by the Sheffield District office and was always conditional on the room being respected and kept clean for passenger use. This arrangement continued until 1987, over 20 years since the closure of Mexborough steam depot. By this time, newspapers were on the fall; they were not sold in the same great quantity as in the pre television days and in the 1987 Railway strike in support of the miners, the newspapers came from Manchester by road and never went back onto the railways. By this time, the majority of the Sunday Newspapers had been taken over and all the wholesalers were given notice to submit new tenders for wholesaling of the papers. Mr Briggs had died and his daughter, Freda Bickerstaffe, assisted by her husband Jimmy and son Peter, had been keeping the business running. They did submit a tender but it was unsuccessful and they lost the Mexborough area, although they did obtain an outlet in the Barnsley area. Peter ultimately sold the Barnsley business to concentrate on his retail business "Newstime" located in one of the new units on the High Street built in conjunction with the Mexborough relief road.

It has always been human nature to earn a little extra and make a little on

Early Sunday morning. Frank Briggs and an assistant, John Hickling, a Swinton newsagent, unloading newspapers from the parcel van at Mexborough station.
Courtesy Freda Bickerstaffe.

the side, if such an opportunity occurred. It sometimes did for one local character, who used to assist Mr Briggs on Mexborough Station. By 2-20am, the newpaper train had departed, but occasionally, a steam passenger train would then follow it into the platform. This could be either a late excursion returning from the west coast or a football special on its way home. The train would stop for water which it took from the water column at the end of the platform. He would take an armful of papers and stroll along the platform shouting "News of the World". Up would go the carriage blinds, people were eager to buy. For those who didn't have the correct money, he took what was offered, apologized for having no change but said he would return within a few moments; and down the train he would continue. He knew however, the train wouldn't be long in taking water and then it would be off right away. He wouldn't have time to return with the change and so as soon as the train began departing he slinked off to count his little profit. It was usually enough to keep him in beer for a day or two.

Finally, and this is probably more for the ex trainspotter's interests than retired engine drivers and firemen, I have recorded engine types and numbers which were allocated to and serviced by the Mexborough depot.

MEXBOROUGH'S ENGINES

Mexborough was essentially a depot for freight locomotives serving local collieries and industry. It had none of the gracious Pacific type locomotives engaged solely on main line passenger duties, and whilst Mexborough did provide engines for local passenger services, they were typically the D9 4-4-0 in the 1920s, the D11 Directors in the 1940s and finally the B1s in the 1950s.

The various classes at Mexborough in the early 1920s were:-

CLASSIFICATION	LOCAL NAME	WHEEL ARRANGEMENT
O4	Superheater or Rod	2-8-0
Q4	Tiny	0-8-0
B4	Fish Engine	4-6-0
B5	Fish Engine	4-6-0
J11	Pom Pom	0-6-0
J10	Claddies	0-6-0
N5	Tanky	0-6-2(T)
D9	Passenger Pom Pom	4-4-0
L1	Crabs	2-6-4(T)
S1	Daisy	0-8-4(T)

The S1 engines were specially built to work at Wath marshalling yard. The D9 passenger engines were diagrammed to work between Sheffield Victoria and Penistone to Doncaster, Cleethorpes, New Holland, and at a later date, Hull Paragon. The J11 Pom Pom was a useful multi purpose engine and despite small wheels, it was a good steamer and would be used on excursions to Leeds and Cleethorpes. Other engine classes arriving at Mexborough in later years were:-

CLASSIFICATION	LOCAL NAME	WHEEL ARRANGEMENT
D11	Director	4-4-0
V2	Green Arrow	2-6-2
K3	Rib Buster	2-6-0
B2	Sam Fays	4-6-0
B1	Springbok	4-6-0
8F	Derby Eights	2-8-0
N2	Dive Bomber	0-6-2(T)
N1	Beaufighter	0-6-2
Q1	Doodlebugs	0-8-0(T)
U1	Garratt	2-8-8-2
WD	Austerity or Aussie	2-8-0

Locomotives allocated to Mexborough (Shed Code 36B from 1948 to 1958) in 1950 were:-

CLASSIFICATION	YEAR INTRODUCED	NUMBERS
B1	1942	61165 61166 61167 61168 61174 61194
O4/1	1911	63611
O4/2	1925	63682
O4/3	1917	63668 63672 63774 63779 63791 63813 63898
O4/7	1939	63775
O4/8	1944	63612
O2/1	1921	63927
O2/3	1932	63969 63970 63971 63972 63975 63976 63977 63978 63979 63980 63981 63982 63983 63984 63985
O2/4	1943	63924
J11	1901	64288 64296 64302 64319 64334 64356 64377 64400 64403 64404 64432 64449
J11/3	1942	64283 64352 64442
J50/1	1929	68890
J50//3	1926	68946 68960 68974
N5	1891	69264 69297 69314 69316
S1/1	1907	69900
S1/2	1932	69901
S1/3	1932	69904 69905
WD	1943	90104 90108 90120 90144 90146 90150 90153 90154 90161 90166 90189 90190 90195 90196 90209 90211 90220 90223

90229 90232 90246 90250 90252 90255
90270 90280 90285 90286 90290 90296
90301 90311 90340 90383 90400 90401
90410 90421 90521 90537 90538 90550
90583 90587 90590 90594 90596 90597
90598 90612 90618 90653 90696 90700
90709 90714

The allocation in 1955 was:-

CLASSIFICATION	YEAR INTRODUCED	NUMBERS
B1	1942	61112 61165 61166 61167 61194
O4/1	1911	63586 63593 63611 63693 63698 63757
O4/2	1925	63730
O4/3	1917	63666 63668 63672 63701 63753 63764 63774 63779 63791 63813 63897 63898
O4/7	1939	63775 63843
O4/8	1944	63612 63828
J11	1901	64356 64374 64377 64400 64432 64449
J11	1942	64352
J69/2	1950	68520
J52/2	1897	68833
N5	1891	69280 69297 69306 69357
U1	1925	69999
WD	1943	90005 90015 90024 90053 90066 90085 90104 90118 90119 90120 90130 90144 90146 90150 90153 90166 90189 90190 90195 90209 90211 90220 90229 90250 90252 90255 90270 90286 90290 90304 90311 90330 90340 90358 90400 90401

Robinson 0-6-0 Class J11 introduced 1901 standing on the sidings at Mexborough shed on Sunday 25th May 1956. It's tender is loaded with coal, ready for the Monday morning and no doubt it will also be full of water; the Tender capacity being 3250 gallons; approx 14.5 tons. Courtesy G Oliver

90410 90421 90495 90498 90506 90521
90526 90580 90582 90587 90589 90590
90597 90598 90612 90668 90700

By 1959; this was a year after the new Divisional formation of British Railways at Sheffield, and when Mexborough's shed code was now 41F, the total allocation by class was:-

Class B1	61112 (transferred from Lincoln) 61165 61166 61167 61194
Class K3	61836 61839 61850 61867 61868
Class O4	63586 63593 63611 63628 63666 63672 63673 63684 63701 63723 63730 63753 63756 63757 63764 63774 63779 63791 63798 63812 63813 63828 63832 63841 63843 63891 63894 63897 63898 63908
Class J11	64377 64393 64402 64406
Class J69	68497 68623
Class N5	69308
Class WD	90119 90136 90139 90153 90190 90195 90203 90209 90211 90220 90250 90252 90270 90286 90290 90301 90304 90311 90330 90358 90384 90400 90401 90410 90421 90491 90495 90499 90506 90521 90526 90567 90580 90582 90587 90590 90608 90612 90668 90700

Stationary boilers at Mexborough MPD, including one from Class N2 0-6-2T No 69573, located at rear of Pump House on 5th January 1964. J Raybould Collection.

The three periods, summarised into Locomotive Classes allocated to Mexborough were:-

		1950	1955	1959
B1	4-6-0	6	5	5
O4	2-8-0	28	23	30
J11	0-6-0	15	7	4
J50	0-6-0T	4		
N5	0-6-2T	4	4	1
S1	0-8-4T	4		
WD	2-8-0	56	53	40
J69	0-6-0T		1	2
J52	0-6-0ST		1	
U1	2-8-8-2T		1	
K3	2-6-0			5
TOTAL		117	95	87

ST denotes Saddle Tank

Mexborough had stabled upwards of 150 locomotives but the electrification of the Wath – Woodhead – Manchester route in 1952 had seen the transfer of footplate crew to Wath and a re-allocation of many locomotives to other depots. At closure in 1965, most of the remaining locos had been transferred to either Canklow (41D) or Staveley Barrow Hill (41E).

CHAPTER 6

MEXBOROUGH'S FOOTPLATEMEN –
CLEANERS, LABOURERS & PASSED CLEANERS

It was never a hard task to persuade a railwayman to recall his personal experiences and share them with me in a tete a tete whilst in the comfort of their own home. I have reproduced in this chapter, some of their accounts. They are totally unstructured, they were written by myself exactly how I heard and understood the conversations and so the topics discussed are quite random and varied and are sometimes sprinkled with a bit of light humour.

I mention first however, a gentleman called George Potts. He became an engine cleaner at Mexborough Shed on the 11th December 1922. He would have started with the Great Central Railway as the new grouping under the LNER didn't commence until the 1st January 1923. Ten years after starting as a Cleaner, he became a regular fireman, going through the various links, including lodging links, at Mexborough. During the war years he became spare driver, then regular driver, but bade farewell to steam when he transferred to Wath to work on the new electrics when the Wath to Rotherwood to Manchester route was electrified in 1952/3. After subsequent promotion and re-appointments, he retired from an Inspector (high grade) post at York Headquarters in 1971 having served a 49 year career on the railways. George Potts is best remembered by non railwaymen for the book he wrote in the seventies, called Bankers and Pilots – Footplate Memories.

One specific account of his, I have reproduced. It concerns his first firing duty as a passed cleaner in January 1927 but preceding this, he makes mention of the economic climate prevailing at the time. He goes into wonderful detail and it is rich reading.

"1926 was a black year for everyone, for then occurred the General Strike, when for two or three weeks, the country was almost at a standstill. The railwaymen's leaders decided eventually that their men should go back to work, which left the colliery workers on their own. Their strike lasted from May to December, which in those days was a very long time for men, women and children to do without reasonable food, clothing and, in some cases, heat for the home. I remember in our household, although my father and brother were working three days a week and I was on the dole, we had plenty to eat but, nevertheless, it was my job to keep the home fires burning with wood that I scrounged and from trees that were sawn down purposefully by the colliers to keep the fires going. There were the odd clashes between the authorities and the wood gatherers but no summonses were issued. It was also a regular ritual, humiliating though it was, for them to go to food kitchens run by charities: churches and chapels helped

greatly, as well as the Working Men's Clubs and local councils. Otherwise I am afraid that there would have been looting of food shops and rioting.

By January 1927, the situation had returned to normal and everyone was glad to be back at work. I was still doing my fire-bar laying but I tried to spend as much spare time as possible with the engine cleaners, listening to their various yarns which were always interesting and, as often as not, very humerous. It was during this year that the Unions and Shedmaster decided that the few men who started in 1922 should be "passed out" for firing duties if required and this meant doing a bit of swotting at the Improvement Classes. Eventually, we all went to see the Loco Inspector, with a certain amount of trepidation, I might add, as we didn't expect to be passed out so soon. However, due to the boom we were now experiencing, there was more work for the depot and we all got through, thereafter waiting keenly for our first firing shift. I remember one of the cleaners' foremen saying as he looked us over, "another dozen bloody good cleaners spoilt now they are passed out.!"

It wasn't long before my opportunity came and I got my first firing shift. I had booked on at 2pm and happened to be the senior cleaner; fortunately for me, a fireman had gone sick and I was told by the foreman cleaner to go to the enginemen's room and report. There I was given

Class O4/1 introduced in 1911. This was the first of the Robinson GC design with small Belpaire boiler (so named because it runs into a square firebox, as opposed to a round firebox), steam and vacuum brakes. Standing on the Cripple sidings at Mexborough in April 1960. Seen on the left hand margin are the platelayer's cabin and the buffer stops for No 2 yard. This loco is identical to the one George Potts did his first firing turn on.
Courtesy Great Central Railway Society.

instructions by the Running Foreman to go to engine 5386 (an O4), working the Moorhouse – Herculaneum Docks. Hell, I thought to myself, this sounds important.So I asked rather diffidently who my driver was and he said with a slight smile, "Bill Hooper – and he eats three passed cleaners for his breakfast, so hurry up and get off the shed!"(This loco, incidentally was built in 1911 and was renumbered in BR days to 63611).I hurried to the messroom for my snap tin and coat, then to the lamp stores for headlamps and a firing shovel. I saw on the engine board that the engine I wanted was outside the shed on No 6 road, so off I went to find it. This didn't take a moment and I put my headlamps in the position for light engine, put my tin and coat in the cupboard and then introduced myself to the driver, who was oiling the eccentrics in the motion. When he came out from between the frames – which were entered over the top splasher – he looked at me and said, "What do they call thee? Has tha been out afore?" I told him who I was and added that this was going to be my first firing shift. "Bloody hell, I do gerram! Anyhow has tha fetched tools?" I shook my head, somewhat dumbstruck. "Tha'd better fetch 'em then." Having hurried back from this little errand, I started to sweep the footplate up, clean the gauge glasses and check that we had a full complement of fire irons, ie long and short slack shovels, straight and bent darts, which could best be described as long pokers for removing the clinker off the firebars.

I was fortunate that the steam gauge showed 100lbs, as I was late getting to the engine but there was a good fire under the door ready for pushing forward. The allowance time for preparing an O4- which we called superheaters- was one hour from signing on to being booked out at the Top Pit cabin. After Bill had finished oiling round he decided that we should go up to fill the tank with water, and then we were away to the outlet signal. I quizzed him as to where we were going. "Tender-first to Moorhouse on the G.N. main line Doncaster to Leeds", I was told. "The signal box is Hampole and Frickley is the colliery from where we are taking 45 wagons of coal for the Herculaneum Dock at Liverpool." I saw myself at the Docks and us putting off the wagons and returning light engine to Mexboro, but to make sure, I asked Bill how far we would be going with the train. "If the shunters and guard get cracking, we might go as far as Penistone. If not, it will be bloody Mexboro!" I happened to say that this didn't seem very far and I always remember his reply. "This isn't a bloody aeroplane tha knows! We can't go'er fields wi' this lot and besides, there's other buggars on't railroad besides us, so we've to take us turn!" After that, I decided to keep my mouth shut....

We left the depot and trundled through Mexboro station towards Denaby Crossing but we came to a stand at the home signal at Denaby; so, after waiting the prescribed time, I proceeded to the signal box to carry out Rule 55, which meant protection by the signalman of our engine at that home signal. I shall always remember that particular box, as my father was the signalman there for about three years. I informed the bobby where we stood, where we were going and asked if he had protected us. He assured me that he had and told me that at the next box, Lowfield Junction, the tail end of the train of empties was 'stood out foul' of the main line and as soon as he cleared we would be going. When I got back on the engine, I could see that Bill had been throwing buckets of water about to slack the dust, simply because I had no slacking pipe, which in those days was not provided as a fitment to the injector. Moving away after the signal was pulled off, I soon found out that it was not as easy firing up running as it was standing in the shed. It was a matter of spragging your backside up against the engine seat to keep one's balance. Working hard at this, I glanced up now and again to see we were passing through Lowfield Junction – for the Hull & Barnsley Railway to Hull via Sprotboro and Brodsworth – and Conisboro station, a place of nostalgic memories for me, as practically my whole childhood was spent here until the family moved to Mexboro in 1927.

All the signals, including Cadeby distant, were off, so we knew we were alright to Cliff signal box beyond Conisbro tunnel, approximately 100 yards long. This line running over the top of the tunnel was the Dearne Valley Railway, worked by the L.&Y.R. They ran pull-and-push trains between Wakefield and Edlington, also coal trains to the Wakefield area. Passing Cadeby box, we saw Cliff distant, underneath Cadeby's starter in the off position, so we were alright to Warmsworth. Everything in our favour, we kept moving at a good 25mph, with me putting a bit on, and, often enough, missing the firehole door. We only used a little water, although it is a rising gradient from Conisborough to Hexthorpe Junction. The latter was the junction for the Doncaster avoiding line to Hull and Yorkshire Main Colliery, G.C. side. As we passed the junction, Bill shouted across, "Tha can shut thi damper for a bit, cos I'm going to shut regulator. Its downhill to Doncaster and I know tha's got a big fire on. She'll be blowing bloody top off if tha leaves the damper open!" I did as I was told, which conserved the fire already in the firebox – and as Bill said, prevented her from "blowing bloody top off".

As we dropped down to Cherry Tree signal box without steam on, I seemed to notice the clanging of side rods and the passing over facing points and V- crossings more. Yet we made less noise and negotiated these more easily than I had imagined possible with a heavy 120 ton engine. When we arrived at Cherry Tree, the home signal was on; a guard came out of the box and climbed onto our engine, saying to Bill, "I'm your guard and there is a brake at Moorhouse." We proceeded towards St James Junction and on to Doncaster Central signalbox where the goods line took us behind the station. As it happened, we got past Frenchgate box without further delay and went onto the Leeds main line. "Tha can open t'damper now. We're going to move a bit smarter – mun't stop any of their bloody crack trains!". I felt a bit peeved at him, telling me what to do; I'd been doing my best to look like an old hand in front of the guard.....Anyway, I opened the damper and put a little bit on.

At our destination, Hampole box, the signalman put us inside and then the shunter put us on one side for the time being, as he already had another engine on hand before he could deal with us. During the time that we were waiting, I kept cleaning the faceplate down, wiping the injectors, polishing this and that, until Bill eventually exploded. "Sit thi self down, tha'r gerrin on my bloody nerves! Atha like this at home?"

So that settled that and I had to be content listening to his horseracing talk with the guard. When the latter left to look around some wagons, Bill and I got into conversation about the various places he had worked to, types of engines he had worked on, and so on and I, of course had plenty of questions to ask. I might add that at this time I was in no position to judge whether a man was a good or a bad driver; however after having been with Bill a little longer, I realised he was one of the good ones – not all hell and no notion – and weighed everything up very carefully, such as stopping at signals, moving away gently so as not to break couplings or knock hell out of the guard and so forth.

Eventually our guard came to tell us that we would now be preparing our train. With this news, I decided also to prepare my fire, opening the front damper and putting some coal all round the firebox, with a little extra under the door. But it was apparent that, in my eagerness, I had put too much on because the O4 started blowing off at the safety valves. "Shut thi damper and put injector on to quieten her. I can't hear what bloody guard's saying ," Bill shouted at me. "But don't fill her too full, else we shall have the old buggar priming and tha knows what damage that can do.!" I had to confess I had no idea "She would be throwing water all o'er place, that's what, and we might knock a cylinder end out". As we started to get our train ready, I realised how important it was to know what the hand signals meant that the guard was giving on my side of the train and which I had to relay to Bill. These involved a great deal of shunting, due to some crippled wagons, but at last the guard walked up to give Bill the necessary information – 48 wagons full load, and an assisting engine from Doncaster through to Dunford. Then he went off to tell the signalman that we were ready to depart. Eventually the signal was lowered for us to proceed, Bill gathering the train up nice and gently. I started firing up enthusiastically but after a minute or two he interrupted me. "Steady on a bit. There'll soon be no coal left for thi relief and its not too bad to Doncaster, nice and level". Just then he acknowledged the guard's tip by giving a blast on the whistle. Two light firings took us to the Doncaster goods line and as we passed Central box the signalman showed Bill a green flag and pointed to our assisting engine at the other end of the goods line.

It was another O4 and from Doncaster to Wombwell it had to be attached at the front, so along I went to take my headlamp off the bracket on the buffer beam while the fireman off the assisting engine went in between to couple on and take his lamp off. When he saw me he said with a grin, "Does thi mother know tha out at this late hour? We shall have to get thee home reight sharp!" He happened to be a regular fireman, so he was doing a bit of showing off and this deflated me a little after feeling so important on my own engine. By and by our signal was lowered, both drivers acknowledged with the whistle and Bill allowed the driver on the leading engine to gather the train up and tighten the couplings gently until he felt the whole train moving. Then he opened the regulator gently, while looking back to see the guard giving us the tip that the train was following complete.

From Doncaster to Hexthorpe Junction is an upgrade, so I started firing again I had already got three quarters of a glass of water and therefore had no need to give a heavy firing; moreover, Bill was soon ready to tell me when I had put enough in the box. I might add, because I kept missing the firehole door, there was coal all over the footplate, Bill finally being driven to comment, "I'll have that bloody hoil made bigger for thee or else I'll get thee a little shovel!" Going up the grade to Hexthorpe Junction , it was necessary to open the regulator wider and the blast from the exhaust gave a very white appearance in the firebox, with flames licking round the firehole door. I started firing up again, this time with not too much on the shovel. Consequently, I was managing very well not to spill coal all over the footplate, when all at once, through not watching the steam gauge, she blew off at the safety valves. As I only had half a glass of water, there was plenty of room in the boiler, so on went the injector to quieten her down and get back to three quarters of a glass. I got what I expected from Bill, another little dig. "I expect tha knows tha's wasting energy and bloody coal, so I think what tha's got in't box will tek thee o'er top at Hexthorpe Junction and then its practically downhill to Mexborough." Naturally Bill was right. After getting through the steep cutting at Warmsworth both drivers gently closed the regulators and we were being pushed along by the weight of the train, probably at about 20 mph; it was great to sit there on the seat, injector singing away, damper closed to deaden the fire slightly, past Cliff signalbox and through the short tunnel at Cadeby, then onto Conisborough with all the signals in the off position. As we entered the platform at Mexborough, a guard walked by shouting that he was going to relieve ours; Bill closed the regulator and I slipped the injector on. When we came to a stand, the relief stepped on and things could not have been any better – a full head of steam and three-quarters of a glass; proudly I told the fireman that she were a good 'un. Bill gave the relieving driver all the information about the train while we stepped onto the platform and waited for the guard to come up to retrieve our running statement, which we called a ticket. As we walked across to the Loco shed, I asked Bill about the assisting engine. He told me it would stay on the front to

Wombwell, then uncouple and move to the rear of the train.

We arrived at the enginemen's room at 8-40pm and had only been in about five minutes when the foreman lifted his sliding window and shouted through for Bill to dispose of an engine on the top pit. My mate grumbled somewhat but I felt really well suited, so off we went. I saw that it was a Pom Pom (J11 0-6-0) and I had to clean the fire, rake out the ashes underneath and empty the smokebox of ash, after which we moved the engine down to the sand hole to fill the sand boxes. By then, it was 9-40pm – twenty more minutes and our day was up – so we walked back to the enginemen's room to sign off. My home was in the opposite direction from Bill's but he did say before we parted company, "Tha's done well, lad! Tha'll make a fireman someday."

In reading his book you will see that he was back to cleaning duties the next day giving detailed accounts to his mates of his first firing shift. At this period, 1927 onwards he would from time to time, pick up the odd firing duty but it was another 10 years before he became a regular fireman.

All footplatemen started their careers as a Cleaner, and, as with George Potts, it was a long "apprenticeship" before a regular position of fireman was attained. There were periods in later decades however, when economical and political influence created real shortages of men, particularly firemen, on the railways. I will illustrate this by Vic Parkes' own account of his early days on the L.N.E.R.

Vic had worked at Wath Main Colliery for 3 years before joining the L.N.E.R. in July 1937. The seam he had been working on had become exhausted, and all the men who worked on it were given a week's notice. He didn't relish seeking another mining job however, for he would never forget his awful experience of seeing his best friend killed in an underground accident. So Vic, and four of his colleagues responded to calls for Cleaners on the railway. There was a shortage of firemen and management were looking specifically at new recruits of 17 years and 9 months in age so that they would become eligible in 3 months time (on attaining the age of 18) to be promoted to a passed cleaner. Vic was of the right age; (being only 5'6" tall was not a problem), his colleagues weren't and he was the only one recruited. This was an unusual policy. The railways had always operated on seniority but Vic became a passed cleaner at 18. The actual exam required Vic, with an Inspector, to join the footplate crew of a Doncaster to Sheffield passenger train at Mexborough station and with a little bit of guidance from the fireman, he fired the engine to Sheffield. It was not an automatic pass; you had to show self initiative as to when to put on coal, spread it around the firebox and add water to the boiler. There were also many Rules to learn. As passed cleaner No 185, he continued to do cleaning duties but in the event of firemen not reporting for duty, he would take their place, and with over 300 firemen at Mexborough, this was quite frequent

By early 1938, there were the beginnings of a slump and many Cleaners were dispersed from Mexboro' to different depots; Vic himself, going to Doncaster. This was good experience. Whilst on cleaning duties, he recalls cleaning "Mallard" before it went on its record breaking run on 3rd July 1938. 5 Cleaners were required to clean a Pacific. The usual format was to toss a coin to see who did which section of the engine. The 1st pick (or winner) would take the right hand side of the boiler, frame and the right hand side of the tender and tender wheels, the 2nd pick would take the corresponding left side, the 3rd would take the top of the tender and engine wheels on one side, the 4th the corresponding left side whilst the loser would take the smokebox, buffers, footplate (inc cleaning all the brass pipes) and the back of the tender. To put 5 people in order with just one coin required many "throws" and the system would be open to "fiddling" as the foreman cleaner used to find out.

Another temptation to the cleaning gang would be, that is if they were cleaning a Pacific and it was cold (ie had no fire in it), they would hurry up the cleaning to save time. Usually, two hours were allocated for a clean, but with rushing, they could do it in an hour and then they would all scramble into the large firebox; rig up a lamp and play cards. One day they were caught by the Foreman; who promptly closed the fire door and left them shut in the firebox for a good hour.

Vic was still a passed cleaner at Doncaster but the difference was that when he was put on firing duties, he was either firing Pacifics or sometimes the Doncaster station pilot loco. He recalls in those days, seeing locomotives coming through Doncaster Station with as many as 24 coaches behind them. The slump continued and Vic was then transferred from Doncaster to Neasden (N London). Others were disposed to such as Frodingham and

Driver Charlie Walker and Fireman Vic Parkes sat in the passageway leading to the Enginemen's room, Mexborough in 1940. Courtesy V Parkes.

Norwich. There hadn't been much choice in the matter; it was a management decision and if you didn't want to go, you were given your "cards". These were times of hardship, for there was no subsistence and out of his Passed Cleaner wages of £1-16s-0d per week; he had to pay lodgings of £1-5s-0d, Mum, who was widowed was sent 5s-0d and the rest is what Vic survived on. The approach of war in 1939 altered things; some of the Cleaners had to go on National Service and Vic was transferred back to Mexborough. Work on the railways increased dramatically; there was a need for more drivers; and so old firemen in their fifties were promoted. This had a knock on effect right through the grading structure and at the bottom; more recruits had to be taken on as cleaners. The railways were so starved of manpower yet the demands for additional freight and troop carrying had to be met. The normal progression of entrants to the footplate grade just had to be bypassed.

One such account of this is Dennis Porter's. He joined the LNER at Mexborough in 1939 just before Christmas. (Retired 10th May 1983 after a career of 43 years). His father Cliff was already a driver at Mexborough having previously transferred from the Immingham depot. Dennis started as a Cleaner on a Monday morning and that same afternoon he was up in front of his Inspector and regraded Passed Cleaner. By Thursday he was doing his first day's firing. This timescale was even more exceptional but it demonstrates the short cuts that management were prepared to take. Of course, Dennis had been well tutored by his father, and he knew Rule 55, the protection of trains, off by heart. Dennis remained a fireman until 1951 and we will later return to some of his stories. No training was ever given as such for firing duties and the Passed Cleaner learned his job from conversations with other cleaners and firemen, also by the myriad labouring jobs he did, eg firelighting, steam raising etc; and when he had a firing turn, by instruction from the driver he was with. Much later on, 1956 onwards, cleaners were sent on a short training course to learn firing

A gathering of fellow comrades on the front buffer beam of a Gresley K3 No 3818 on Mexborough Shed circa 1943. Left to Right Top Row - L Franks, Jim Rodway, Tony Early, Harry West, Ronnie Fareham. Second Row – Walt Harris, Sid Ellis, H Brown, Wilf Hankin. Third Row – Alf Skirrow, Dennis Porter. Bottom row – H Fern, Harold Cook. Photograph taken by Cyril Morley. Courtesy Dennis Porter.

duties. Eventually, when regular firing vacancies arose, passed cleaners were promoted to firemen but in strict seniority order. They were then allocated to a regular driver who they would stay with for a period lasting from six months to several years. Wally Smith and George White both started as cleaners in 1944. This was still a good time to start and their progression was very quick. Both left school never thinking for one moment they would soon be starting a 40 year career on the railways. Their early stories are very different.

Wally had left school at 14 and went to work in Kilnhurst Co-op in the Cobblers Department. It was war time, leather was scarce; they just couldn't get enough of it for all the repairs and he was moved into the "flour place". Striving to earn that bit more and being disenchanted with the Co-op life, he went to work at Dale Browns for about £2 per week, but it was becoming well known that you could get a Cleaner's job at Mexborough Loco for nearer £3 per week (because of the shortage of men due to the war). So Wally joined the LNER in October 1944. It took him only 3 weeks to become a Passed Cleaner but he couldn't go out as fireman until he was 17. He didn't have long to wait. As a cleaner, he would clock on and then make for the canteen where, more than likely, he would be told by the foreman cleaner to go and "fire". Although he had clocked on as a cleaner, the driver would have to put the name of his passed cleaner on his ticket so that he would be paid the firing rate.

George White's railway career was one he'd no regrets about, but it wasn't the one he'd set out to pursue when he left school. His parents felt that he could better himself by not working on the railways or in the coalmines like most young lads did, but by working for his great uncle; Mr Jack Harry White, the undertaker on Bank Street. That did not last long however; he was soon to see his first body laid out and that was it; off he went home without a word of explanation. Nevertheless, keen to establish himself in the right job, he tried his hand at the Queen's Foundry, then as a bricklayer at Tyas Guest Monumental Masons, then as a builder with Trowbridge Property Repairs before finally, successfully applying in January 1944 for a job on the railways. He was then 16. Fortunately, he was a big tall lad and met the then entrance requirement of 5' 11". Of course the reality of working on steam locomotives was far removed from the starry eyes of youngsters at school who had dreamed of nothing else. Most jobs were physically demanding and dirty; the footplate was a much harder, harsher, more unforgiving environment than we could ever imagine and it took great strength of character to put up with the working conditions of the vast majority of enginemen. The footplate bred strong characters, strong men; more so, men with great pride in their work which galvanised into a tremendous spirit of comradeship.

At 19, George became a passed cleaner which meant that he could be used on fireman's duties as and when required. On firing occasions, his weekly wage in his first year was £4-13s-06d, (decimal £4.67½) an increase over cleaning of £1-15s-06d (£1.77½). The drivers, who were "god" and "kingpin", did exert some influence on who was to be their stand-in fireman while their regular was off and George, being a tall lad, handy with the shovel was often allocated fireman's duties because a driver had requested his services. Being so young of course, George knew all about "burning the candle at both ends". Getting up in the middle of the night wasn't easy. He recalls living in a "two up and two down" terraced house on Thomas Street, Swinton. His mother would shout up the stairs "come on George; its time you were getting up". "I'm on my way mum", would come the reply down the stairs; albeit he hadn't been in bed too long and he was half asleep.On one occasion, he recalls coming down, the kettle was on the gas ring, and his mother made him a cup of Camp coffee to have with his sandwiches before he set off. George took a sip. "Mother, its dreadful, there's something wrong with it". His mum had a sip. "Ooh George, I've made it from brown sauce". She was tired out; ready for bed, but couldn't go until George was on his way and she had mistakenly taken the wrong bottle from the cellar head.

Cleaning locos was a very dirty, oily job and apart from washing his hands at the end of the shift; he had to go home in work clothes which reeked of paraffin. His weekly reward was less than 60 shillings (£3); hardly enough to live on, but over the years, and being quite money orientated, he would look to supplement his income with overtime, an abundance of which was always available. These would be labouring jobs of which there were so many. This was because a Cleaner was also regarded as a Utility man and could be used for any kind of labouring job on the depot. They would be allocated out by three Foremen Cleaners, namely Herbert Kelshaw, Joe Bullitt and Bob Lewis. There were 3 firedroppers per shift, for instance, and if one didn't turn up; then you could work an extra shift on overtime as a firedropper on labourer's pay. It could also be working on the coal stage; emptying coal wagons into a tub, or shovelling coal which had spilt down onto the banks of the lime pond back into wagons at the top. Working in fireboxes which had to be entered through the little firing hole, legs and bottom first, to clean, remove and replace firebars was another regular overtime duty. And yet another overtime job George used to do was visiting railwaymens' homes as the Knocker Upper. This was not a pleasant job. It necessitated walking the streets in the early hours of the morning, hanging around in bus shelters waiting for the next knocking up; there were no street lights, blackout conditions still prevailed and it took a brave man to get round. For George, if he'd got time to call in at home in Swinton, he would, to collect his dog; a white bull terrier called Peter. He recalls one morning, knocking up a driver; a batchelor, who came down the stairs to open the door in his pyjamas. Peter growled, and in a flash, the driver was "flying" back up the stairs. Usually, one had an hour from being knocked up to signing on duty. By the time George was passed for Fireman in 1947, telephones were becoming more available, (hitherto, it had been cheaper to pay Knocker Up wages than install a telephone) and knocker ups had been dispensed with.

All of these duties were slightly higher paid and it was therefore a bonus if you were labouring instead of cleaning within your shift but the incentive was always there, particularly for the married men, to do labouring jobs on overtime. This work was often hard and physically demanding. Rates of pay for Engine Cleaners in 1946 were:-

Age	£ -s-d	Equivalent Decimal
16	£2-0s-06d	£2.02½
17	£2-6s-06d	£2.32½
18	£2-15s-0d	£2.75
19	£2-18s-0d	£2.90
20	£4-5s-0d	£4.25
21	£4-5s-0d	£4.25
22	£4-5s-0d	£4.25

No matter which cleaner, fireman or driver I spoke to, they would all have experienced or witnessed an accident or incident which occurred to them or their mates at some time in their career. I have recorded a few but I will start off with Alf who was on this day, firing as a passed cleaner.

A training manual issued to footplate crew. Many retired locomen still have these as keepsakes. Kindly loaned by Dennis Porter.

Alf recalls a particular braking incident. On this particular day, he was firing for a driver called Mervyn Bell. The train had come from the Birkenhead area via Manchester and they took it over at Barnsley Junction. It was headed for Scunthorpe. Coming from West Silkstone to Wentworth is a down gradient of 1 in 40. Alf said to Mervyn "the backboard's off" (this is a distant signal meaning the whole of the signalman's section is clear). Mervyn replied "it bloody well wants to be; I can't stop these". These happened to be tank wagons carrying petrol. At any time, bulk liquid was a precarious load because of the swilling effect. At this time (1940s), these trains were not fully fitted but loose coupled. From West Silkstone down to Stratford crossing, they used to drop the wagon brakes down and pin them, but on a petroleum train, they could only drop them; they couldn't pin them for fear of sparks, so the brakes just clattered away. The driver eventually got hold of this train but it certainly denoted to him how serious an incident it could have been.

The working conditions of an engine cleaner were really quite deplorable. The job itself was an extremely dirty one, working overalls at the end of a shift, in which one had to walk home, were badly stained, stank of paraffin and not until the later British Railway days were there any showers or washroom facilities at the depots. The incentive for any junior recruit however, was that career progression would ultimately make him an engine driver and British Railways would encourage them through the issue of training manuals. I have inserted below an extract from a Manual issued to Footplate Crew. This was titled "Locomotive Management" "Cleaning – Driving – Maintenance – 9th Edition Price 10/-".

SECTION 1 GENERAL
The Junior Engine Cleaner who has started his career to become an Engineman on British Railways is expected to take an interest in locomotives, to fit himself to take charge of them when he is promoted. Whilst working as a Cleaner he must make himself aquainted with the general arrangement of the various types of locomotives and learn the names of the various locomotive parts, eg frames, cylinders, steam chests, wheel arrangements, boiler, firebox, smokebox, safety valves etc. He will receive tuition from Chargeman Cleaners, Firing Instructors and Inspectors. He should take the opportunity to supplement the information in this Handbook by asking questions of Fitters, Drivers, Firemen, Foremen, Inspectors, and by attending Mutual Improvement Classes and lectures in the Mobile Instruction Trains, where provided.

NOTICES AND RULES
In addition to obtaining a knowledge of locomotives, it is essential that he should become fully acquainted with the Rules and Regulations which apply to him.

A study of the Permanent Notices and Rules 1 to 16 in the Rule Book will instruct him in his personal conduct and safety, and a knowledge of the following rules will prepare him for the time when he will be called upon to act as a Fireman:-

Rule Nos. 34-49	Fixed Signals
Rule Nos. 50-51	Hand Signals
Rule Nos. 55-56	Detention of Trains
Rule Nos. 126-8, 141-3	Working of Trains
Rule Nos. 178-181	Protection of trains stopped by accident, etc

Of course, there were always recruits who couldn't take to the job and would leave after a few days or a few weeks. Joe Raybould would have been one of these but he wasn't allowed to leave and he went on to serve 48 years on the railways. Joe had gone to the new Mexborough Technical College in 1940. At 16, he couldn't easily get a job; women were used in many industries while the men were at war, and the only option he had, was to be a miner. This wasn't really a chosen occupation however, for someone who had been to the "tec" where the slant on education was towards engineering. Joe therefore went to the labour exchange and he was offered a job as a cleaner at Mexboro Loco Shed. He started in 1943. After two years of engine cleaning, his step-brother secured him a steel erection job at the new Gray's Bridge Power Station in Mexboro'. His application was accepted by the builders but he couldn't get released from the railway because of the Essential Works Act. He had to continue cleaning locos at £3 per week.

Into the fifties and still in the era of steam, nothing really had changed. Promotion from Cleaner to Fireman was still quite rapid, overtime was abundant so making for a good wage, but until the arrival of the diesels, the nature of the work remained hard and physical.

Dick, now retired from GNER in 2003 is the youngest footplateman I interviewed. He attended Kilnhurst C of E school and took his first job in April 1954 as a messenger lad in Mexborough Goods Yard on Rowms Lane. This, being the only goods yard in the area, it was quite a busy one, particularly with customers such as Woolworths, Dale Browns, and virtually all the other large trading concerns in the area. Most goods, including beer and cigarettes were delivered by the railway in those days. His work was clerical in nature; checking ledgers with goods etc and his boss; he recalls, was Joe Cartledge from Barnsley.

It didn't last long however, the young banter about Mexborough Loco was filtering through, and Dick transferred into the Loco as a Cleaner in March 1955. He started like everyone else; at the foot of the ladder; as a Junior Cleaner. Until he had gained some seniority, the foreman cleaner would allocate him the filthiest part of a loco to clean; the motions, which were the wheels, pistons and connecting rods and so on. It was very manually intensive work, every part of the engine and tender was done by hand with cotton rags and wipes soaked in paraffin. There was no driving it through a train wash like the modern diesel.. It would take a team of five or six cleaners to complete, on average, two locos per shift depending on size. As seniority was gained, Dick would be allocated, first a boiler side, and then the tender, whilst another junior cleaner would have been allocated the motions. The most frequently cleaned locos were the passenger B1s and that would be every other day. The foreman cleaner was very fair but strict. No driver enjoyed driving a dirty engine and if he, the foreman cleaner, found any part of a cleaned engine still looking grubby; he would make the cleaner go back and do it all again.

In his early days, Dick found himself working more on nights, starting at 10pm, than days. Sometimes he was allocated a labouring job, like cleaning out the ash pits, working on the coal stage or fire lighting, but these jobs were also available to him on overtime if he so desired. It wasn't long; 2-3 months, before Dick was told quite out of the blue, by the foreman cleaner that he was going out as fireman for the first time. It wasn't a permanent position; the next day he would be back as Cleaner but over the next 12 months, he would be gradually called on more and more to fire, and on the 19th May 1955, he was finally certified as a Passed Cleaner. He then took regular firing jobs on nights. His first regular mate was driver George Clifford Peat with whom he worked for about 6 months. Then, when Barnsley MPD closed, and some drivers were transferred to Mexborough, he had a spell with Driver Jack Perry. Jack could have gone into the main line at Mexborough, but preferred instead, to stick to his old routes around the Barnsley and Grimethorpe collieries and therefore Dick also did a lot of this work too.

Time moved on as a Passed Cleaner, and he finished up back with Driver Clifford Peat in the Annesley Link (Nottingham Area), relieving York men at Mexborough No 1 signal box on locos of various types and sizes, ie V2s, K3s, 8Fs and 9Fs (spaceships). In those days steam was steam; no training was given on each type of loco; if one was passed for steam; it covered every loco type. The controls in a steam loco were much the same, but motion was very different although this did not matter too much to the drivers.

CHAPTER 7

FIREMEN – TASKS AND TALES

All firemen were issued with a British Railways Rule Book. The one I have quoted from was for the year 1950. On Firemen's duties, the rule book stated:-

"Good timekeeping is an essential part of a Railwayman's job. After signing on duty at the right time and reading the notices, the Fireman should then join his engine. His first duty is to examine the water gauges and notice the steam pressure. If the water level is satisfactory he should give attention to the fire, level it down and raise the steam pressure, to enable the injectors to be tested as early as possible. [The injector is an ingenious device which feeds water from the tender into the boiler. It is operated by steam from the boiler].

He should satisfy himself that the fusible plugs and tubes are satisfactory and that the brick arch and firehole deflector plate and protection ring are in good condition, also the smokebox door is screwed up tight.

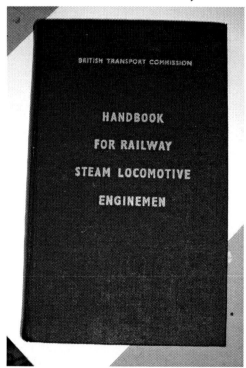

One of the handbooks issued to Firemen. A careful study of this book would assist firemen to become proficient in their duties and prepare them for their examination to pass as a driver. The examination comprised of an oral and a practical examination. Loaned by Dennis Porter.

It is the Fireman's duty to draw tools and equipment from the Stores, where tools are locked up, and to clean and trim the lamps, where required to do so. He must make sure that the required number of flags and detonators are carried and, where these are contained in a sealed cannister, ensure that the seal is intact and the "date" indication correct.

Careful preparation of the fire is half the battle. He should start by spreading the fire over the grate evenly with a fire iron, running this over the bars to clear the air spaces. Some classes of coal require the use of broken firebrick, limestone or shingle, which prevents clinker adhering to the firebars. This must be thrown on the bars before spreading the fire.

The fire should be built up by adding small quantities of coal. Large coal must be broken to lumps little larger than a man's fist. This exposes to the action of the fire a greater surface of the fresh coal than would be the case if large pieces were used.Firing should continue at intervals, giving each charge of coal time to ignite properly, until a bed of fire, well alight and suitable for the class of train to be worked, is obtained. The damper should be open and blower carefully applied sufficiently to avoid smoke.[The aim was to start with a fire in the middle of the box, and let it spread slowly across the grate over an hour or two. In this way, the firebox is heated gently and strain on the boiler due to expansion is minimized. Once the fire has spread over the grate, if there is some pressure the blower can be put on to stop smoke coming out of the firehole and to create a draught to draw the fire.]

He should be particular to sweep the front platform and the foot framing clear of all loose ashes and sand, which would, if not removed, present an untidy and unkempt appearance, and, moreover, would blow into the motion and cause increased wear.He should satisfy himself that the ashpan has been cleaned and that the dampers are in working order. The sand boxes must be filled, the fire irons properly stowed and the coal safely stacked on the tender.

He should see that the cab, boiler fittings and tool boxes are kept clean; it must be remembered that a good Fireman takes a pride in the cleanliness of the footplate.Any difficulties experienced or defects noted during preparation must immediately be brought to the notice of the Driver. The

Class O4/3 No 63701 at Mexborough Shed on 7th April 1957. The engine is standing on the Cripple Sidings, coaled and watered ready for duty and ready for the Monday morning light up. It was built in 1917 as a ROD loco; purchased by the LNER in 1925 and withdrawn in August 1965. Courtesy Great Central Railway Society

Driver is in charge of the locomotive and the Firemen's duties are carried out under the Driver's control and supervision".

There were of course, many characters amongst the realm of engine driver and many had different views on how to drive a steam locomotive. This, of course, had a great bearing on the fireman's job; some drivers would be a dream to work for, others would make the job doubly hard.

One driver in the passenger link had his own theory about clearing all the dirt and deposits out of the boiler. He would pick up the newspaper train at Mexborough and on the run down to Doncaster, he would tell the fireman to fill the boiler right up, to get as much steam as possible so that when leaving Doncaster station the engine would start priming. (Now priming was not a healthy condition for a locomotive to be in. It was caused by the boiler being overfilled and also by the use of "hard water". When the regulator was opened, the excess water would be carried to the steam chest, then via steam pipes to the cylinders, from where it would be exhausted via the blast pipe to the atmosphere along with all the dirt and soot it had picked up along its journey. Imagine an engine priming whilst stood at a station; - that would be an "unforgiveable" offence for a driver; the platform, passengers and everything else would be covered with sooty water droplets. Priming could also cause serious damage to the engine's cylinders. Water doesn't compress like steam and as the piston moved along the cylinder, it could often result in the cylinder head and cover being forced off. One way of trying to alleviate the pressure was by opening the cylinder cocks, or taps" as they were known.) By the time they were approaching Thorne, the priming had meant that the water level in the boiler was low. The driver would be feeling very pleased with himself that he had given the boiler a good clean out. He would then say to the fireman, "right, over to you now". That's when his work had to start. The fire would need building up to raise steam as soon as possible, because without steam he couldn't use the steam injectors which were the means of refilling the boiler with water from the tender.

To explain further: using the power of steam, the injector accelerates water to a speed of one mile in three seconds and its pressure is increased above that of the boiler from where the steam came. The water can be 'injected' into the boiler, through the clack valve. To operate the injector, the water valve is opened first, and water runs from the overflow pipe. Then the steam is slowly opened and the injector would begin to 'sing' with a low whistling noise, indicating that water is being injected into the boiler.

The power of steam and the way it has been utilized to move men and machinery has always fascinated me; I find it incredulous that on a Pacific locomotive, three or four "smallish" cylinders of steam measuring about 18"x 26" at 250lb of pressure can create so much power as to pull 12 coaches weighing upto 475 tons at speeds over 70 mph. It was only when I read an article in an old magazine, Trains Illustrated No 2 1946 on the subject of boiler pressure that it "brought it home" to me. It said "Boiler Pressure is defined as the force resulting from compression of steam inside a closed container. Because steam, like any other gas, is elastic, it is therefore compressible. Boiler pressure in the abstract has no definable limits and can be as great as the boiler is strong to resist it. The more steam you stuff into a boiler, the more the steam already inside it will shrink in volume and gain in pressure, and this sequence, if not checked, will continue until the pressure explodes the boiler. This is not a practicable way of raising steam. In practice you fix a limit to the above process according to the work you want your engine to do, make the boiler safe for that particular pressure and fit a control in the form of an automatic safety valve to ensure that the limit is not unduly exceeded. Now back to the tales…

Dick recalls one day when he was fireman on a WD Austerity taking 30 loose coupled coal wagons from Wath to Frodingham. The driver decided that he would show him how to fire. For much of the time, Dick was driving and the driver was sat in the fireman's seat smoking a woodbine. Very little coal went on and at Lowfield Junction Dick queried the driver's tactic. "We're allreyht kid" was his reply, by which time after they had climbed up to and through Conisborough tunnel, the steam pressure had dropped to 80lbs and they were coming to a halt. Furthermore they were getting to a point where there wouldn't be enough steam to operate the brake. I'll do the bloody firing", said Dick now feeling quite alarmed. There was no further dissent, the next two hours was sheer toil to get a good spread of fire across the whole grate and regain full steam pressure.

During his time as fireman, Dennis had two periods of teaming up and firing for his father. One was a 6 month period in the passenger link when they were doing the Sheffield to Hull train. Of course, he got absolutely excellent tuition and experience came quickly. On a Saturday morning when there were fewer officials around, dad would take the fireman's seat and tell Dennis, he was driving. He recalls one little incident, in 1951, whilst driving "under tuition" when they were returning from Cleethorpes and entering Doncaster station. Approaching the Frenchgate bridge; Dennis could see an approaching train crossing the line well in front of him. Although not yet seen, he knew the signal must be at red. Dad however, being in the right hand fireman's seat had a clear view of this signal; it was actually amber, but from that side he could not see the crossing train. He felt the engine stopping; Dennis was applying the brake but Dad was shouting at him to go on. Fortunately when Dennis stopped the engine, Dad had realised why. At the time, an inspector was also travelling on the footplate. He told Dennis not to move the train until he had walked to the signalbox to call the signal fitters out. Clearly this had been a fault for which the signalman could not be responsible.

Alf was also a fireman in this period. On this particular shift he was firing for Eric Smith on a football special which was travelling from Bishop Auckland to Wembley. They relieved the North East crew at Mexborough No 1; it was a large engine; either a Pacific or a V2 and they set off for London Marylebone at 3-30am, arriving at 7-30am. It was a very hard trip. The engine was badly clinkered up; trying to liven the fire up needed his constant attention and it wasn't steaming right. Furthermore, the tender was half empty and it required Alf to climb onto the tender and shovel the coal forward while the driver had to shovel it into the firebox. At Marylebone a football supporter had a can of beer in his hand and he said to Alf, "could you do one?" to which Alf replied " I cud yet that wi a knife and fork.". The supporter then said "here then an one for your mate". Alf said that his mate didn't drink and so he stood on Marylebone station and "supped" em both. Even today, Alf still likes his pint. When he got into the dormitories at Kentish Town, he asked everyone if they had seen a khaki shirt so wet with sweat; it was saturated. On the return trip, Alf said it was a different "ball game". He cleaned out the fire, gave it a good "cobbing" (plenty of coal all the way round) and got it well burning. They took the engine under the hopper at Neasden and filled the tender up. The return journey was a treat. Just outside Nottingham, Eric the driver said that he could go all the way to Newcastle on this engine; Alf replied he would go to Timbuktoo.

George recalls one of his first stints firing for a driver nicknamed "Gunboat". It was a full coal train coming from the west and they had relieved the Gorton crew at Barnsley Junction near Penistone. From here, they took the Worsborough Branch (a line built in 1880 to avoid Barnsley. To railwaymen, it was known as the "Plevna" because the 4 years it took to drive the two Silkstone tunnels coincided with the siege of Plevna in the Russo Turkish war). At 1 in 40, this was a steep gradient and all trains had to stop at the top level, before descending, so that the guard could pin (put brakes on) the first six wagons and then, every other one for the rest of the train. He drove over the hump and onto the descent very slowly until the guard shone his green light to signify all brakes on. Then, the regulator was opened and they were on their way. Before long, the engine was rolling; coal shaking out of the tender and George felt a little uneasy for his safety. "Aren't we going a bit too fast", enquired George, to which the Driver, sitting comfortably on his seat, burst into song "there is a happy land far away, where they had bread and jam three times a day". He was not concerned in the slightest.

Most drivers I spoke to could recall experiences as a fireman, of coming down Worsborough bank. Of course it was much easier coming down; the fireman could get his feet up, rest and have a smoke. Vic relates to one driver as they were on their way down the bank when he enquired and trying to remain polite, "We're going fast aren't we?" "Aye", he said, "we're running away, I can't do nought, put hand brake on and we'll start whistling as we're going down through Wentworth". As he blew the engine whistle, the signalmen manning boxes with level crossings would open the gates as quickly as possible, because he knew the train was in trouble. They shot through Worsborough crossing, Worsborough Bridge, Glasshouse, and they eventually managed to pull up at Lewden. Not enough wagon brakes had been put down, and although the guard has a brake in his van; he can't apply it heavily because the wheels would then just slide.

If an engine ever ran out of steam; then things came to a halt. It wasn't often; but it could occur if an engine had come a long distance and its bars were clinkered up. If it happened, the driver would request a signalman to put him in a loop or sidings so the fireman could clean the fire out.

George White had one recollection of this when he was firing for Jack Bates on a Sheffield to Scarborough excursion. They relieved the Sheffield crew on Mexborough station; the engine was a K3 and they soon noticed that they only had 120lbs of steam (working pressure 180lbs). This wasn't expected for the engine had only come from Sheffield. However, with ten coaches and a poor fire, they struggled and struggled and struggled. This was the hardest day's work George had done in his life; but just outside Scarborough, near Seamer, pressure had dropped to 110lbs and the vaccuum brakes went on. The Driver walked to the signalbox and asked the signalman to give him 30 minutes to clean the fire out. Being on the main line when he stopped; obviously meant he needed train protection. The engine was very badly clinkered up; (clinkers were termed "horses heads"), obviously it had been used before and had not been properly prepared for this run. The Driver refused to take the engine back; it was left at Scarborough and they were given another K3; but this time with a good healthy fire and a full head of steam; there was even time for George to put his feet up for a while on the way back. Firemen had preferences on which engines were considered better for steaming. It wasn't down to individual engines but more to engine types. The Robinson O4 superheater was always considered the fireman's friend, the WD Austerity with its large firebox likewise, then the J11 Pom Pom and the Derby Black 5s. The hardest were the K3s.

CHAPTER 8

DRIVER REMINISCENCES.

Everything in this chapter has been written from conversations with retired drivers. It includes memories of working practice as well as a few personal stories. It is very variable in content and not in any particular chronological order.

Dennis Porter and Ron Fareham passed for drivers in 1951.Their promotion had been pretty rapid, starting out as cleaners in 1939 and 1940 respectively. They were still only in their late twenties, they still had their boyish youthful looks about them and the older York and Sheffield men who had taken half a career to get to driver, would when relieved at Mexborough by Dennis and Ron, be very sceptical at leaving the locomotive with such young people. Dennis explained to me that variety in the work came from driving different locomotive types, from taking slow, mixed or fast freight or passenger, or from the different routes that the driver was signed up for. Some drivers would opt for the colliery workings, others would go onto the top express links. Dennis himself, was keen to get several routes under his belt; they were short of drivers withYork station route knowledge and he soon volunteered to learn this route after being approached. (there were actually 16 different routes which could be taken from one signal outside York station). He was allowed two days for studying the route, being tutored & examined by Inspector Smith at York. This gentleman had the task of training all drivers from all regions. If you didn't learn this route, then of course you couldn't get to Scarborough, Newcastle or other places beyond York. Once passed; you "signed the route card".

Many interesting trains would come down from York on the S&K (Swinton & Knottingley Joint Railway); but instead of going onto Wath Road Junction and Sheffield, they would branch off at the Dearne Junction and drop down onto the Great Central line at Wragby Row, before stopping at Mexborough West Junction to be relieved by Mexborough men. A relief cabin outside Mexborough No 1 box provided shelter whilst waiting for up or down trains on the Woodford, Annesley – York routes; - usually, I was told; with a rat or two in attendance. Many of these trains were fast freight coming from the North of England down to London; the South or South West. From Mexborough, they would be routed down the GCR to Darnall and on to Woodford (near Banbury), where the Mexborough men would be relieved. Some drivers had route knowledge down to Wembley and would pick up through football specials at Mexborough. Newcastle United were in the cup final in May 1951, 1952 and 1955. Bringing all the supporters down to Wembley usually meant running up to a dozen trains from Newcastle. The operation had to go like clockwork and would first commence with Gateshead Loco Depot sending a Pacific locomotive (A3 or V2) light engine down to Mexborough on the day before. The first football special would arrive at Mexborough West Junction in the early hours of Saturday morning. The engine and crew would come off and the light engine with a Mexborough crew would take over. They would go all the way to Wembley after first picking up an Inspector (who had the route knowledge) at Leicester. The unhooked Pacific would then be 'whipped' into the sheds for coaling, watering, ash & clinker removal, fire building up, and lubricators filling with oil. This was then ready to go onto special no. 2 which would be arriving at Mexborough West Junction. The whole process was then repeated for the engine which had been unhooked from special No 2.

Dennis Porter and Ken Butterfield were supervising this operation one year. Everything went to plan until Special No 8 arrived. The train came to a halt well before it got to Mexborough Junction and the driver , with 21" of vacuum showing and falling, knew the communication chord had been pulled. (when the brakes are full off, there is a 30" vacuum. When the communication chord is pulled, about 5" of vacuum is left in the brake pipe to allow the driver to move the train on; should it stop in a tunnel for instance.). There wasn't much time to investigate but Ken had to walk the length of the train to see which chord had been pulled and identify the emergency. It was pretty apparent that this was not going to be easy. In every compartment the Magpie supporters were in great merriment and much laughter and drinking was going on. No emergency became apparent; there wasn't time to investigate further, not that many would have been in a serious state of mind to co-operate anyway, and rather than waste much time in seeking out the culprit, Ken decided for quickness to hop onto the roof of the last coach and reset the communication chord butterfly assembly from there. All else went quite smoothly with this operation.

They would also work the returns as far north as York. The Newcastle , York to Bournemouth passenger train was a Saturday only summer working. This would come down to Mexborough West arriving at approximately 11-20am. It was a trainspotters ' dream. The engine was invariably a Pacific, V2, A3, even a rare A4, pulling a long rake of green (Southern Region) coaches. Mexborough men would relieve the crew and then the train would be routed via Darnall. It did not touch Sheffield, because another train ran from Manchester to Bournemouth via Sheffield. There were also occasions when the main east coast line was blocked and trains would then use the S&K route via Mexborough rejoining the main line at either Potteric Carr or via Darnall at Retford.

Vic Parkes was promoted to driver on 10th August 1959 along with colleagues Ernest England and Lionel Hand. He was now aged 40 and had joined LNER in 1937. Firemen were always joking with drivers "when are you going to retire", for it was a fact that it was the drivers who were stopping promotion. He gave me accounts of working the Worsborough branch and the Beyer Garratt. I have included them in this chapter. (Ron Fareham has also covered these subjects in great detail and these can be read in his chapter).

The Beyer Garatt engine no 2395 was a solitary class U1 2-8-0 + 0-8-2 designed for banking duties on the Worsborough incline and built by Beyer Peacock & Co Ltd at Gorton. It was built in 1925 and was the most powerful steam locomotive ever to run in this country. It was basically a pair of class O2 three cylinder 2-8-0s under one boiler. After nationalisation, it was renumbered 69999. It had a long period of use but it was ultimately displaced by electrification. The loco was returned to Gorton for conversion to oil burning and in 1955, it was sent to do banking duties on the Lickey incline, near Birmingham. It did not prove successful; it was returned after 3 months and it was finally condemned on the 23rd December of that year.

Although the Garratt was stationed at Mexborough, when it was working and not in for repair, it was only returned to the depot at weekends. On a Sunday night, the two crew assigned to this duty would prepare the engine; ie firing, watering and oiling and then take the engine up to Wentworth Junction on the Worsborough branch. The same Mexborough men would do the first banking duty of the week, but on their return, they would be relieved by Barnsley men who would then man the engine for the remainder of the week. Banking involved pushing loaded coal trains up the 1 in 40 bank from Worsborough Junction to West Silkstone; a distance of about 2¾ miles and a round trip of about one hour if there were no delays. The most unpleasant part of this journey was going through the two Silkstone tunnels. On the heavier trains, there would be two pulling engines and at the rear, either two Robinson O4s or the Garratt. The smoke and steam was so thick, you were compelled to take whatever action you could to facilitate breathing. One driver always had a top coat with him; even in the middle of summer, and when entering the tunnels; would put the coat over his head to protect his airways. Returning light engine; they would often sit on the footplate floor because the steam had the effect of pushing the smoke upwards. The Garratt would then return to Mexborough on Saturday, after banking as many as 60+ coal trains in the week.

From Wath Yard, there would be a coal train of 60 wagons plus leaving every hour to go to Mottram or Manchester. Additionally, there were all kinds of cross country freight trains; eg fish, newspapers, meat, fruit and steel etc which meant that there were always trains going up and down the Worsborough branch. On leaving Wath, there would be one loco at the front and one at the back. On arriving at Wentworth Junction, another engine would hook on at the front and another would bank, unattached, from the rear, making four engines in total. Onwards and upwards they would go to West Silkstone where the train would be stopped in a loop. The leading engine and rear banking engines would then unhook and return down the bank together. Even on a Sunday, Vic has known as many as 10 trains stacked all the way back from Wentworth to Lewden.

Time on the railways didn't matter. Put simply, the job had to be done and some of these crews would work a 10, 12 or 14 hour shift. Irrespective of the number of hours worked, no train crews could sign on for duty again until they had 12 hours off duty. If one, say, worked as many as 14, one had to have 12 hours off before reporting for further duty. Therefore if you were booked on for 8am starts; and worked 14 hours, you would start the next day at 10am. At weekends, if say on a night shift starting at 10pm and not finishing until noon or afterwards on the Saturday, you would get the Saturday night shift off; albeit you would be paid for it. This was a popular dodge for the younger men and if possible, they would do anything to string out the shift into the afternoon so they could have Saturday night off; with pay!

There were some inglorious tasks attached to a footplateman's job. For instance, on arrival on the ashpits, the driver would report to the clerk in the foreman's cabin (known at Mexborough as Paraffin Villa). All engines arriving or departing the depot would be booked in or out of here. On booking in, if his shift was not up, he would be instructed to dispose of his engine (ie to put it away). Vic explained that an hour was allowed for this. If the loco was due for boiler washing or firebox repairs, then all the fire had to be removed, if it wasn't, then just the ash and clinker would be removed, leaving just a good clean fire in the firebox. This information would be given to the driver when he booked in.

So the fireman had to first clean the fire out. There were three methods of doing this, depending on the type of loco. Some had drop bars, which, when operated by handles would push the clinker into the ash pan, others had rocker bars but on locos where neither were fitted, the fireman had to remove the clinker through the firebox door using a clinker shovel (also known as a dart). This was a steel shovel with an 8 foot long handle. This was a hard job, but then, so was the removal of ash from the ash pan with the first two methods. The fireman had to enter the pit and rake the ash out with a long rake. This was a dirty job, particularly if the wind was blowing towards you. After cleaning the fire and ash pan, the next job was cleaning the smoke box of soot, ash and grit. Some locos, mainly GCR ones had a small trap door in the box and when opened the grit emptied out of it; on others it had to be shoveled out. Finally the sand boxes had to be filled. This involved a long walk to the sand pit which was located near the coaling stage but it often meant a 400 yard walk from the engine being worked upon and that could be repeated 3 or 4 times if several buckets of sand were required. Whilst the fireman was thus engaged, the driver would be examining the loco for any defects. If a fireman had a good driver, he would give him a hand with the disposal. Putting an engine away was a very tiring job; coming at the end of your shift.

There were also some men graded labourers and called firedroppers who did nothing but cleaning and dropping fires, removing ash and cleaning the smokeboxes. At the Mexborough depot, there were four, post war; Joe Caress, Jack Tingle, Arthur Goldspink and Jack Oliver. They were allocated to do so many locos, and that constituted a shift. After that, they could do other locos (different loco types had different times for disposal) which amounted to overtime. These men were so adept at disposal, they could do above 20 engines per shift. A driver could be informed, when he booked in, that there was a firedropper available. In that case, the crew were told to examine and sand the loco. This was known as "Sand and tapping". The "Tapping" was because the driver tapped the various parts of the loco with a spanner. This was to detect flaws in the motion side rods and other moving metal parts. A dull sound would confirm a flaw. This was similar in principle to the wheel tapper who would walk down the length of a passenger train tapping the wheels to detect flaws. Coaling, watering and relighting was the job of the shed staff.

Similarly, on booking on for duty, a driver had to read a book showing where all the line cautions were on the route he was going on. An hour was then allotted to prepare the engine. The driver would take the number of the engine he was allocated to from the roster board; and then go to the oil stores for half a gallon of oil. The driver would then oil all the motion; side rods, connecting rods etc and of course this entailed going under the frames and oiling the inside motions as well. (Some drivers would get their firemen to do this if they could). The axle boxes also had to be oiled and this meant having to prize the box lids up. They were often full of water and this had to be pumped out with a small pump before oil could be applied. Meanwhile the fireman had to go to the lamp room to collect two lamps; one for back and front; and which had to then be cleaned and filled with paraffin. Next the gauge lamp had to be filled with rape oil. This has a low flash point; because the lamp would get quite hot as it was hung from the footplate steam pipe. Then there was a whole host of tools the fireman had to collect from the stores, the shovel, the coal hammer, the darts (for cleaning the fire if they were not on the loco), the bucket, cloths, gauge cock spanners, gauge glasses, rubber washes (gauge glasses were prone to breaking and the fireman had to be prepared to cut off escaping steam and replace the glass; a job which could be done in a few minutes if he had the tools). He would then go to the engine and build up the fire.

All procedures were documented and here I will quote a few extracts from the British Railways Rule Book 1950 which further illustrates the above.

"On arrival at the locomotive, the Driver should test the water gauges, satisfy himself that the fusible plugs and tubes are tight, note the condition of the fire and steam pressure, and see that the Fireman is correctly attending to his duties." [Fusible Plugs were a safety device. They were fitted into the crown plate on the top of the firebox. If the water in the boiler got too low, a lead plug would be exposed to the heat of the fire. This would melt, and any water left in the boiler would crash down onto the fire and put it out, preventing an explosion.]

"He should see both injectors tested and himself test the brake and sand

gear, and if any defects are observed, take steps immediately to have them remedied."

"In making his examination and oiling of the locomotive, the Driver should have a definite system and always work to it. He should be acquainted with the differences in the layout of the various classes of engines with which he may have to deal in the course of his duties. By commencing at the same point, and always in the same order, he will deal with the various parts methodically."

The Rule Book was also a bit like the Highway Code but a Railway Code. Nothing was left to chance and the modern reader with so much traffic and technology around him, would think that with so many things, it was stating the obvious. However, there were no training classes as such; a Driver's knowledge was acquired from exchanges with older Drivers throughout his fireman years and the book simply served to emphasise these things. A couple of extracts read as follows:-

"A Driver should have a thorough knowledge of the route over which the train is required to travel and have signed his Route Knowledge Card to this effect. If he is not fully conversant with any section he should obtain the services of a competent conductor".

"The Driver must have with him on his engine a complete set of lamps, not less than 12 detonators and two red flags and such tools as may be described by the Motive Power Superintendent. He is responsible for seeing that the prescribed lamps etc., are exhibited and in good order and lighted when necessary. He must keep a good look out when the engine is in motion, sound the engine whistle when necessary, especially as a warning to persons on the line and frequently when passing through tunnels, see that the proper signals are exhibited, observe and obey all signals, and all speed restrictions, have his fireman disengaged when passing signalboxes, start his train carefully and proceed along the proper line, stop his train with care, paying particular attention to the state of the weather, the condition of the rails and the gradient as well as the length and weight of the train."

Imagine the difference that the Diesel or Electric Locomotives made. All that was necessary was to turn a key to stop or start the engine or put up the pantograph for the electrical supply. 15 minutes from booking on would be the maximum time for preparing the diesel or the electric. The savings in manhours would be immense. With steam, because there was so much preparation time, punctuality was important. If one was only 20 minutes late reporting for duty, the likelihood would be that someone else would have been allocated to your job with the probability that you would not get another job. One could not afford to be late; so nearly everybody arrived on time. It was strict; but everybody knew what they were doing; the driver knew what he was doing, the fireman knew what he was doing; they knew what time they were leaving; if going to Wath Yard, the guard would be waiting; he would direct the engine to the train and hook it on. Mexboro Loco Shed was indeed a well run organisation.

Then there were those drivers who, in moderation, did like their pint. One such was in a queue of trains waiting to be banked up Worsborough Bank. He was in the habit when he knew there would be a big hold up of leaving the fireman on his engine and slipping off for a pint. On one occasion, he was in a pub in Worsborough for an hour; he'd calculated there were six trains queueing and each would take half an hour. When he returned, he couldn't find his train. He immediately thought his fireman had took the train on and he jumped onto the next train to get a lift up the bank to Penistone. He still couldn't see his train. What had actually happened was that the line was congesting with more and more trains and his train had been put on the Colliery Branch Line at Wentworth Junction. Most of his shift was therefore spent looking for his train which fortunately had been in safe hands with his fireman.

Stealing was a disciplinary offence and was punishable by instant dismissal. It rarely happened. Coal however was in limitless quantities; and supplies were maintained at the depot to fill up to 100+ engine tenders per day. There were a few eccentric drivers who took advantage of that and used to give a few lumps of coal away as a service to mankind or in lieu of a favour rendered. It was condoned; because it wasn't missed; these drivers were looked upon as "little gods" and whatever their fireman was asked to do, it was carried out. There was always a driver who looked after himself. One fireman was with such a driver over a long period. It was typical that when he was putting a large lump of coal in the firebox , the driver would say " eh, don't throw that on't fire", and he would have to stack them up on the footplate until he was told to throw them off onto the side of the track; not a "million miles" from where the driver lived.

It was on one link, when the crew would run light engine from Mexborough to Milford to pick up a southbound freight train , (they would be relieved at Mexborough) that one driver would be known to stop at several remote railway cottages on the way up. He would tell his fireman to go to the house, knock and tell them I've brought them some "coil", and then they will give you some eggs. It was customary to receive a dozen or two. This driver became very friendly with many of the cottage occupants; and in 'waltzing' down their path to greet them; a little embrace was never out of the way. On one occasion, he was even known to have returned to the footplate with a live cockrel; the bit of coal he left there must have been appreciated!

Another roster was to leave the shed at Mexborough and go to Kilnhurst light engine and wait at the back of the station for a Sheffield to Mottram freight. On arrival, the engine would then go to the back of the train and bank it up to Dunford. The story goes .... on one occasion when waiting for the freight train, the driver told his fireman that he and the stationmaster were going into the Ship Inn for a pint. "While we're away" he said, " throw 'coil' off into't stationmaster's'coil' place". The engine had been conveniently positioned for this. After quite a bit of coal had been transferred from the tender to the coal house, the fireman went to the pub and told the driver he had finished. The driver came out of the pub; had a look in the coal place, and said "tha'nt thrown enough coil off, fill't bloody coal place full". So the coal house was filled to the top. The fireman returned to the Ship and the stationmaster bought him a pint as well. The time was being idled away of course because they were still waiting for the freight train, which was often delayed. The fireman kept popping out; checking on the engine, the signals and for the arrival of the freight. He would then pop back into the Ship. Two or three pints were drunk; all paid for by the stationmaster, and on leaving, a 'ten bob note' was pushed into the palm of the driver's hand as further appreciation for filling the coal place up. On arriving at Dunford; much coal having been used in firing up the bank to raise steam; the fireman said to the driver, "eh up Fred; we havn't enough coil to bank another train upto Dunford". (This additional banking turn was part of the roster.) "Oh", he said, "it doesn't matter", and he promptly went to phone Mexborough shed to say they would need to come back for coal. The foreman was in disbelief; because he knew that all engines were sufficiently coaled to do two trips up the bank. They therefore returned to Mexborough to coal up. The driver was disciplined with a Form One; but nothing was said which would explain the "mystery". In those days, everything was easy going; the drivers were like "little tin gods"; many doing things which could get them into trouble; like leaving an engine and going for a pint; or taking three hours to get to Frodingham instead of one; but as long as the job got done; discipline would go no further than the issuing of a form one; which several drivers could have papered a bedroom with; they had that many.

Rates of pay on the railways in steam days compared less favourably with other industries of the time. Joe Raybould printed the rates of pay for footplate staff in 1946 in his book.

RATES OF PAY FOR FOOTPLATE STAFF 1946

Engine Cleaners	Shillings/Pence	Decimal
16 Years	40s 6p	£ 2.02½
17 "	46s 6p	£ 2.32½
18 "	55s	£ 2.75
19 "	58s	£ 2.90
20 "	85s	£ 4.25
21 "	85s	£ 4.25
22 "	85s	£ 4.25
Drivers		
1st Year	113s 6p	£ 5.67½
2nd "	113s 6p	£ 5.67½
3rd "	115s 6p	£ 5.77½
4th "	115s 6p	£ 5.77½
5th "	120s 6p	£ 6.02½
6th "	126s 6p	£ 6.32½
Firemen		
1st Year	93s 6p	£ 4.67½
2nd "	93s 6p	£ 4.67½
3rd "	96s 6p	£ 4.82½
4th "	96s 6p	£ 4.82½
5th - 10th "	102s 6p	£ 5.12½
11th year onward	107s 6p	£ 5.37½

All these rates of pay were all for a 48 hour week. Prior to the 1939-1945 war top rates of pay for the following were....

Cleaners 22 years old 48s = £2.40p
Firemen 11 year onward 72s = £3.60p
Driver 6th year onward 90s = £4.50p

Rates of Pay – Courtesy J Raybould.

This has been reproduced in the picture on the previous page. Some drivers still have their P60s from the 68/69 tax year. A senior driver earned £1,230.1s gross and paid £113 tax. His net weekly pay would have been £21.9s.7d.

George White passed for Driving at the age of 35 and became a regular Driver at 40. He had had nearly 20 years on the shovel; it had been a long apprenticeship, but after so long a time, you certainly knew your job, he said. He was now able to pass onto his Firemen what he had learned from his Drivers who were always wanting to share their countless experiences with you; be it on loco handling or route finding. There were so many drivers who could not be faulted at their job, they knew the sounds of every crossing; every bridge, every sleeper; and they had you looking out for every semaphore. He didn't go in the passenger link (although he was required to do the occasional special); most of the routes he learnt were the pits, Gorton and Frodingham links and an LMS route to Toton. The night shift, George recalled, could start at any unearthly hour; sometimes it was midnight and George's wife would, in that case, be cooking a dinner at 11pm before he went to work. What she then packed him to take to work would be best described as a festive board; bacon, ham, eggs and onions; all of which could be cooked on the footplate. The injector exhaust was very handy for boiling an egg or an onion. These would be tied into a rag which would then be hung up onto the ejector pipe. The wheel would be cracked open for just sufficient steam to come out and permeate the rag. In no time at all, the cooking was done. Bacon would be wrapped in foil and cooked on the shovel in the firebox; indeed, potatoes, bread or anything which needed roasting or toasting would be done this way. Of course, as George reminded me, when you left for work, the last thing you would say to the wife was "expect me when you see me", and so having a good snap tin was important. One driver, he recalls, only ever had one thing in his snap tin; bread and cheese and the usual customary greeting when he met George on the footplate, would be "What's tha got for snap Whitey?" Despite the long and uncertain hours, routines had to be attended to at home and this is where his wife Barbara would give her support. Many people, just after the war, kept allotments to grow produce, and keep small livestock. George kept pigs. They needed feeding and if he was working abnormal hours or overtime, then Mrs White would harness their little black pony and do the rounds collecting potato peel and other kitchen food refuse. It would then be down to the allotment to light the boiler and boil the mashings into pig swill for feeding. Her two children would accompany her.

Of course, there were some perks as well. The L.N.E.R. Club on Rowms Lane would annually run a day trip to Cleethorpes when all the children would receive ten shillings in an envelope. The train would start from Mexborough and George would occasionally be rostered for fireman. On arrival at Cleethorpes, out of the train would get Mrs White and their two children. They would then walk up to the engine and give George his bag of fresh clothes. He would then go into the station and change into his seaside clothes so that they could all spend the day on the beach and in the pleasure gardens until it was time for George to return to the engine, change back into his boiler suit and prime the fire to raise steam for the journey home.

A forty year career also didn't go without memories of the more untoward experiences. These ranged from a fatal accident when at only 17, wartime and pitch black, a shed labourer walked out of the depot and across onto the junction where he put his head onto the main line. Another he recalls when on banking duties; on the Worsborough line. As second man on a Bo-Bo electric which was pushing from the rear of the train; they had got to the summit at Dunford. The train then continued towards Manchester and as distance emerged between the coal train and the electric, which was about to return down the gradient for the next banking duty, he saw the body of a man who had been fatally injured. Sadly, on this morbid note, he also recalled returning from York in 1983; this time on a diesel, when nearing Frickley, he saw a man with no shirt on, jump in front of the loco and put his head on the line. There was no time to stop to avoid the inevitable fatality. George stopped the train a few hundred yards down the line. He then had to walk back to assess the situation before reporting it. You had to be a hard man to take those terrible shocks which a few other drivers also experienced. Other memories are of that severe winter in 1947 when, as fireman for Fred Gascoigne, they were trapped in snowdrifts near to Woodhead

Dennis Porter brought the Bardic Lamp to my home to show me how it worked.

tunnel for 16 hours before a train equipped with a snowplough could get them out. He was never one to have been frightened whilst working on the railways, but probably the nearest to that was on a moonlit night when taking a fish train to Guide Bridge. Just before rounding the corner to cross the viaduct at Godley, he looked back out of the engine and noticed an axle box on fire. They were travelling very fast and sparks were flying. He hoped and prayed that the fish wagon would not come to grief whilst on the viaduct; he had visions of getting derailed and the loco plunging over the viaduct. He was lucky.

All drivers were personally issued with a Bardic Lamp. This was a practical torch which the drivers, could not manage without. It wasn't envisaged in the steam days, but a driver wouldn't dare to go to work on diesels without it, for the engine compartments and electrical cupboards were too dark. On steamers; they were used a lot to check water gauge levels as not all footplates had electric lighting and there were some long tunnels; the Dore & Totley being over 3.5 miles long. These lamps could be turned to red or green; they could be used as a train light in an emergency; their use was so versatile. When a driver retired, it was customary for him to retain the lamp if he so wished. Many of them can be picked up these days in railwayana auctions.

CHAPTER 9

THE WAR YEARS

Because of its location, "a junction to anywhere", the war years proved very busy ones for the Mexborough Depot. Not only was it business as usual with serving all the collieries and local industry, but so much more east, west, north and south traffic was routed via Mexborough. There were troop, ammunition, ambulance, POW trains, and then freight trains carrying anything from tanks and other military equipment to gas cylinders for the barrage balloons; many of them required Mexborough relief crew and engines. Inevitably, in discussing old times with Mexborough footplatemen, each and every one would relate to an experience in the war years and I have therefore decided to focus all these little tales under one chapter to try and recapture the adrenalin of those days.

Many recall the long trains of American Troops passing through the steeply curved Mexboro West junction at a slow 15mph on their way to York; they would be stationed at Harrogate. It was amazing how the "silent telegraph" worked so effectively, for all the trains would be cheered by hordes of Mexborough women who had collected by the railings to give them a waive, for they knew, in return, the Yanks would throw them chocolates or cigarettes.

In the war, there were certain procedures for warning footplatemen of air raids. They were often experienced on the Hull link because that city suffered so much bombing. Vic recalls being brought to a near stop (by signals) at Stainforth and the signalman would show a purple lamp from his box. The driver would give a toot on the whistle to say he had seen it. Purple meant there were possibilities of air raids. Passing Staddlethorpe, the signalman was showing a yellow light which meant that an air raid was imminent. Nevertheless, the train had to keep going. At Brough, the signalman was showing a red light, which meant there was an air raid in Hull; but even so, the train kept going; even though they could see the glow of fires in the city. (The reason the trains kept going was that if they stopped, they stopped the whole system; that is, all the trains behind them). They ran into the Dairycoates goods yard. They came to a stop and it was the guard's job to then walk to the front of the train and unhook the engine. On this particular night, there were bombs dropping all over. Their engine was a Geordie type with a wooden roof over the footplate; and whilst tending to things; they could hear bits of shrapnel dropping onto the roof. The driver asked Vic to go to the rear of the train to see if he could see the shunter. For protection, each footplateman was provided with a tin helmet and a gas mask., but Vic never used to take his. On this night, the guard said "I've got my tin hat, I'll go and have a look". He was just stepping down off the footplate when a bomb exploded not 200 yards away. He was back on the footplate in a flash! Once hooked off, they were off to the shed. Regulation was that in an air raid, the firebox door had to be kept closed, so as not to throw light; but even on this night when there was so much burning, the driver wouldn't agree to opening the firebox door. No coal could therefore be put on the fire and the engine had to limp to the shed under a much reduced steam pressure of about 50psi. Whilst dropping the fire in the shed, there was light everywhere:- bombers dropping flares; anti aircraft guns firing "flaming onions". Once in the office and booked off, there were several sets of Mexborough men waiting to go back. A bomb dropped close by and the fierce explosion caused the window blinds to roll up. One driver, nicknamed "sausage Jackson" shot straight underneath the table like a dog that had been scolded.

During the war, Alf recalls firing for Mervyn Bell. They had relieved a crew from York and picked up a Green Arrow V2 at Mexborough No 1 box. The train consisted of gas cylinders for barrage balloons. It was night. There was no moon; blackouts were in force and they were running under the signalman's warning known as "air raid red". This meant that the glow of the engine fires had to be suppressed. On the V2, a tarpaulin stretched across from the roof of the cab to the tender and this was supposed to obliterate the fire glow; but in practice, it didn't really do the job. It was difficult to hear anything above the

The Great Central Railway erected a plaque on Mexborough Station commemorating the railwaymen of Mexborough who gave their lives in the First World War 1914-1918. Courtesy Giles Brearley.

sound of the engine, but on this night, shortly after leaving Mexboro, the driver said to Alf that he could hear an aeroplane above and it didn't sound like one of ours. They reached their destination, Annesley Yard (just north of Nottingham) and then took the loco to Annesley shed. There, they were to learn that German planes had dropped bombs on Nottingham. Had they been following Alf's train at any time, he wondered? – quite possibly.

Dennis recalls firing for driver Albert Spring. They had also picked up a southbound freight consisting of RAF lorries, each with 45 gas cylinders for barrage balloons, loaded onto flat wagons. It had come from Haverton Hill, 90 miles north of York and was destined for Ashford in Kent. The train was worked by a Green Arrow V2 4812; it would have been too heavy for the lighter B1s or B16s. It was daytime and they had got as far as Tinsley loop when the air raid sirens commenced. They could see the aircraft and the bombs dropping and in sheer terror, they jumped off the loco and scrambled underneath it for shelter. It was a fortunate ending for after the air raid they emerged unscathed and got back onto the loco. It was then they noticed that across from them, a land mine which had been dropped some 10-15 yards away was swaying in the breeze suspended by its parachute chords on nearby telegraph wires. They quickly restarted the train and took it into Sheffield Victoria station where they again left it and took refuge in an air raid shelter. By 5am the next morning the blitz was over and on crawling out of the shelter, a quick survey of the scene revealed a whole rake of passenger coaches had been hit and were burnt out. They quickly rescued their own engine and hastened back light engine to Mexborough.

One driver that Jo fired for had signed the route to Hull and so Jo went there quite often during the war years. He recalls:- All locos were fitted with blackout sheets that fitted from cab to tender and many also hung down at the cab sides. In addition the cab windows were partly painted to eliminate any light escaping, you had to peer between the sheet and the cab side to see the signals. The sheets were OK in winter but on a warm summers night, they were a bit much. Many times he has walked down Hessle Road from Dairy Coates shed and later on passed piles of rubble which previously had been houses, pubs or shops. Often, you would be walking and suddenly hear an explosion; then the warning siren would sound, followed almost immediately by the all clear. They were what we called "Hit and Run" raiders. They used to fly in low over the North Sea; drop their bombs and be away. When Sheffield was blitzed, Jo mentions in his own book, one driver from Mexborough was working in that area and was injured during the blitz. He lost a leg.

1943 was a bumper year so far as new 2-8-0 designs were concerned. The LMS 8F engines were being built by, and used on the LNER; then in the early part of the year an American Army 2-8-0 design began making an appearance and the Ministry of Supply Austerity 2-8-0 followed later in the year. Ron Fareham, as you will gather from the next chapter, took a keen technical interest in the design and efficiency of different locomotive types but it might be interesting here to include his own account of the American S160. None were allocated to Mexborough, but many Mexborough drivers and firemen had to operate them as relief crew. 400 of them were loaned by the U.S. Army Transportation Corp. to British Railway companies to cope with the extra traffic as D-Day approached. The L.N.E.R. received 168 engines, of which 25 were based at Woodford.

"In February 1942, I was appointed officially as fireman, as distinct from being a passed cleaner or spare fireman. My first regular driver was Cliff Porter, and this was a good start for me. Cliff was then 48 years old and very active: he was a good engineman and light with the regulator. He signed a good many roads and was an all round good railwayman.

One night in June 1943, Cliff and I were given a Sheffield to Hull special to work forward from Mexborough to destination. The engine number given to us by the loco foreman was 1834. This number was new to me and I made comment on it. Cliff said "Oh it's either a K3 or a standard J39" and as I didn't know all the LNER number groups, I didn't argue. We reported at Mexborough No 3 box and the signalman, Bert Parr, said, "He's approaching the home signal but I can't run him yet. You can relieve him at the signal if

WAR REPORT

The S160S were all transported across the Atlantic as deck cargo, secured by heavy chains and bars. The ships were in convoy escorted by the Royal Navy and other locomotives can just be made out on the deck of the sister ship further out. Many of the ships were from Norway, and its seamen remained loyal to the Allied cause, though their country was occupied by the Germans. A special Norwegian Merchant Navy was established in England, "Nortraship", which became the largest shipping company in the world. Ships conveying eighteen US locomotives were lost by enemy action, despite being in convoy you wish". At that, we made our way to the signal gantry. The night was pitch dark and of course the blackout was in operation, but as we approached the engine I could see its dim outline. What I saw was unfamiliar. At that time, I had been taking the Railway Magazine for over two years and had read about the USA 2-8-0s arriving in Britain. There was also a photograph of the cab interior accompanying the article. As we drew level with the locomotive, I could see the very wide cab window as it framed the reflection of the firelight in the cab; and then it struck me. "It's a yankee engine", I said. Cliff didn't seem to be too pleased about this. "Oh I don't know anything about those" he said, and the fact that there were no cab steps didn't make things any better. We both clambered cautiously up the unfamiliar tender steps – it was really a ladder; and into the cab.

The first thing to meet us were vertical canvas curtains hanging down from the back of the cab roof and which could be drawn across the rear of the cab in case of "air raid purple", instead of the more normal overall sheet attached to the tender. The Sheffield crew then set about instructing us on the whereabouts of all the equipment.

The firedoor, which opened with a latch, was oval in shape and seemed a crude affair to me; it looked more like the door on a domestic "copper" (wash boiler) found in most English kitchens. I later found out that it could also be secured on the first latch; and so admit a secondary amount of air to the fire. There were also small round holes which could admit air. The

ATLANTIC TRAIN

Ship of S160s and tenders arriving at Cardiff docks in November 1942.

Ships of S160s and tenders arriving at Cardiff docks in November 1942

boiler water gauge was something quite new to us. There was only one at the fireman's side, and this comprised a heavy metal frame with a thick glass front; the back of the interior surface was facetted and coloured silver. The water inside the gauge showed up black. To compensate for the lack of a second water gauge there were test cocks, such as the Great Eastern engines had. The US engine had three cocks arranged in a sloping row and when used, discharged into a small trough with a drain pipe. The water gauge steam, water and drain cocks were operated not by small handles, but by wheels made of heavy gauge wire. The steam cock was high up near the cab roof, but with typical American practicality, the operating spindle for this cock was coupled, via a universal joint, to a very long extension rod so that it could be shut off by the driver from a distance, in case of a burst.

This water gauge steam valve was, literally, a death trap, because a number of lives were lost on the LNER and GWR owing to the cock being closed and thereby showing a false level of water in the boiler. The outcome here was a boiler explosion and collapse of the firebox crown sheet. The cause of these disasters was the boiler water gauge steam cock being closed. With British boiler water gauges, these cocks were fitted with handles, and one could see immediately whether the cock was open or closed. With the American gauges, operated by wheels, one had to operate the wheel to check its position. There was of course always the possibility that an "out of sight out of mind" syndrome could develop with both footplate and fitting staff and apparently, this is what happened. Of course, wartime and unfamiliarity could have played a part; there was no training of footplate crews and word of mouth was thought to be sufficient.

There were actually three boiler explosions while the class S160s were being operated by British crews. The first occurred on November 17th 1943 at Honeybourne on the GWR when the 2-35pm Banbury to Margam was being worked by US No 2403, one of the ALCO batch. Three sets of men involved; the first a Banbury crew who worked only 20 miles before being relieved; the second set worked a further 15 miles before they too were relieved. All three drivers said that they tested the boiler water gauge just after getting into the cab. Only the second set seemed to doubt the operation of the water gauge because of some "bubbling" in the glass, but after draining the glass they seemed satisfied. On approaching Honeybourne, the firebox roofplate collapsed, seriously scalding the fireman. This did not stop him from walking nearly a mile to the next signal box, but he died later the same day.

A second explosion occurred on 12th January 1944 with US No 2363, one of the group built by the Baldwin Co. In this case, the crew had heard a bang in the firebox but on examining it, could not see anything amiss. The driver then made provision to stop at Thurston, between Haughly Junction and Bury St Edmonds to examine the firebox more thoroughly. The crown collapsed before they arrived. Both survived though injured. The men said they had tested the gauge.

The third case was the worst of all in that both members of the crew were killed. This occurred on the Great Central section of the LNER with US No 1707; another of the Baldwin Group. The date was the 30th August 1944 and the train was the 0245 Neasden to Woodford. The engine had been prepared for the crew working the train and the preparation men said they had tested the boiler water gauge. The train was late leaving Neasden and had gone only a few miles along its journey when the firebox roof collapsed in the middle of South Harrow tunnel. The explosion was of such violence that it forced the firebox roof plate down into the ash pan between the wheels. The smokebox door, firebars and arch bricks were found along the ballast. In the tunnel, the effect would be similar to that of a bomb going off. The crew suffered serious injuries and severe scalding. The fireman died within a few hours and the driver some days later.

It was of course, wartime, with only certain items being published in the newspapers. News of the explosion on US1707 however, passed very rapidly down the footplatemen's grapevine and everyone was put on their guard. The testing of the boiler water gauge, after the news, was performed very thoroughly indeed.

After these boiler incidents, some depots refused to work the US engines and there was considerable alarm in management circles. Boiler explosions had been thought things of the distant past. Large drawings of the US water gauge and full instructions as to its correct operation were hastily produced and exhibited at all LNER sheds and special glass fronted cases were made to contain the notices. At Mexborough shed, the notice was

USA S160 Class 2-8-0 No. 1846 near Quorn Leicestershire on an up mixed goods train. The locomotive is built to an American design with air brakes; the air pumps being fitted to the front of the smokebox. These are the locomotives which Mexborough men relieved on, during the war. Courtesy of Great Central Railway Society.

fixed above the fireplace in the enginemen's room in a very prominent position during the summer of 1944. I made a last nostalgic visit to Mexborough shed in 1965 (by that time I was locomotive inspector) just after the shed had closed and there above the fireplace, covered in dust, was the faded drawing of the American water gauge, 21 years after the last American 2-8-0 had left the shores of Britain! After the war, there were many firebox collapses in Europe and Asia as other railways made the painful discovery.

Apart from the water gauge, the Yanks were regarded as good engines; light on water, big firebox, good steamers with well protected and comfortable cabs; a wooden fold down seat for the fireman and an upholstered one, on the right side for the driver, but the layout of the cab equipment was understandably, different to British practice. The one universally condemned feature was the position of the sand box. There was only one, of large proportions and placed on top of the boiler! This, I know, was normal American practice but "over there" special arrangements for sand filling existed. The S160 on the other hand, was intended for operation in Europe, where such arrangements were not provided. There was plenty of room inside the frame for sand boxes (as with Thompson & Gresley practice) and the filling pipe and lid could have been placed on the framing. Each 80lb bucket of sand had to be lugged up 14' and seven steps to the sandbox lid: only one hand could be used, the other, perforce, having to grip the various handrails to prevent a fall. The language when a large amount of sand was needed was certainly ripe, and the designer's parentage constantly in doubt.

A very good feature of the design was the tender, which was a large one for a 2-8-0. It was a double bogied vehicle with a water tank capacity of 5400 gallons, 26% more than a Robinson O4, a loco of very similar power. This gave some drivers a false impression – they thought the Yankees were light on water, the truth being of course, that there was a good deal more water to go at. Some of the older drivers were never interested in how many gallons a tank held; their yardstick (precisely so) was the depth of water in a tank; measured as full tank, half tank, quarter and so on. In the aforementioned trip to Hull with 1834, the Sheffield driver had filled the tank at Tinsley, some seven miles before reaching Mexborough. Cliff Porter and I took the train the further 48 miles to Hull without further replenishment. On looking in the tank at Dairycoates shed on arrival in Hull, we still had a good half a tank left. I mentioned this and Cliff was most impressed. I reckon we had used just over 2000 gallons for the 55 mile run; ie 37 gallons per mile. Of course the line from Doncaster to Hull is all but level. Using the tank depth as a guide, one had a fairly large safety margin as the bottom half held much more water than the top half. This was certainly so with the Yankees, as the coal space took up a lot of room in the top half of the tender.

The total number of class S160 engines built in America was 2,120; almost 800 were sent to Britain, some to be worked here, others to be stored. Just over 400 were to be worked by the four main line railways, with the rest put into store awaiting the Invasion in June 1944. The working engines were divided between the four main companies as follows:- GWR – 190, LNER – 170, LMS – 50, GWR – 6.

These figures are rounded as there were some transfers between the companies; mainly GWR and LNER, and also between depots. It is therefore difficult to be hard and fast with the figures. As far as allocations to individual sheds are concerned, I can only give the LNER numbers with anything like accuracy. They were as follows:-March 50, Woodford 24, Stratford 25, Newcastle (Heaton) 25, Leeds (Neville Hill) 20, Edinburgh (St Margarets) 20 and Manchester (Gorton) 6. In total 170.

All the locomotives sent to Britain had to be passed through a main works for commissioning. All the LNER works were involved in this; Doncaster, Darlington, Gorton, Cowlairs and Stratford. Some attention was given to the wheel flanges, a British type hand brake was fitted on the tender, vacuum brakes were fitted as well as the steam brake equipment and screw couplings.

The locomotives to be stored presented a serious problem – where to put nearly 400 engines? An arrangement was reached with the GWR to store most of them in South Wales. There had been a number of competing companies involved in the coal trade and each had transfer sidings where coal from one company to another had to be stored awaiting movement. After 1923, many of these were redundant. However, the first batch of Yanks was stored on little used double tracks of the old Barry Railway with the up line used for storage and the down one converted to a single line arrangement. 119 US S160 engines were placed buffer to buffer on this piece of track, to a total length of 1 mile 660 yards, presenting a sight never seen before and one unlikely to be seen again.

After the war, the S160s were spread far and wide. As well as the near 800 sent to Britain for forward movement to the Continent, many others were shipped direct from USA to such places as Italy, Yugoslavia, Morocco, Austria, Tunisia, Algeria, Greece, Turkey, Hungary and Spain. Others were later sold to Poland, Czechoslovakia, South Korea and China. Others were sent to India and the Soviet Union. The American engines sent to Britain were built by three large companies as follows:- Baldwin 340, Lima 190, American Loco Co (ALCO) 266. This was a total of 796. 18 engines were lost at sea owing to enemy action.

Returning to that February night in 1942,, with so many 2-8-0s lost in transfers from the LNER, the arrival of 170 Class S160s was a godsend. The shortage would also be alleviated by the arrival of the WD Austerity class later in 1943, Mexborough getting a large tranche. All the S160s and Austerities were sent to the Continent in early 1944 and in 1946 some

Austerities came back to Britain. They were very run down. No Yanks ever came back; they were distributed around the partly ruined railways in Belgium, Holland and the rest. No S160s were ever allocated to Mexborough, but many continued to pass through and were relieved by Mexborough crews. I had plenty of experience on them, and liked them. The last one I saw was at the Keighley and Worth Valley Railway at Haworth, little enough could I have foreseen such an outcome in 1942. There I went on the footplate and spoke with the fitters. All the faults with the boiler water gauge steam cock appeared to be still present, but the staff were well aware of the situation".

Cedric Lockwood also gave me a similar account. He remembers firing for Bill Reynolds and they had to relieve a train coming from Woodford and going to York. The engine number was always displayed on the shed board, but Bill didn't recognise this one. They were walking upto Mexborough No 1, it was pitch black, it was the middle of the night, just puzzling what this loco might be. It was a USA S160.

As a fireman, Dennis Porter recalled signing on at Mexborough Loco and with the driver; they were allocated a V2 (a Gresley Green Arrow 2-6-2 of which two or three were allocated to Mexborough in the war years to handle the large heavy freights). They were to hook onto a train heading north at Kilnhurst station. On their reporting brief was a strict instruction to go no faster than 25mph. They were obviously very interested to know what was on the train. On arrival at Kilnhurst, they could see that the wagons were large flat loaders. The cargo was not covered up; it was there for all to see; a submarine. They were met by a Naval Officer who reiterated the instruction.

They got to York safely but it was very difficult keeping a V2 below 25mph and at times, the speed did creep up towards 50mph! Was this a Tirpitz connection?

It was July 1945, the war had just finished in Europe, although it continued in Japan until August. It was a time when everybody was in celebratory mood, and street parties proliferated. It was also a time when a tragic railway accident occurred involving Mexborough men and locos. Three engines had been on banking duties pushing laden coal trains up to Dunford. These were individual workings and as they were each approaching the end of their shift, they then set off light engine for Mexborough. The first loco to return was waiting a signal at Oxspring and then the second and third engine arrived. The drivers decided to hook up for the rest of the journey back to Mexborough. The three then proceeded to West Silkstone which is at the top of the bank (where the Garratt came off after banking). There was a caution on the signal. This signal was there for a specific reason. Although it was permissive block working, one train couldn't follow another but a light engine could follow a train. It was peculiar to Worsborough and it was done

110

so that the banking engines returning from West Silkstone to Wentworth were not unduly delayed having to wait for freight trains which were coming down the line all the time. The regulation with this arrangement was that the light engine had to stop at the signal so that the signalman could inform the driver what was on the line in front. On this particular day, the signalman explained in a correct manner about the train which was in front (and which would be on the same section once the light engines set off). And so they set off. As they were approaching Wentworth Junction they could see their next signal. It would normally be to the left of the track but because of the curvature on this section; it was sited on the right of the track but it was a very high signal so that there was always good sighting of it. However this accident occurred about 25 wagon lengths before this signal. A train coming up the bank had just set off after attaching a banking engine at each end. There was lots of smoke and steam as the four locomotives struck out. The driver of the leading light engines saw that this home signal was off. This could have been for the train in front and what should happen is that the light engine driver should see the signal reversed; that is put back on and pulled off again. However, because of all the smoke and steam from the train coming up, the light engine driver didn't see the signal drop and pull off again nor could he see the train in front and he mistook the signal in the off position as being for him. They were approaching the steepest part of the bank not knowing there was a short train getting ready to set off because the signal had been pulled for that train and not the light engines. This train incidentally, was full of supplies for Catterick; everything from food to blankets but it didn't set off immediately because the guard had to unbrake the wagons which had been previously pinned to come down the bank. Because of the amount of steam and smoke puthering out of the four engines coming up the bank, it probably helped to camaflage the train in front of the three engines. The driver of the leading light engine accepted the signal; took his brake off and 300 tons of locomotives on a 1 in 39 down gradient really "flew". As he rounded the curve, there was the train in front. The driver slammed his brake on, sounded his whistle, and told the fireman Cedric Lockwood to jump. Both Cedric and the driver jumped. The driver of the last locomotive also jumped. This was a hot summers evening about 7pm.

When Cedric came round; for he hit his head so hard on the ballast and temporarily passed out, he saw wagons piled up on top of his loco. Close by was the driver of the third engine who was in a bad way. He had split his head open on a rail and sadly, he died in hospital about 4am the next day. Neither Cedric, nor his driver who jumped and the other crew were so badly injured but he did feel that something was not right about his head; feeling it; there was thick black matted blood in his hair and several cuts on his head. He then felt an excrutiating pain in his neck as he tried to get up; unbeknowing he had broken his collar bone clean in two. Cedric then collapsed and the next thing he remembered was waking up in Barnsley Beckett hospital with bandages around his head. The guard on the train in front was fortunately "picking up" (unbraking) wagons; had he been in his guards van; he would most certainly have been crushed to death. The three engines had run through 8 or 9 wagons.

CHAPTER 10

RON FAREHAM

Ron started as a cleaner at Mexborough in January 1940. He had a distinguished career of over 40 years; progressing through the footplate grades, then taking further advancements as Running Foreman at March and Mexborough MPDs, as Controller at Rotherham Control Office, and Locomotive Inspector at Sheffield. In the early days of dieselisation, when all steam engine drivers had to go on conversion courses, he was instrumental in the organising and the running of those classes. His last promotion took him to Leeds where he became an Assistant Area Manager to the Area Manager Bob Oliver, with specific responsibility for Motive Power at Leeds Neville Hill MPD and the Leeds signing on points. His office was in Leeds station. He subsequently retired in 1984 at the age of 62..

Ron was one of the keenest and most conscientious of railwaymen. He "walked, talked and slept" railways. He took his job very seriously. He learned the "ins" and "outs" of each type of locomotive; how one compared in performance and handling technique with another, he was an absolute boffin with a steam locomotive, but he always wanted to share his knowledge, and in this respect he ran the Mutual Improvement classes at Mexborough which were designed to help colleagues further their technical understandings. He was also a prolific writer and he has contributed many articles to Railway

Ron Fareham in retirement, enjoying home life. Courtesy Mrs M Fareham.

Journals. I was never fortunate to meet Ron, he sadly passed away in January 2001. He will always be remembered for his deep interest in the railway, much of which he has put into words; some published, some not. His wife kindly donated his files to the archivist of the Great Central Railway Society and I am very grateful to Mrs Fareham, the Society and Irwell Press Limited, the publishers of British Railways Illustrated in giving me permission to include some of his work in this book. The Titles included are:-

1 Thoughts on entering a working life – 1935
2 And Quiet Flows the Don – Mexborough and its 3 engine sheds
3 The Busiest Branch ?- The Worsborough branch
4 Moving the Coal to Manchester
5 Wath Yard
6 A Personal View of the B1
7 Mutual Improvement Classes.
8 The Sheffield Division of British Railways

THOUGHTS ON ENTERING A WORKING LIFE : 1935 - R FAREHAM
On leaving school at 14 to start work, all young people deserve thoughtful handling, and help, to enable them to settle into what is in reality, a new life. At school, which commenced at 9 o'clock in the morning with various breaks, and finished at 4 o'clock in the afternoon, a youth was supervised, instructed and encouraged by people who were, for that time, well educated, kindly and understanding. At 14, one left this cosy world and entered the real one – childhood was finished.

When you entered a factory, in my case an iron foundry, where my father worked, the reception technique, in 1935, was non existent. You put a brass cheque through a slot in the time office wall, sometime before 7 o'clock: exactly at that time, a large card was put up in the office window with 7-30 printed upon it. If the cheque went in after the display of the card – then you were deducted 30 minutes pay. Such was the time discipline in 1935, and a very salutary beginning, for someone destined to follow a footplate career on the railway.

On reaching your station in the works, you were given a barrow made of sheet steel with an iron wheel; you then went into whichever moulding shop to which you had been assigned, to collect all the castings made by 16 moulders on the previous day and transported them to the fettling shop. The barrow turned the scales at 1½ cwt [approx. 76.2 kg]. and when filled with rough castings, was just about the limit of what a 14 year old boy could lift, and wheel the necessary 200 yards to the fettling shop. Here the castings were wire brushed and all the "flash" metal removed by either a grinding wheel or a file. After that, they were examined for defects – which was my father's department.

Despite the combined weight of barrow & castings, the "wheeling out" boys used to have contests to see who could get the most weight into a barrow. This game eventually resulted in my having to have three days off work with a bad back- I couldn't straighten up!

The entry into the trades of the Foundry was dependent upon two factors:-

(a) when it was your turn to make the move

(b) the trade in which the vacancy occurred

There was no choice of trade- if it was your turn you went. After 10 months "wheeling", I was given a place as an apprentice in the moulding shop. This was interesting work, and the technique was, initially, something of a mystery. In simplified form, damp sand (Greensand) was rammed around a wooden model (pattern). The pattern was then lifted out, leaving a void. Into the voids were placed "cores"- also of sand, but baked hard in a large oven – so as to be capable of being handled. Into the resulting mould, molten metal was poured and then allowed to cool. It was eventually removed from the sand and sent to be fettled as outlined previously.

After 3 years of moulding; I learned from my brother Eric that engine cleaners were wanted at the LNER Locomotive depot at Mexborough – some half a mile away. Eric had worked as an engine cleaner since July1937. This occurred in late August 1939, and, together with five other youths, I underwent a medical examination at Doncaster and was accepted for railway employment. However, before we could start work on the Railway, the second world war was declared and my brother brought home a letter for me, which stated – "owing to the current international situation, your services will now not be required" – nothing more!

This situation was, of course, very disappointing as I wanted to follow my brother into the locomotive department of the Railway – which I thought was a very interesting and rewarding job. However, some 4 months later, in January 1940, another letter arrived asking if I still wanted Railway employment and I commenced what was to be my life's work on Monday 29th January 1940.

EARLY MONTHS ON THE RAILWAY

I shall never forget my first morning on the Railway on January 29th 1940; it was two foot deep in snow, and I had to be at the depot, half a mile from home, at 0600 hours. This time was a good deal earlier than starting at the Foundry, but one soon became used to early hours.

Reporting at the depot time office window, the telephone attendant Fred Smeaton, showed me how to use the time clock and the attendant time card. Fred then took me into the engine shed to the premises which doubled as a Foreman Cleaner's office and a lamp room. There were three people in the place; Bob Lewis, the foreman cleaner; Frank Wilde, the lamp man; and Percy Croyden, a cleaner who issued rags and cleaning material, and who rejoiced under the name of the "Rag Lad".

My brother Eric, who had been a cleaner for the previous three years, and was always a clean and respectable young man, was obviously a favourite with Bob Lewis. After I had told Bob my name, and that I was Eric's brother, he asked me "Ar thar as good as your Eric?". I was determined not to be put down, and my answer was "Yes, better"! "Oh aye" said Bob," We'll see about that". Bob never held this encounter against me – so he must have been something of a psychologist.

I was told to get some cleaning rags and paraffin and join another new starter, Cliff Meggitt, on locomotive No 4637, a class K2, (ex GNR). Although strictly a mixed traffic engine, these K2 engines were used at Mexborough as passenger locos: there were 5 at the shed in the early 1940s – nos 4632/34/36/37 and 4638. Within six weeks they had all been reallocated to the GN Section and K2s were never again allocated to Mexborough. They had been there 10 years.

Goods traffic on the railways increased enormously during the early months of the war, mainly I suppose to conserve supplies of petrol for the Army, and cleaners were being set on every few days: six more were started on the following Monday 5th February. Two of these recruits I remember, Tony Early and Claude Dale, two pals from Brampton, wore trilby hats during the first two weeks- a most inappropriate headgear in an engine shed. I was an engine cleaner for a week! Because on my fourth day of employment I was examined for firing duties by Inspector Horace Wigglesworth of Doncaster – and was from the following Monday graded as a "passed cleaner", ie a cleaner passed to perform firing duties ; Wigglesworth's first question to me was "Show me your Rule Book", and I had to tell him that I hadn't yet been issued with one. (The Rule Book had 240 Rules in it; 241 if you included Rule 55A.) At this, the Inspector went into the Depot General Office and a fierce row developed with the Chief Clerk, Jack Walker, regarding my not having a Rule Book. Inspector Wigglesworth came out of the office with a battered copy of the LNER Rule Book – one which had obviously been handed in by a retiring driver, and handed it to me with the remark that "And I don't suppose it is much good asking you any questions about it". My brother had given me some tuition on the book and the Inspector seemed quite pleased with the extent of my knowledge – seeing that I had not had the advantage of possessing a book. Of course, I didn't tell him about my brother.

He demonstrated the hand shunting signals and went through the preparation and firing of a steam locomotive in general terms – also how to conduct oneself, with safety, in an engine shed' operating hand points etc – and then left.

Four days later, on the second Monday 5th Feb 1940, just a week from starting, the foreman cleaner – Walter Johnson – came and asked me if I was passed to go out firing. I said I had been examined but was not given a result. Twenty minutes later, after enquiring at the General Office, I was told that I had, in fact, passed and that I should "clock out" for firing duties. I was now officially a "Passed Cleaner". I must explain here that when one "clocked in" for cleaning duties the time was registered on a time card. This meant you had to "clock out" when going firing – as the time thereafter was shown separately on the driver's daily ticket.

On this, my first firing trip, I was told to go onto engine No 5744, on number three road in the shed, with Driver Alf Bostock, and work the Junction Pilot. This loco had come into the shed to do daily "Loco" duties; ie have the fire cleaned and everything oiled etc. Bostock's own passed fireman had obviously been taken off to do driving work.

Junction Pilot was a considerate work job for drivers with a medical history of incapacity of one sort or another. Alf had a stiff leg from a previous accident and was unable to walk very far. When I arrived at 5744 he said "who are you then"? I told him that this was my first firing turn. "Right", he said. "The first thing you can do is to oil this shaft for me – as my bad leg prevents me from getting up onto the framing". He then put an old sack onto the engine top framing and indicated to me what was required. This involved me removing the corks from the oil receptacles on top of the big ends and eccentric sheaves and filling them up with oil from a feeder (oil can).

When I saw that in order to do this job I had to lean, full length , into the machinery in order to reach the corks, I was terrified. What if the engine moved whilst I was in there oiling? I should end up as a mangled fireman, and this on my first trip. However, nothing came amiss during this exercise – and I had the pleasure of knowing that, after only a week on the railway, I had not only been firing, but had also performed some of the Drivers work whilst oiling the engine.

Class N5 No 5755 on Mexborough shed circa 1932. This engine was renumbered 69302 after nationalisation and was withdrawn in 1957. Courtesy Great Central Railway Society.

The second day, which I found more interesting, was on the "Top Yard Pilot" with Driver Jim Courts. Now old Jim was something of a philosopher and very easy to get on with, he kept a close eye on things and saw my mistakes before I did; his advice was invaluable. The engine was one of Thomas Parker's 0-6-2 tank engines, No 5757, LNER Class N5; it was already 40 years old in 1940.These were very good shunting engines; comfortable, adequate for the task and with, for a good shunter, a large cab. They had been designed originally for short distance trip work in the late 19th century and Mexborough at one time had more than 40 of them on the books – mainly for colliery jobs. They were also used at Barnsley on local passenger work to Penistone and Doncaster. Jim Courts was a bachelor and at one time had lodged with old Mrs Jackson, only a few doors away from me. He was always kindly to young people and was well known to me; he was permanently on this pilot for reasons of defective eyesight. After 8 hours on this job, I went home with a feeling of satisfaction knowing that I had done a fair days work. One incident I remember clearly on this day, was that one of the shunters came on the footplate, during a lull in the work, for a warm. His name was Len Hartley. He had been a guard in the past but had been demoted for some misdemeanor or other. He said "ar don't know thee lad",

A page from Ron Fareham's diary in 1943. He recorded for each shift his clocking on & off times, span of time worked in hours & minutes and the engine number. Over this ten day period he didn't have one day off; in fact his diary shows for the month of May 1943, he only had off Sunday 2nd, Sunday 9th and Sunday 30th May. June was no better – just three days off!

so I told him my name and that this was only my second firing turn. His reply was "Ah, tharl be aw reight, thars gorra a job for life ere-an it's a continuous claddy wi pay".This attitude was quickly corrected by Jim Courts, who had a rather low opinion of Len.

My third day was spent on the Loco Pilot. This engine did all the internal movements required in the depot.. These consisted of such things as shunting the empty wagons off the coal stage and placing loaded ones back; setting and moving wagons on the two ash pit; marshalling the Breakdown train when required and everything else that wanted moving in the shed. The locomotive was 4125 – an old GNR 0-6-0 tender engine, class J3. The difference between this engine and the previous two was dramatic. 4125 was, like all other GNR engines – uncomfortable; the footplate was crude in the extreme- a classic example of Victorian stark ironmongery. A foot square piece of wood as a seat- which occasionally collapsed if not set properly. A Sterling pull out regulator – usually with the gland blowing, and a large "Pole" type vertical reversing lever, very little in the way of cab roof and, generally speaking, miserable to work on. To add to the discomfort was the driver, old Harry Pendlebury, who was another medical case and on this job permanently. I never saw this man smile; he never gave you any directions or encouragement and shouted at you if things went wrong; his conversation

FACTS ABOUT BRITISH RAILWAYS

EMPLOYMENT

The railway industry comprises a great diversity of occupations. An indication of the wide range of departmental activities may be gathered from the following:—

Accountancy, advertising, architecture, canals, cartage, chemistry, civil engineering, commercial matters, docks engineering and dredging, docks traffic, electrical engineering, electric train services, estate management, goods traffic, horse management, hotels, legal, locomotive running, marine engineering, mechanical engineering, passenger traffic, police, photography, rating, refreshment rooms, road traffic, secretarial, staff management, staff welfare, statistical steam train services (passenger and freight), stores (purchasing, storage and issue), surveying, traffic operating, warehousing, wireless operating, etc.

The total number of railway staff is 555,337, including the following main grades:—

67,000 clerks.
35,000 drivers and motormen.
33,000 firemen.
50,000 permanentwaymen.
40,000 porters.
17,000 shunters.
23,000 signalmen.
106,000 workshop staff.

The total amount paid in salaries and wages in 1940 was approximately £123,000,000.

PEACETIME STATISTICS

Passenger Journeys	(number)	1,158,318,000
Parcels forwarded	"	90,556,000
Freight Tonnage	(tons)	254,496,000
Passenger Train mileage	(miles)	284,946,000
Freight Train mileage	"	133,440,000
Total Passenger and Freight Engine mileage	"	583,007,000
Road Vehicles:—		
Passenger Motor vehicles in which Railways are interested	(number)	15,000

Road Vehicles—cont.		
Railway Parcel and Goods Motor vehicles	(number)	10,367
Railway Horses	"	11,163
Railway Horse vehicles	"	24,823
Containers	"	15,521
Steamships:—		
Railway-owned Steamships	"	130
Gross registered tonnage	(tons)	176,145
Docks, Harbours and Wharves:—		
Places where situate	(number)	76
Length of quays	(feet)	501,402
Rolling Stock:—		
Steam Locomotives	(number)	19,577
Diesel Oil Locomotives	"	35
Rail Motor Vehicles—		
Steam	"	86
Electric	"	1,888
Diesel Oil	"	28
Passenger carriages	(number)	42,575
Seating capacity	(seats)	2,513,000
Freight wagons (Rly.-owned)	(number)	646,479
Carrying capacity	(tons)	7,783,000
Wagons of 20 tons and over (included in the above)	(number)	45,059
Mileage:—		
Total mileage, single track (including sidings)	(miles)	50,555
Total mileage, electrified track (including sidings) (in the above)	"	2,013
Total route mileage	"	19,131
Total electrified mileage (included in the above)	"	806
Equipment:—		
Signal Boxes	(number)	10,220
Water Troughs	"	141
Tunnels	"	1,049
Passenger Stations	"	6,698
Goods Stations	"	5,908
Houses owned	"	49,774
Weight of rail per yard (Standard) (Main Lines)	(lbs.)	95
Weight of chair (Standard)	"	46
Sleepers per mile	(number)	2,112

16

17

Ron Fareham's working diary was always an ASLEF issue. The first few pages were always a "mine" of information. Here's one such page from his 1942 diary.

was all but non existent and I was glad when the relief arrived at 2-0pm.

After these episodes, I was either cleaning or firing – but mostly the latter. However, when on cleaning duties one didn't always clean steam locomotives. In the second week I was given the job of "bar laying"; this involved going feet first into the fireboxes of cold engines that had been washed out and cleaning the interior of the boiler with water jets and rods. The job of the Bar Lad was to get in and examine the firebars, replacing any in the grate which were worn or damaged. The ends of the firetubes had to be checked and any accumulation of "birds nests " removed. The latter were pieces of fused ash which attached themselves to the tube ends and if not removed, would eventually block the tube; this would then impair the steaming capacity of the boiler by negating the action of the tubes. Roof bolts and brick arch had also to be cleaned down.

Bar laying was a filthy job and one I thoroughly disliked. One had to use a carbide lamp on this duty, and the smell of the lamp in the confines of a firebox was somewhat sickening and nauseating. However, there was one very important benefit to doing these duties; you obtained a first hand knowledge of the innards of a locomotive boiler and the reasons why a clean grate and tubes was the first essential to good steaming.

At the end of the second week, when I drew my first wage, there was a letter accompanying the wage tin. The letter stated, "This is to confirm your appointment as Engine Cleaner (Supernumary) as from 29-1-40". Although I had seen the word supernumary before, I had only a hazy idea of its true meaning. To solve my problem, I consulted my immediate superior, the foreman cleaner Bob Lewis, and sought his advice as to the meaning of the offending word. Bob said "It means thar a casual employee, they can sack thee wen't war's over". I was somewhat despondent at this remark as I had given up a permanent position at Queen's Foundry to come on the railway. Incidentally, the "supernumary" status was never officially cancelled – so in theory the rest of my 44 years of railway service were casual employment. I gradually came to feel that Bob Lewis knew about as much about "supernumary" as I did in 1940.

Another duty was "Coal Stack": these stacks were, of course, a hedge against any sudden interruption in the normal supply of coal, such as a miner's strike. A well built coal stack consisted of large lumps, built up as dry stone walls, behind which all the smaller coal was placed. The stack remained down for some years and was then lifted and used up. The reason for the intermittent lifting was because, in time, the coal weathered and its quality declined if left down for too long a period. It was for this reason that only the best quality coal was "stacked", as the weathering process was therefore slowed down. At Mexborough shed the"stack" coal was usually of much better quality than that normally used because the majority of the depot's work was slow coal and goods trains, and so didn't need the best coal, even though the district was surrounded by a high quality coalfield.

There were two large stacks at Mexborough in 1940 containing thousands of tons of coal. Lifting a stack was usually the job of the engine cleaners – as they were always the floating reservoir of labour at an engine shed. Stack lifting was a hard and dusty job, and when the large lumps were disposed of into wagons, by hand, there then remained the small stuff and the dust. This had to be thrown up into the wagons, from track level, and of course clouds of coal dust were everywhere, with no water supply on hand to lay the dust. The situation can well be imagined on a hot summer's day, as it was in 1940.

There was another chore that cleaners had to perform occasionally; this was "Pick up Coal", which originated in the hump marshalling yard at Wath, some three miles to the west , and was the result of spillage from wagons of coal during the marshalling process. The Railway Company was responsible for the loss of the weight in the wagon and had to indemnify the customer. Obviously, having to pay for the coal lying on the ground, the Railway was going to make some use of it and the stationery boilers at Mexborough shed were fired exclusively with this "pick up" coal. As the war progressed, Italian POWs who were held in a POW camp at High Melton were used to pick up the coal.

There were two large hoppers at the shed – built up of old sleepers- holding something like 50 tons each, and when wagons of "pick up coal" arrived from Wath, it was the job of the engine cleaners to empty them into the hoppers. It was, as with all aspects of coal handling, a dusty task, and a long hosepipe was provided at the side of the boiler house to lay the dust. It can be imagined what would happen with eight or ten youths on this job on a hot summer afternoon, with a hose pipe handy. Of course, boys being boys, they sprayed the coal and then they started spraying each other with the hose pipe. One day someone was playing about with the hose pipe and Cyril Morley- whose father was the depot examining fitter and a local councillor- was drenched. He picked up an old bucket which was lying nearby and hurled it at his tormentor. Of course it missed and went straight through a glass window in the adjoining pumphouse. The day after this episode, we were all paraded in front of the Shed Superintendent (no shed masters in those days). This gentleman was a First World War officer named Major A Clear, whose father had been Assistant General Manager of the Great Central Railway in the days of Sam Fay. We were all thoroughly admonished and threatened with dire consequences if there was any recurrence. Major Clear was really a kind boss and eventually progressed to District Loco Superintendent at Norwich.

When things were busy, or staff were on annual leave, cleaners were sometimes used on the coal stage. This consisted of shovelling coal out of a wagon into 10 cwt steel tubs: these were trundled across iron plates to a tipping deck and onto the locomotive tenders. The main coaling device at Mexborough until 1961, consisted of the Steam Breakdown Crane tipping end door wagons on a high tipping deck. The crane lifted one end of the wagon and the coal shot out of the end door on to the loco tenders, the wagon end being dropped by the crane when the tender was full. This was a much quicker method than the stage. However, when the Breakdown Crane was needed for its proper purpose, ie derailments etc., then engine coaling had to revert to hand shovelling on the coal stage and a significant slowing of the whole process. In this case, extra cleaners were drafted onto the coal stage, especially during the evening and night when most of the allocated engines were returning to depot.

CHAPTER 11

AND QUIET FLOWS THE DON

MEXBOROUGH AND ITS THREE ENGINE SHEDS
BY RON FAREHAM
PUBLISHED IN BRITISH RAILWAYS ILLUSTRATED
VOLUME 10 NO 4 JANUARY 2001.

By the year 1850, Mexborough had progressed in startling fashion from a village of some 500 souls to a small town of about 5000. The factor making this possible was (largely) the arrival of the Sheffield and South Yorkshire Canal in 1829. It put Mexborough in direct communication with Sheffield, Barnsley, Doncaster, Goole and the sea, and industries were quickly established. A second form of transport arrived in 1849 with the South Yorkshire Railway, connecting the Great Northern at Doncaster with the Midland at Swinton. These were to become major trunk routes from south to north and a great deal of traffic was secured for the S.Y.R.

Two boat yards had been established on the canal and two substantial glass works built but the railway did not take all the canal traffic; much of it in fact – gas works, brick kilns, glassmakers and potteries – continued to use the canal for many years. Railways in the Mexborough area were intended to carry coal, though not a single colliery existed in Mexborough – and never did! There were many however, on the immediate outskirts – large pits such as Manvers, Wath Main, Barnburgh, Denaby, Cadeby, Kilnhurst, Swinton Common, Elsecar, Cortonwood, Aldwarke, Roundwood, Lidgett, Wombwell, Mitchells Main and Darfield, all within 5 miles. The centre of the South Yorkshire coal trade was really at Wath, three miles to the west where eventually a very large marshalling yard served by Mexborough, was established.

The South Yorkshire Railway began operations on 10th November 1849, with a branch to the Elsecar Collieries opened on 2nd March 1850; by then the main line to Barnsley was under construction, together with the Worsborough Branch. 0-6-0s and 0-4-2s served at first and were "stabled" in the old literal railway meaning- that is, fed, watered and looked after- in the South Yorkshire Railway's first Mexborough engine shed, a single road structure at the north side of the line. It had doors at each end and a "preparation pit" throughout its length; on the south side was another road, in the open with a disposal pit at the east end. Each of the roads would hold about six engines, fuelled by men shovelling the coke directly out of the wagons onto the low tenders of that time. This shed was in use for the first few years only but the site was known to generations of railwaymen afterwards as "back line cutting".

The main line to Barnsley was finished in 1851; with its attendant branches

(Elsecar 1850. Worsborough 1852, and the Chapeltown Branch to the Midland in 1854) it tapped 14 collieries. The nine engines (four of those were second hand) and the little shed were fast becoming inadequate for the task in hand. With more collieries being sunk, the S.Y.R. decided to order more 0-6-0s; there was also a further 0-4-2 from a cancelled Russian State Railways order, which was presumably a bargain. Wagons were proving a problem too. At first, the S.Y.R. did not have any of its own, using those of other companies, mainly the Great Northern, but a hundred were ordered in 1851 and a further 250 in 1854. This fleet had expanded by early 1856 to 672. The number of engines also grew to sixteen by 1856.

It was a time of great expansion and the company soon acquired a larger plot of land on the south side of the line, in the "v" of the junction up to the Midland Railway at Swinton. The signal box was named Mexborough Junction, later becoming Mexborough No 1 . It was on this site that a larger two road engine shed with a two road repair shop was built, in 1854-55. Indeed, two locomotives were actually constructed in this shop some years later; Nos 20 and 22., they became Manchester, Sheffield and Lincoln Railway Nos 171 and 173, doing yeoman service until the turn of the century. The new premises butted directly onto White Lee Road, which was then at ground level. By 1864, the last year of independent operation, South Yorkshire locomotive stock had grown to 28.

The South Yorkshire Railway was leased to the Manchester, Sheffield and Lincolnshire Railway in 1864 and the engines numbered in the M.S.&L. series, but though they got M.S.&L. style number plates, the letters S.Y.R. were embossed upon them. This was altered to M.S.& L. in 1874 when the latter took over the S.Y.R. lock, stock and barrel and its identity disappeared.

Having built the two steam engines, Nos 20 and 22, the modest collection of buildings was rather grandly known as "Mexborough Plant". (Mexborough's Plant Hotel was so named because of its close proximity to the Plant.) In 1875, plans were made to widen the three running lines at this point to five; the line and the Swinton Branch were to be bridged and White Lee Road raised so that the crossings could be replaced by bridges, avoiding endless inconvenience thereby. It meant demolishing all the buildings – the two new lines (they would be the main lines) are shown in dotted form on the shed plan of 1870. As can be seen, the new up main line was to take the line of the No 1 road of the second engine shed. Before this could be done, it was clearly necessary to build a third running shed, to replace the one to be demolished.

When the building of this third, much larger building commenced, is somewhat obscure, though a South Yorkshire Railway Board minute of 17th August 1872 records: "The MS&L Railway [has] asked the SY Railway to construct an engine shed and siding accommodation at Mexborough". The question was adjourned until the next meeting for the production of plans and estimates. A fortnight later, an estimate of £47,186 was 'carried'. Nothing further appears in the SY minute books regarding this third Mexborough shed before the disappearance of the SYR into the MS&L ,but it is recorded at an extraordinary general meeting of the Board and shareholders on the 30th July 1873. Its sale to the larger company was again 'carried': this received the necessary parliamentary approval in July 1874 and the new shed opened in the same year. Its erection is thus credited to the SYR. After this, part of the triangular site of the earlier (second) shed and works was left vacant until wagon builders and repairers Burnett & Co put up their premises about 1890. The siding at the south side of Burnett's works was known as "the old plant siding" up until the 1970s- nearly a hundred years after its demise. Nos 20 and 22 lived on! William Gittins & Sons also had the old Plant Works for wagon repairs.

The men engaged at the old premises must have been truly looking forward to July 1874 and the opening of the new Mexborough shed. It lay half a mile to the east, adjacent to the new station and for the time, was very large, with a long two road wagon repair shop, three road engine repair shops and fifteen shed roads. There was standing room for over 90 of the small engines of 1874.

The new shed, as we have seen, was situated in the heart of the burgeoning South Yorkshire coalfield, becoming one of the richest in the country at the time. Not surprisingly, it supplied the great part of the railway traffic of the area. In 1874, the capacity of the shed was much greater than the number of engines stationed there but the planners were far sighted; further expansion of the coalfield was seen as inevitable. More collieries were sunk, the lines to

GCR 0-6-0 No 572 became LNER Class J13 No . 5572 seen here at Mexborough in September 1932. It was fitted with what was considered to be an ugly LNER flowerpot chimney.
Photo published by Photomatic Ltd Hatfield.

London and Banbury opened at the turn of the century and by 1910, there were 230 engines stationed at Mexborough. At weekends the place was chock-a-block with locomotives, with some pushed out into the surrounding goods sidings.

During the shed's lifetime, 1874-1965, it had five owners; SYR, MS&LR, GCR, LNER and BR and over that long time (the best part of a century) its main role in life never changed – shifting very large tonnages of coal. There was always some general goods traffic arising in the area such as glass, iron and steel, sand and so on but this was miniscule compared to coal. In later years there was always a considerable amount of ordinary merchandise freight flowing through Mexborough from all and to all points of the LNER compass. It has to be appreciated here that, from 1879 onwards, Mexborough stood on the very border of the 'North Eastern'; first the railway of that name, then the NE Area of the LNER and later the NE Region of BR. The junction was Mexborough West and beyond that point lay the S&K (Swinton & Knottingley) joint line leading to York and the north. The amount of traffic to and from the 'North Eastern' was always substantial and during the two world wars- especially the second- it was truly enormous.

The 1874 shed had five roof bays covering three roads each, with pitched slate roofs and two large circular openings set into each of the bay gables. The purpose of these was to help keep the interior of the shed clear of smoke though the structure was 'blind backed' (open at one end only) and chance wafts of breeze were the best hope of getting smoke out.The only hope at the rear of the building was a passage leading to the offices and other rooms. The front of the shed faced North West and the prevailing wind was usually from the west; at the weekend when engines were making plenty of smoke after being lit up from cold, the smoke pouring from the east end of the

A view of the whole of the shed front with the water softening plant towering above, in July 1958. This is looking east, with K3 No 61867 on the "new pit". (so named with incontestable logic, for it was built after the "old pit"). The coal wagons on the right are empty and loaded respectively.

126

passageway, propelled by the west wind, was an extraordinary sight. There were also three long sidings outside the shed on the North side: these were at one time part of another shed, for the repairing of wagons. On the GCR, carriage and wagon work came under the overall management of the Locomotive Shed Superintendent (later – Shed Master) and at Mexborough, it was part of the same premises. The wagon repairers were moved out after the First World War to the Wath and Rotherham Road yards and the Mexborough wagon shop demolished. This released the three long roads for engine stabling. Inevitably they retained the name associated with wagon repairs – the "Cripple Sidings".

The development was obviously part of forward policy because at the time, 1919-1924, some forty odd small J10 and J12 0-6-0s were being sent away in exchange for a large number of 04 2-8-0s, from the War Department's surplus fleet. There were three more long sidings, at the south side of the shed, for storing loaded and empty coal wagons. In the days when 200 and more locos were allocated, there was never enough room on the shed roads proper to accommodate them all; many had to stand over the weekend in the three coal sidings, while others were put in the "New Junction" freight yard next door. The complement in 1922 (LNER Class designation) was thus:-

04/05	2-8-0	58
05	2-8-0	6
D8	4-4-0	3
D9	4-4-0	3
J10	0-6-0	15
J11	0-6-0	16
J13	0-6-0	6
N4	0-6-2T	13
N5	0-6-2T	40
Q4	0-8-0	41
Total		201

On a warm still Sunday evening in the summer, after all the engines had been lit up for departure on the Monday morning, a pall of smoke hung over the shed. As a child and youth, I lived only half a mile away and witnessed this event every weekend. Mother always dusted heavily on a Monday morning.

In the ninety odd years of its existence, Mexborough was organized on traditional lines and these arrangements remained in force until the end. Engines entering the shed were signaled in from Mexborough No 3 box straight on to one of the two ash pit lines. These were of the simplest sort, a brick lined trench between the rails – Mexborough (until the very end that is – see the ill fated coaler scheme, later) never had any of the modern aids to ash and clinker removal sometimes found at more important sheds.

On these pit lines the engines were 'disposed'. Fires were either cleaned or dropped: smokeboxes were opened and all the char removed with the firing shovel and the ashpans raked clean of ashes using a seven foot iron rake. There were a number of 'firedroppers' employed at the shed for this purpose, but it was a labouring, not a footplate grade and they were on piecework. When their 'stint' (a mere twenty engines!) was completed for the day, they went home and remaining engines were disposed of by footplate staff. These were not duties for weaklings and the heavy nature of the work was one of the reasons why the starting age for firing duties was eighteen years. The tool for cleaning and dropping a locomotive fire was a nine foot clinker shovel, made of wrought iron and weighing about half a hundredweight (25 kg). The fire, ash and lumps of metallic clinker in the firebox were drawn back through the firedoor and thrown through the 'doorway' gap between the engine cab and tender, onto the ground. The manoeuvering of a nine foot iron clinker shovel in the confines of a locomotive cab can best be left to the imagination. Some engines were easier than others, those with a high tender front and any tank engines - with their enclosed cabs - were obviously the most awkward, though 'awkward' hardly begins to do the task justice...

Disposal duties also involved the driver examining the engine for faults, spotting repairs on wearing parts such as brake blocks and so on. He had to go underneath the engine to check items such as springs, large and small ends of the connecting rods (if there were inside cylinders) cotters and wedgebolts. Meanwhile the fireman, after cleaning the fire, would be filling the sand boxes from special spouted buckets. When full of dry sand, these could weigh anything up to 80lbs each, and had to be lifted up onto the engine framing and the contents poured into the sandboxes. In winter, when

Class S1 "Daisy" 0-8-4T under repair on No 5 road, 19th May 1952. H.C.Casserley

rail conditions were bad, an engine could use anything up to ten buckets of sand per day.

If a firedropper had gone home, or was on leave or (more likely in later days) there simply wasn't one, a fireman lumbered with disposal was looking at a day's work of six engines or so. After such exertions (it involved much more per engine – sanding and so on) he went home tired to his bones, with a soaking shirt. There were no shower baths at Mexborough and in 1940 there was just one small wash hand basin, with cold water, in the enginemen's room! A few more sinks were provided after the war, 1947, and some hot water.

An aid to fire cleaning, on the later Gresley engines, was the drop grate: the front portion of the grate was hinged at its rear so it could be tipped forward using a screwed shaft which extended backwards into the cab. When in the tipped position, the fire and clinker could be pushed forward into the ashpit by means of the long clinker shovel, instead of being lifted out through the fire door. This did away with most of the heavy lifting work and also speeded up the process of disposal.

A later arrangement, copied from the American Army 2-8-0 S160 class which arrived in Britain in the middle of the Second World War, was the 'Hulson Rocker Firebar and Hopper Ashpan' combination. With this apparatus the firegrate sections were tipped vertically, one half of the grate at a time, so that the fire and clinker fell straight through the now wide open grate, through the open hopper ash pan and into the ashpit. This proved a very beneficial development for footplate and disposal staff. The same US engines were also fitted with the self cleaning smokebox. This meant that, except for the sandboxes, the time for disposal was reduced from an hour to

Two of Mexborough's lumbering giants on 19th May 1952. An old Mexborough stalwart Class O4/2 63774 stands on No 8 road and behind it, the original "Daisy" No 69900.
Photo H. C. Casserley.

the few minutes necessary to open the ashpan and operate the rocker bar levers. Nevertheless, by the early 1940s, there was still only one engine at Mexborough fitted with a drop grate, K3 No 3818; there were non at all fitted with rocker bars, though by 1947 there were five B1 4-6-0s with drop grates, 1164-1168.

The smokebox was normally emptied of fine ash by lifting it out with the firing shovel. One or two attempts were made over the years to ease this task and a few GC engines, mostly passenger types, were fitted with Robinson's smokebox ash ejector. Riddles and Thompson self-cleaning smokeboxes followed, though neither was 100% successful and they both inhibited steaming to some extent. The best arrangement was Robinson's smokebox ash hopper fitted to the class O4 2-8-0. This was a deep hopper on the smokebox floor, with a heavy cast iron bottom door operated by a treadle behind the left hand pony truck wheel. In this case the ash was raked into the hopper and down into the ash pit.

The ash pit roads at Mexborough were separate and some distance from the shed roads proper and from eight in the morning the 'ash fillers' (yet another labouring grade) began to shovel all the ash and clinker out of the pit on to the ground above. Wagons would then be placed on the pit line and the ash fillers would throw the ash up a second time, into the wagons. This double handling involved a five foot throw out of the pit, followed by a seven foot throw from ground level into the wagon. During this process the ashes were blown all over the place – it was a stupifyingly awful job by any measure!

Engines usually took water on the ash pits but for some reason, at

Mexborough in the 1950s, with a typical mix of old G.C. Pom Pom 0-6-0s and modern era WD 2-8-0s, along with a couple of B1s. This pair of water columns between roads 7,8 and 9 served most of the engine requirements. A third water column can be seen on the far right.

Mexborough watering took place when the engines were ready to leave the shed. There were columns on each of the pits, but they were seldom used. The two main water cranes, between roads 7, 8 & 9 were the ones in constant use. These bore the name of the maker on the base, under many layers of paint in cast iron letters 'BARKERS FOUNDRY, MEXBOROUGH', a firm no one could remember. There are records of a Barkers Pottery, so did it serve a dual purpose I wonder?

[I can explain this. Samuel Barker was born in 1802 in Burslem, Staffordshire and his family moved to Mexborough following the pottery trade. They were an industrious family owning the Don Pottery at Swinton and Mexboro' Pottery - the site of this would be between the former Ben Bailey offices and the relief road roundabout and extending down to the canal. The family lived in "Mexborough House", a large mansion type dwelling on the present Post Office site in Main Street, Mexborough. The Mexborough Pottery closed c1844 and Samuel and his son in law John D Beckett, who had operated the works as a partnership re-opened it as an iron foundry and railway wheel manufacturers. Samuel died in 1856. The works were then continued by sons Henry and Samuel (Jnr) and in 1862 they became known as H&S Barker, "Don Iron Works" and they traded profitably for many many years.]

The next operation was coaling; at most sheds this was done first, but at Mexborough it followed disposal. From 1874 to 1961 the task was done from the coal stage, either from the traditional shelter built on it or, more usually, from the curious 'wagon tip' provided on the stage itself, some yards beyond the shelter. The coal shelter was of conventional design, single sided with a pitched slate roof and there were two tipping decks for four wheeled tubs filled and pushed by hand in time-honoured fashion. This was disagreeable compared to the 'wagon tip' and most engines were coaled using the latter arrangement. The 'wagon tip' was quicker and less men were needed; it was a special, possibly unique and certainly much quicker Mexborough arrangement, whereby a measure of mechanisation was imparted to an otherwise unmechanised, hand-worked operation. Remarkably, a wagon turntable was installed on the end of the coal stage, beyond the shelter and the steam breakdown crane was propelled up the stage and through the shelter, there to stand and up-end coal wagons, an extraordinary sight. These had to be end door wagons, and were turned through 90 degrees on the little table so that they emptied directly onto the loco tenders. If this arrangement was ever approved 'higher up' than Mexborough itself, history does not record..... The breakdown crane, in steam, with a driver, had the virtue of being almost always 'on tap'. The drawback with this (unique?) 'wagon tip' was that, when the breakdown crane was needed for its proper purpose, the work had to cease. All engines had then to be coaled at the stage by hand shoveling, and extra labour drafted to the task – usually engine cleaners with the promise of a few extra bob.

By 1960 the old stage was in poor shape and something drastic had to be done, for it was well past repair. I suppose the management were hoping that it would last out steam traction; dieselisation after all was very much on the horizon in the Sheffield District but some spending was inevitable, and urgent. The Authorities decided, at long last, that Mexborough Loco was to have a coaling plant and one was therefore built and commissioned in 1961. This was fairly astonishing given that diesel locomotives had already begun to arrive at Mexborough in small numbers and the life of the coaling plant was destined to be short – easily the briefest ever. There were many ironic (to put it briefly) remarks among the footplate staff about this; one story going the rounds was that the contract to knock the plant down was let while it was still being built!

In the days of the coal stage, a number of drivers were required to move engines and set them under the stage, or 'wagon tip', to be coaled. After that, engines were brought on to the 'ladder' road and left there. Two other drivers, with firemen, then placed the engines in the shed roads either for immediate further work or for washing out, repairs, or an 'X' day. The latter was an LMS idea and became a BR standard procedure in the early 1950s. The 'X' stood for examination and the examining fitter went over the engine with a 'fine tooth comb', booking all the repairs he could find. These were supposed to be put right in the 24 hours allowed. The basis of the scheme was that any items not of a serious nature could be deferred until the 'X' day. Brake adjustment, injectors and sand gear were, of course, done as necessary and were never deferred. The scheme worked reasonably well though not perhaps as well as on the company of its origin, where it had been honed over many years.

Mexborough shed on 4th April 1957, and a coaled up Class J11 Pom Pom waits outside. Someone is coming back later – note the up ended oil can draining its last drips into the lubricator. Courtesy Peter Groom.

The problem of marshalling the engines in the shed for next morning departures had, as at all single ended sheds, to be done in reverse order, the last engine out had to be the first one in, and so on. This demanded a fair degree of skill on the part of the driver in charge of shed shunting on each shift so as to avoid constant remarshalling.

The policy adopted in the case of the twenty or so colliery pilots (Robinson 2-8-0s) was to use the two long cripple sidings at the north side of the shed. These held about a dozen engines each; during the evening, each was filled with 2-8-0s, one road for 'engine first' departures, the other for 'tender first'. When each road was full they were booked out in the order in which they stood. This was called 'shunting engines on paper'. It was very successful and cut out a lot of work. All the tenders had to be filled by the shed staff before being placed in the 'cripple sidings' as no water column was available on these roads before departure.

Mexborough water was very poor in quality, and was notorious for causing priming – the carrying over of water with the steam when working hard. The well was sited at the back of the shed, hard by the river Don, a once noble stream by then regarded as little better than an open sewer. In fact it was worse than a sewer, for added to the offensive organic matter was the variously chemical and mineral outpourings of every industrial undertaking upstream. The river passed through the heavy industrial parts of Rotherham and Sheffield and the damage was well and truly done by the time it passed the shed at Mexborough. In the early years of the last century it was decided that a water softening plant should be built, and a substantial lime/soda plant was installed both at the shed and Wath Yard before the First World War.

The biggest headache for the shed staff came on Sundays. Most of the allocated engines, and many from other sheds, were on the premises and much remarshalling and tank filling became necessary. Unfortunately 95% of the fires were dropped and the engines were 'dead' with no steam. In this case, one of the 2-8-0s was steamed up and used as a pilot. Mexborough shed was also the home of the LNER Beyer Garratt locomotive; it was the most powerful in the country and was used for banking (pushing) heavy coal trains up the very steep portion of the route to the west – the 2.5 miles of the Wentworth incline near Barnsley. It was stationed at Mexborough for the great part of its working life. It was never liked by footplate staff, for it was really two engines rather than one, so far as the fireman's work was concerned. The same held true for the fitters of course. It was scrapped in 1955 with many a dry eye.

In 1961 a large proportion of the Mexborough footplate staff transferred to the new 'Mixed Traction Depot' which had been established at the erstwhile Wath Electric Shed, together with a new building in the middle of Wath yard called the 'service shed'. This was a clumsy arrangement with a lot of locomotives moving between the two establishments and much walking for the loco crews, for the places were half a mile apart. Neither shed was ideal and some of the equipment was badly sited. For instance, the fuel pumps at the service shed were inside the building and this meant that any two 'multiple' diesel locomotives (that is, coupled together and controlled by one driver) requiring fuel had to be uncoupled and then fuelled individually, and later recoupled. This involved the parting and recoupling of control air pipes, vacuum brake pipes, air brake pipes and finally electric jumper cables. The job could sometimes take the best part of an hour, when ten minutes would have sufficed if the layout had been properly designed. I suppose at this early stage of dieselisation that there were few, if any, among the design staff with any experience of what was involved in shunting and coupling of diesel locomotives in the confines of a depot The steam equivalent of placing fuel pumps inside a shed would be placing a coal stage at the bottom of a shed road; imagine it!

A B5 4-6-0 at Mexborough on 11th April 1948; 1686 was one of half a dozen at the shed during the First World War, given to the small 'Banbury Link' of that time for troops and ambulance trains from Yorkshire to the GW. The large expanses of daylight so obvious through the decayed ventilating holes ('holes' does not seem a good enough word, for they are beautifully fashioned in brick) and the poor state of the smoke 'pots' reveal that by now the roof is in very poor state. In fact, it was under renewal even as this photograph was taken. The roof covering the fifteen roads was massive and stately, made up of ancient wooden baulks covered in slate but in time the mightiest oak must come to a ruinous old age. Traditional railway neglect allied to decades of smoke and blast and the tender mercies of too many South Yorkshire winters meant that the proud timbers eventually rotted and failed in the damp and smoke. By 1947 the attractive roof with its fine brick gable ends was 73 years old, and sagging in odd places. The decision was made to re-roof the shed in asbestos sheeting, which was supposed to resist the effects of smoke(if not blast). The task took over a year to complete, during which time various roads were stopped off. It was generally regarded as a neat job and was finished early in 1948. Photograph MB.

134

In 1964, steam traction disappeared from the area and the remaining staff were transferred to Wath. The Shed Master and his clerical staff hung on for a few more months into the next year until their accommodation was ready. They then followed the rest of the men to Wath. So ended ninety-one years of work at what was latterly called Mexborough Motive Power Depot. At the time of writing (1999), Wath Yard and Depot and the four track main line to Barnsley have all long been lifted – nothing is left! This has been brought about by many factors, in the main of course, the closure of so many of the South Yorkshire pits – accelerated by the miner's strike – and also the radical transformation of the coal trade in the wake of North Sea gas. It was, as we have seen so many times over the years, the sad end of an era.

ROUTES WORKED BY MEXBOROUGH MEN

In 1880, when the coal traffic to Manchester was expanding, the Worsborough branch had been made a through route, avoiding Barnsley (it had previously been a dead end route to Moor End Colliery). Further and longer routes were added to the Mexborough Shed knowledge roster, destinations such as Northwich in Cheshire and a number of places in and beyond Manchester. The then twelve hour day enabled train crews to work to these places without the necessity of lodging overnight before returning. In 1886 there was no lodging work at Mexborough. In fact, the only lodging work on the MS&L at that time was an Ardwick (Manchester) turn from New Holland shed, fourteen turns at Gorton and two Hull passenger turns at Brunswick shed in Liverpool.

You might have thought that, with the immense coal traffic to the Manchester area, lodging work on that route would have been substantial. The main reason for *not* working through to Manchester was that the coal was tripped to Barnsley Junction (Penistone) with Gorton men working similarly from the Manchester end – this was the origin of the 'Barnsley Juntion Turn Back' jobs at Gorton. In 1886, Mexborough had eleven such turns, and Sheffield two. Another way of helping traffic along on the Manchester route was that trains could take bigger loads on the long downhill stretches beyond Dunford. Traffic was therefore staged upto the summit at Dunford to allow trains to make up to bigger loads from that point. The safety of such heavier loads was assured by the dropping of wagon brakes on leaving Dunford.

Three Mexborough-Barnsley Junction jobs involved three trips from the Wath area to Barnsley Junction in 1886, each turn averaging sixteen hours a day. Come the ten hour day in 1900, these sort of shifts could not be contemplated so the workings then went through to the Manchester area and the crews lodged at Gorton 'barracks'. There was at the time no special link for lodging work at Mexborough. It was spread throughout the roster and was compulsory. When the 'New Line' was opened to Annesley and then beyond to both London and Banbury, traffic for the southern companies, for London, the Great Western and the LNWR, transferred on to the new Great Central Line. Coal traffic for the Great Northern proper and also for the Great Eastern continued to go via Hexthorpe Yard, Doncaster.

Mexborough shed was one of the main beneficiaries of the extra traffic generated by the 'New Line' – it was still called that in the 1950s. Coal trains were originally worked through to London by Mexborough men (173 miles), lodging in private digs at Neasden. This did not last long because of the excessive overtime involved and the coal train working was eventually cut back to Woodford (104 miles) with the crews lodging there. In 1919, again because of a reduction in working hours, this time to eight per day, the coal train workings were cut back to Annesley (43 miles), again with a lodge.

With the coming of Sam Fay as the GCR General Manager in January 1902, traffic to the GW via Banbury increased substantially. Mexborough men started to work down 'the branch' to Banbury with trains of general merchandise, then light engine back to Woodford to lodge. This route developed even further in 1940; a special train began to run from the Great Northern Yard at Ardsley (the collecting point for traffic from the West Riding) conveying van loads of woolen cloth for the West Country and also for export via Southampton: these specials were called 'Tailors' Trains'. A Mexborough crew then worked through to Oxford – initially with a conductor from Banbury – lodging at Oxford. This work was performed by a small link of ten men but some of the drivers were only in their late twenties, because of the sharply increased promotion caused by the extra traffic. Each driver had a brand new class 9H (later LNE class J10) allotted and some were so proud of having their 'own engine' at such a young age, that they arranged for a photographer to take a picture. One in this period was George Fred Sadler, who was only twenty seven. His engine was 9H No 120, one of fifteen at Mexborough at the time, all new. Sadler's fireman was another George Fred, the nineteen years old George Fred Lambert. The pair were fearless and went anywhere and everywhere. Sadler was a driver of some prominence in his middle and later years and was the first man to sign the road to Oxford. He worked troop and ambulance trains throughout the 1914-18 War with class 8F (LNER B4) locomotive No 1098, with fireman Tommy Walker, and later to London with the heavy traffic to the 1924 Wembley exhibition, with fireman Jack Bloomfield. The sphere of operations at Mexborough did not then alter a great deal until after the grouping in 1923, when running commenced over the lines of the erstwhile North Eastern Railway to York, Hull and the resorts of the Yorkshire Coast.

The first great change in traction came in 1951, when instructors were sought for the new electrics on the Manchester- Sheffield – Wath scheme. Six Mexborough drivers went down to Liverpool Street and after a few weeks came back to train the 54 drivers needed to work the electrically hauled traffic to the west. Most of this group went to the new depot at Wath while others stayed at Mexborough to staff the 'dual link' for spare electric work and cover for holidays and sickness at Wath.

The next upheaval came in 1960 when dieselisation commenced. In this period 1960-1964 all the remaining footplate staff were trained in diesel practice and gradually, all went to the Wath depot. Mexborough shed closed officially in 1965, when, as described above, the Shed Master and his administration class finally left to join the rest of the men at Wath.

LINKS

Rosters at a large depot such as Mexborough tended to be somewhat fluid over time, making it difficult to form an historical picture. The reason for this is the changing commercial and industrial trends year to year. The link structure at Mexborough had some parts which did not change radically over the years however, and as an illustration, I have selected the main roster for 1940. – the figures in brackets is the number of crews:

Link 1 (14):   colliery pilots ('old men')
Link 2 (14):   colliery pilots ('old men')
Link 3 (10):   Hull and York
Link 4 (10):   York
Link 5 (24):   main line and local trips
Link 6 (24):   main line and local trips
Link 7 (24):   main line and local trips
Link 8 (16):   main line and local trips
Link 9 (30):   Gorton, Immingham, Annesley (lodge)
Link 10 (10): Woodford, Gorton, York (lodge)
Link 11 (10): passenger to Hull, Sheffield etc
Link 12 (3):   Top Yard Pilot ('medical men')
Link 13 (3):   Junction Pilot ('medical men')
Link 14 (2):   Shed Pilot ('medical men')
Link 15 (5):   Shed ('medical men')
Link 16 (1):   Local trips ('medical men')

Outstations rostered from Mexborough were:
Wath Yard Pilots (12 crews):   Mexborough & Wath Yard
Rotherham Road Pilot (3 crews):   Rotherham Road Yard
Aldham Pilot (4 crews):   banking work

The grand total on the Mexborough footplate staff establishment was 528; 219 crews and 90 cleaners.

FOOTNOTE

The position of Shed Superintendent ('Shed Master' under BR) at Mexborough was one of some considerable importance in MS&L and GC days, when the shed was second in rank only to Gorton. In those days it was the headquarters of the South Yorkshire District in charge of the smaller sheds at Barnsley, Wakefield, Barnsley Junction and Keadby. It had 15 guv'nors in its ninety or so years, as follows:- J Bell, J Sharpe, J Horsley, A Preston, C Hugill, G White, G Morris, A Fish, W Stuart, A Clear, R Vereker, H Beastall, K Pitts, R Jones, W Rusling. The most renowned were Preston and Hugill who together served thirty three years at Mexborough; Preston 1887-1901, and Hugill 1901-1920.

Algernon Preston was a professional engineer and in 1886 was Chief Draughtsman and Manager of Gorton Works at the time of Thomas Parker's arrival as Locomotive Superintendent (later CME). There was obviously some friction between the two men, as Preston was sent to manage the South Yorkshire District and was not best pleased about it. He departed in 1901 to take charge at Trafford Park, Manchester and was succeeded by Charles Hugill.

Hugill arrived at Mexborough with considerable experience in locomotive running matters. He was born in Sheffield in 1855 and commenced work with the Yorkshire Engine Co. at Meadowhall (Sheffield) in 1874 as an apprentice. Four years later he became a fitter at Neepsend shed and after two years was sent to Gorton Works and became a leading fitter there in 1882, and later foreman fitter. He was obviously a man marked out for promotion and in 1891 took charge of the small shed at Barnsley. Two years later he graduated to the recently opened shed at Staveley. With the opening of the New Line to London in 1899, Hugill was sent to be the first Shed Superintendent at Woodford. Two years later he came to Mexborough, to stay until retirement in 1920.

Hugill was a typical martinet of the Victorian era; he ruled Mexborough with a rod of iron but by common consent was a fair minded man. He had a booming voice and could be heard shouting up the shed roads "Now then, Jackson, what are you on with?" and similar, redolent with threat. At this, people would either discreetly disappear, or quickly get on with what they were supposed to be doing. He was a strong supporter of the St John Ambulance movement and his team won the GCR Ambulance Shield in 1909. He lived at Doncaster and traveled to Mexborough on the train – which of course had one of his engines on it – and woe betide the driver if there was anything amiss. He was, by common agreement, the best boss Mexborough shed ever had, and his reign coincided with its busiest times.

CHAPTER 12

THE BUSIEST BRANCH?

BY R FAREHAM
PUBLISHED IN BRITISH RAILWAYS ILLUSTRATED
VOLUME 5 NO 1 OCTOBER 1995
THE WORSBOROUGH BRANCH 1850-1981 AND THE PROBLEMS OF ITS
OPERATION

In the 1830s the discovery of a very high quality coal in Worsborough Dale started what can only be described as something of a "coal rush" in the general area south of Barnsley. The quality was such that the hitherto daily "taking up the ashes from the domestic firegrate was reduced to a weekly task when using the local coal – and that amounted to only a small shovelful of white powder. In 1849 a small company, the South Yorkshire Railway was formed to tap the coal of this area; the Midland and the Great Northern, were not intended to encroach on Worsborough, so the railway field was wide open to exploitation.

Starting in November 1849, the SYR built a short line to connect the Great Northern at Doncaster and the Midland at Swinton, eight miles away, for passenger trains to Sheffield Wicker station (MR). Coal branches were quick to follow and in February 1850 the line from Mexborough to Earl Fitzwilliam's collieries at Elsecar was completed – Fitzwilliam was SYR Chairman for the first seven years. In June 1850 the South Yorkshire opened its line from Elsecar Junction to the Worsborough collieries. They were, at first, single track lines.

Coal had been worked in a minor way around Worsborough and some of the collieries were actually holes in the sides of the hills (adits) but around Barnsley they were known as "Day Oils". The products of these workings were conveyed to the old Worsborough canal basin by short, narrow gauge tramways or by horse and cart. With sharply increasing demand for good quality coal at that time, the system of horse, cart and canal was found wanting, for the throughput of coal could not sustain demand. The technique of deep mining was developing, along with improvements in the running of railways, and so the stage was set for the exploitation of coal on a large scale.

The original branch of 1850 to the Worsborough collieries, when opened, was single line and remained so, a dead-end branch until track doubling took place in 1876. There were at various times, twelve small collieries, Strafford (near Stainborough) being the largest – given the early regulations for the operation of single lines, the clearing of the pits and other small works could only have been a very slow business. However, not all the twelve collieries were in operation simultaneously, and it would be safe to assume

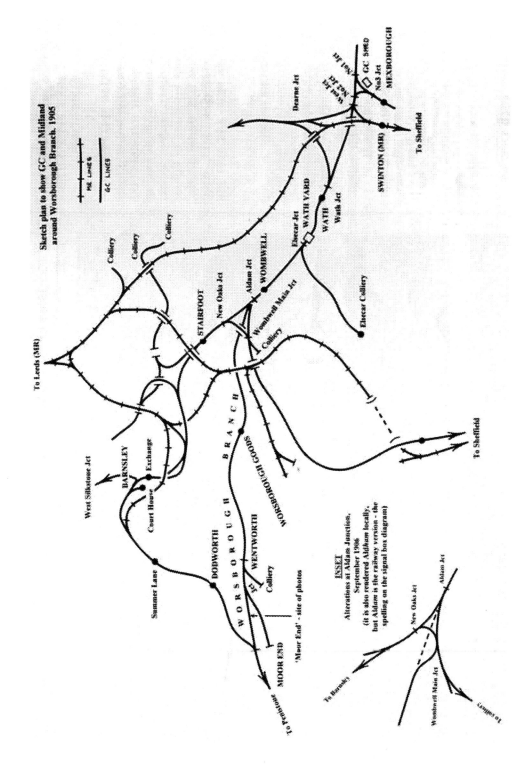

Sketch plan to show GC and Midland around Worsborough Branch. 1905

MR LINES
GC LINES

INSET
Alterations at Aldam Junction.
September 1986
(it is also rendered Aldham locally,
but Aldam is the railway version – the
spelling on the signal box diagram)

Dearne Jct
GC SHED
No3 Jct
MEXBOROUGH
SWINTON (MR)
To Sheffield
WATH YARD
Wath Jct
WATH
Ebecar Jct
WOMBWELL
Aldam Jct
Colliery
Colliery
Colliery
STAIRFOOT
New Oaks Jct
Wombwell Main Jct
Ebecar Colliery
Colliery
To Leeds (MR)
West Silkstone Jct
BARNSLEY
Exchange
Court House
Summer Lane
BOSWORTH
WENTWORTH
WORSBOROUGH GOODS
WORSBOROUGH BRANCH
Colliery
'Moor End' - site of photos
MOOR END
To Penistone
To Sheffield

New Oaks Jct
Aldam Jct
Wombwell Main Jct
To Barnsley
To Sheffield

that five at any one time would be usual. Some of the day holes or adits were essentially of short life. By the year 1886 there were only five left of the original twelve, Swaithe, Worsborough, Strafford, Wentworth and Sovereign.

By the turn of the century, there were left only Swaithe, Strafford and Wentworth, and in the 1930s, Strafford was bought by the Denaby Collieries and closed down. This pit at one time, supplied coal to the Royal households and it came out of the colliery sidings in sheeted wagons! Wentworth pit lasted into the 1970s and its small output was tripped westward to the Barnsley Junction yard at Penistone.

Most of the output of the Worsborough collieries went to the old SYR Hexthorpe yard at Doncaster, to be forwarded from there to the east coast ports of Hull and Grimsby for export, but mostly, it went south to Peterborough, for East Anglia or London by the Great Northern Railway. There was also an increasing tonnage of coal from the whole South Yorkshire area, westbound for Manchester, Cheshire and the South Lancashire region.

In 1864, there had been a partial amalgamation of the SYR and the Manchester, Sheffield and Lincolnshire Railway (MS&LR) and finally in 1874 the takeover was completed. By that time westbound traffic exceeded that to the east and the whole of the west traffic was routed through the middle of the town of Barnsley. The main problem with working heavy coal trains through Barnsley was the severe gradient: starting at Stairfoot at 1 in 76 it steepened from Barnsley Exchange station to 1 in 50 up through Summer Lane to Pogmoor. This of course, meant using banking engines and there was a busy level crossing at Jumble Lane, right in the middle of Barnsley. There were MS&LR passenger services and the Lancashire and Yorkshire Railway (L&Y) also used the station and level crossing, so the slow and complex movement of the coal trains had to be fitted in with the passenger trains. The MS&L management determined upon a solution to the congestion through Barnsley, with its manifold problems and in 1875, with western coal traffic continually increasing, it was decided to extend the Worsborough branch from Moor End to join up with the Barnsley to Penistone line at West Silkstone Junction, two and a half miles away.

This extension was difficult to build, mainly because the driving of two tunnels, Silkstone No1 of 75 yards and Silkstone No2 of 290 yards – took four years to complete from 1876 to 1880. The line was laid to a gradient of 1 in 40, an incline always known to enginemen as "Plevna": in my early days nobody seemed to know the reason for this but research has now revealed that the four years of the construction coincided with the period of the Russo-Turkish War, and during that conflict was fought the siege of Plevna, a town in the Ottoman Empire. The siege lasted for six months and would be of very serious concern internationally. It was, of course, a habit of the Victorians to name structures etc. after important events and this, although the memory of it had faded amongst railway staff, was obviously the reason for the name of a small Ottoman town being given to a short

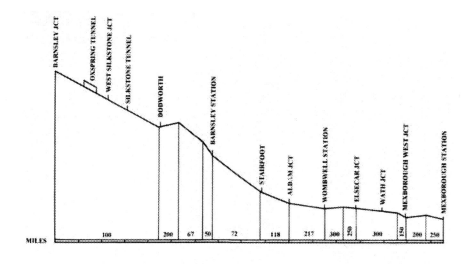

piece of railway in South Yorkshire. The name of Plevna was in use until the Worsborough branch and the whole line to the west, was closed in 1981. Incidentally, the name of the town is now Pleven in Bulgaria.

At 1 in 40 the gradient of this Worsborough extension was somewhat steeper than on the Barnsley route but the hilly nature of the country surrounding Barnsley and the difference in levels left the engineers no choice. Steeper gradients, however, were preferable to the delay, expense and frustration of the Barnsley town route. Having completed the Worsborough extension and established what was a new Barnsley avoiding line, the MS&L management was stuck with the problem of operating the Wentworth incline, not only in assisting trains up the bank but braking them on the way down.

The allocation of engines at the nearest large engine shed, Mexborough, in 1886 (the earliest record available) was 79, as follows:-

No	MS&L Class	Type	Load Class	Load to Penistone (wagons)
5	10	2-4-0	5	17
7	18	0-6-0	5	17
12	22	0-6-0	4	18
26	23	0-6-0	5	17
3	6A	0-6-0	4	18
6	6C1	0-6-0	1	22
6	6C2	0-6-0	1	22
14	18T	0-6-0T	Shunters	-

79 in total. All had rear assistance (banking) from Wentworth Junction to West Silkstone. Class 1 was the heaviest load.

The loads stated in this 1886 list were valid as far as Wentworth Junction;

from there to West Silkstone Junction the train would be banked in the rear, the banker then dropping back to Wentworth Junction for the next train. In 1886 there was only one engine at Wentworth so some delay would be incurred waiting for the banker. Later – and no date is available for this – another engine was supplied to avoid the delay incurred waiting for the banker, though assistance was only one banker per train. This was the norm at Wentworth until the arrival of Mr Sam Fay.

The advent of Fay as General Manager of the Great Central Railway (the name was altered from MS&L in August 1897) in 1902, Alexander Henderson as Chairman in 1899 and John G Robinson as Chief Mechanical Engineer in 1900 led to radical alterations in the burgeoning coal traffic to the west via Woodhead. Firstly, the load was doubled from 22 in the case of the Class 6C to 44 wagons per train – a banking engine would now come behind at Wombwell station. The provision of two engines per train forward from Wombwell station meant that the additional assistance given from Wentworth Junction must also be two engines. We therefore come to a situation unique in Britain, that of four engines per train up the Wentworth incline for two and a half miles.In the years prior to the First World War the train engine, banker and the two additional engines at Wentworth would all be Robinson 2-8-0s of class 8K (the LNER 04). These locomotives were class 7 for loading purposes and the total load for this combination would be 66 wagons of coal. A single load for one class 8K was 40 wagons, again with two bankers from Wentworth.

The correct procedure for a train leaving Wath Yard in 1908 with a double train of coal – I have yet to see it correctly described – was: the two engines (coupled together) would arrive, banker leading, from Mexborough shed. After coupling to the train, the whole went forward to the next signalbox – Wombwell station. (the train was thus double headed only for the first two miles). Here the banker was detached to go into a siding and the train drawn past. The banker then went behind the brake van and exchanged whistles with the train engine; the train would then be on its way with an engine at each end. First stop would be Wentworth Junction where each engine obtained water. (There were two water columns spaced so that the engines could be watered simultaneously). Another engine would attach at the front whilst the train engine got water. Whistles were exchanged and the train moved up to Wentworth Junction starting signal which would be at danger. After the train stopped, the fourth engine would come up behind the train and exchange whistles. The two engines at the rear would not be coupled – and were not coupled to the train. The speed up the bank was very slow – such that one could get off and pick flowers and then get back on board!

On arrival at West Silkstone Junction the assisting two engines were removed and the train went forward with one at each end as far as the summit of the line at Dunford; the banker then returned light engine to Mexborough shed – twenty miles away.

There had been many theoretical solutions put forward for solving the

Wentworth bank problem, including electrification of the two and a half mile section. Another was the provision of three cylinder 0-10-2 bankers with a tractive effort of 47,000lb. Both came to nothing.

In 1910 special double ended engines were being produced at the works of Beyer Peacock & Co at Gorton, opposite the GCR works, and some talks had been held before the First World War regarding a double ended four cylinder Beyer Garratt 0-8-0 + 0-8-0 using, as it were, two of Robinson's 0-8-0s back to back, the object being to save footplate staff wages and to free the 0-8-0s for train work. Two of these Garratt locos were under discussion when the First World War intervened. Because of hostilities nothing was done with any of these projects and after 1918, when the future of the pre-group companies was threatened by Lloyd George, any scheme for the Wentworth line was held in abeyance.

After the Great War in 1920, the Garratt scheme was re-appraised, this time envisaging a pair of Robinson class 8K 2-8-0s in the articulated form. However, in 1923 Sir Nigel Gresley became involved in all matters affecting loco design and the final shape for "the Garratt" involved two of Gresley's three cylinder 2-8-0s instead of the 8Ks(04S). This formula gave a total of six cylinders and a tractive effort of 72,940lb. The locomotive was delivered by Beyer Peacock in 1925 and after appearing in the Darlington Centenary exhibition of that year, it went to Wentworth to start its career as a banking engine.

The Garratt was never looked upon with favour by Mexborough, Barnsley or Wentworth men – particularly the firemen – as they were, in effect, doing the work of two men. Wentworth was a separate 'depot' for promotion, and

This is the classic combination on Wentworth bank - two engines at each end of a double coal train. The train engine is a J39, and the working possibly a Stairfoot - Mottram. Photograph taken in 1948 (no contact wires erected). Photograph E.R. Morten.

No 3888 arriving back at Wentworth Junction 18th April 1947. Photograph H C Casserley.

there were nine sets of men for the three engines involved; ie the Garratt and two 04 2-8-0s. If the Garratt was out of commission for any reason, two more 04s were sent from Mexborough and an extra set of men from Barnsley, the nearest shed. Wentworth was not a 'depot' in the true sense, merely a small cabin for signing on and storing lubricating oil. The men could also wait in there if traffic was light – which was not very often. Water was available in both directions and a small coaling plant was built at the nearby Wentworth Colliery. Wentworth 'depot' was nevertheless a cosmapolitan little place with, in the 1930s, men from distant climes, the likes of Neasden, Ipswich, March, Retford, Northwich and Frodingham stationed there, as well as local men.

Firing the Garratt on two successive days was forbidden so it was an 'every other day' roster and the great engine was despatched to Mexborough shed even for minor defects. The long main steam pipes to the cylinders had flexible connections because of the extreme length of the engine and these regularly leaked steam owing to the flexing of the long frames when passing through the crossover roads (three per trip). Blowing joints were a hazard when such a long locomotive was buffering up behind a train. A further defect when going up to a brake van was the steam brake: the steam pipe to the brake cylinders was necessarily a long one and the steam tended to condense into water below a certain temperature. Because of this feature, the regular Wentworth drivers always went up to a train 'on the regulator' i.e. using small intermittent applications of the regulator at very slow speed.

Taking the Garratt out from Mexborough shed on a Monday morning

This is the rear end of the aforementioned York - Mottram at Moor End; the Garratt fireman is working hard, the object being for the smoke to clear by the time the train reached the first Silkstone tunnel. Photograph E.R.Morten

was always regarded as something to be avoided. This job was in the bottom link (where else?) and the crew signed on at 2-15am. Two hours were allowed for preparation, double the normal allowance, and the departure time from the shed was 4-15 a.m. – to be at Wentworth for the Monday start up at 5 o'clock. (This time varied slightly over the years).

Making up the fire before departure from the shed was like filling a domestic coal cellar, shovelling for twenty minutes and not seeing any benefit on the deep 56.5 square feet of firegrate – it was akin a small dining room! Before leaving shed, the crew always went under the coal stage and topped up the bunker. When the engine arrived at Wentworth the Mexborough men were relieved by a Wentworth crew, and the first job was to go up to Wentworth colliery for coal, so that fuel would last the full eight hour shift. Such was the appetite of the Garratt. My regular driver in the bottom link in 1942 was Cliff Porter and he always had Monday off when it was our turn to take out the Garratt, so I usually had a passed fireman as a driver; for the remainder of the week it was the 12-15am assist Cadeby – Partington to Dunford, an overtime job so Cliff was little, if anything out of pocket. He always declared he would not get up at 1 o'clock on a Monday morning to take the Garratt to Wentworth – "it's their engine – let em come and fetch it". This was of course, impossible, as there was no way they could get to Mexborough at that time on a Monday morning. Cliff always considered himself a gentleman driver, which of course, he was, and he objected to oiling round for someone else.

Ron Silverwood, an eminent old Barnsley driver who had fired and driven

146

The Garratt at the bottom of Wentworth Bank (quite close to Wentworth Junction Signalbox) returning after pushing a train upto West Silkstone Junction. The date is April 1947 and it's running number has been changed to 9999 under the Thompson Scheme of 1946. Photograph H C Casserley

the Garratt for many years, is on record for the statement " The Garratt was 178 tons of nothing!". This was the universal view at Wentworth, Barnsley and Mexborough – though the latter was only marginally involved.

After 1912, the coal traffic along the branch was always heavy, but to this in 1923 was added several new train groups. Traffic from the old North Eastern Railway for Manchester and west had been routed via Normanton (L&Y) or Leeds (LNW) prior to 1923 but was afterwards diverted via Wath Junction and the Worsborough branch. Trains from Hull, York, Teeside and Newcastle, as well as the developing steel traffic from the Scunthorpe area, were all channelled through Worsborough, adding to the coal traffic already passing to the west. The Worsborough branch thereafter must have been one of the busiest branches in the country. – in the middle years of the Second World War there were 47 trains per day going up the bank and 49 coming down; these were timetabled trains and there were many specials too. This winter timetable 1943/44 extract shows:

Ex Wath	15	To Wath	12
Ex Ardsley	7	To Ardsley	4
Ex York	9	To York	15
Ex Scunthorpe	5	To Scunthorpe	4

147

Ex Hull	2	To Hull	5
Ex Stairfoot	2	To Stairfoot	1
Ex Grimsby	1	To Stainforth	1
Ex Wentworth	1*	To Monkton	1*
Ex Stainforth	1	To Hickleton	1*
Ex Cadeby	1*	To South Kirby	1*
Ex Broughton Lane	1	To Pindar	1
Ex Hexthorpe	1	To Cadeby	1*
Ex Manvers	1*	To Mitchells	1*
		To Barnsley	1
Total	47	Total	49

* Collieries

Instructions regarding train loadings along the Worsborough branch and the extra assistance required were quite specific and the following notes from the 1944 Loadings Book are worth recording. If specified loads on single goods trains, class B, were exceeded by one, two or three wagons, then assistance would not be required between Mexborough and Wentworth Junction, and the booked time had to be observed. This did not apply to mineral trains. Locomotive classes 1, 2 and 3 were to be assisted by one pilot, and classes 4, 5, 6, 7 and 8 inclusive by two pilots, or the Garratt from Wentworth to West Silkstone Junction. In the case of double trains (assisted by class 2 through to class 8) the following instruction applied: "Trains conveying these loads to be assisted by two class 7 pilots or the Garratt from Wentworth Junction to West Silkstone Junction. Double trains must be worked without additional assistance from Aldam Junction to Wombwell

A rare sight at Wentworth, a V2, No 889, on an empty stock train - these usually went via Barnsley. 18th April 1947. Photograph H.C.Casserley.

Main Junction provided there is a clear road from Mitchell Main Down Home signal to Lewden crossing." Except in the case of the one, two or three wagons' excess noted above, the general instruction applied that trains be assisted by a pilot from Aldam Junction to Wombwell Main Junction.

An extra pilot was available at Aldam Junction on a 24 hour basis (two during daytime) and when the Garratt was used from Wentworth on a double train, it meant the equivalent of three engines at the back – the normal banker and the Garratt; in this case a flying run could be made beyond West Silkstone, for there was no stop needed to detach the leading pilot. On some brake vans, when subjected to the three engines at the rear treatment for a few weeks, the frames could be seen to be bowed in an upward direction, such was the force needed to get the train up the 1 in 40 gradient.

Coming down the two and a half mile bank there were, of course, special instructions regarding the pinning down of wagon brakes and, as an average, this meant that the first ten and every other wagon brake was applied. A special brakesman was provided over 24 hours at West Silkstone but the guard released the brakes at the foot of the bank at Strafford.

The delays for eastbound trains were – relief at Barnsley Junction 8 minutes; pinning down wagon brakes 12 minutes and releasing them 12 minutes – a total of 32 minutes delay to most trains (there were very few brake fitted trains then). For trains up the bank, delays were: water and pilots at Wentworth 10 minutes, detaching pilot at West Silkstone 8 minutes, relief at Barnsley Junction 8 minutes – a total of up the bank, 26 minutes, down the bank 32 minutes. This situation of delays was a cross borne from 1880

3219, working a full load from Wentworth Colliery to the Barnsley Junction Yard at Penistone, five and a half miles away, 18th April 1947. Photograph H.C. Casserley.

to 1954, when the lines from Manchester to Wath were electrified.

The Worsborough branch was electrified in 1951/52 and the complete scheme, including Sheffield and Manchester, was commissioned in 1954; in these circumstances the authorities were anxious to find other work for the Garratt and various schemes were put forward... In 1949 the locomotive had been sent to Bromsgrove, south of Birmingham on the London Midland Region, to serve as banker on the Lickey Incline. This portion of the old Midland Railway West of England main line was similar to the Wentworth bank both in length and gradient, two miles at 1 in 37.5. There was however, one important difference; on the Lickey all trains were banked in the rear, including passenger trains. Bearing in mind the aforementioned delay with the steam brake application, there were a few accidents at Bromsgrove, mostly when the Garratt was going up behind passenger trains. With this rolling stock, tight coupled, there was no give in the train, only in the springs of the rear buffers, and on one occasion, the rear of a coach was badly damaged. After this, the Garratt was used bunker first, as this placed the driver nearer the point of contact. To help with the problem, a large electric lamp was fixed to the back of the rear water tank, with a Stones steam generator fitted to the side of the smokebox, to provide the power. At all times whilst in South Yorkshire the Garratt was worked chimney-first up the gradient, to protect the firebox crown sheet. Reversing this procedure at Lickey would always put the crown sheet in some danger.

With electric traction there were still two locomotives – one at each end from Wath to Dunford (1954-1958) and the assisting engine was used for additional electric braking from Dunford to Wath (1954-1958). These banking runs were shortened after 1958, to Wath – West Silkstone and return, because of a cut in loading. There were of course, no delays for relief, water or pinning down of wagon brakes as regenerative braking was used. The working of the Worsborough branch was transformed.

An article by The District Commercial Officer for British Rail Eastern region in trains Illustrated May 1961 summed up the electrics on Worsborough Bank thus:-

"Associated also with coal traffic, but in another part of Sheffield District altogether, is Wath Yard. This handles 3000 wagons a day; - nearly all coal wagons. Humping is by standard 350hp diesel shunters which replaced several years ago the massive Great Central 0-8-4Ts. Coal traffic from Wath to the west is disposed of by the Manchester – Sheffield – Wath electrified lines. The change in working this formidably graded route through the Pennines since electric traction replaced steam is remarkable; compared with the weary drag by steam locomotives, the Bo-Bo type electric locomotives seem to glide effortlessly up the long grades into the new Woodhead tunnel, through which there have never been regular steam workings. Over this route westwards out of the Sheffield District pass 86

freight trains per day; 93 is the record."

Following the advent of North Sea Gas the movement of coal (and goods) over the Pennines gradually fell away, almost to nothing, and the Worsborough branch and the whole line from Wath to the west was closed down and the tracks lifted in 1981. What little traffic remained, mainly the power stations to the Fiddlers Ferry plant were re-routed via Healey Mills.

CHAPTER 13

MOVING THE COAL TO MANCHESTER

BY RON FAREHAM
PUBLISHED IN BRITISH RAILWAYS ILLUSTRATED VOLUME 7 NO 8 MAY 1998.

In the middle years of the 19th century some large collieries were opened in the valleys to the south of Barnsley. One of the important areas was Worsborough Dale where in 1861, six pits were tapping the Barnsley and Silkstone seams, some of which were 11 feet thick and of very high quality with little ash content.

The only railway penetrating this area was the small South Yorkshire Railway, whose Chairman for the first six years was the Earl Fitzwilliam, who was a power in the county. Its lines were single and its development moved ahead slowly, in unison with that of the mining technology of the coal industry. Doubling of the lines came in the 1870s. The six collieries on the Worsborough Branch at that time were:-

1 Old Silkstone
2 Strafford
3 Worsborough Park
4 Swaithe
5 Edmunds Main
6 Darley Main

The working timetable for 1861 shows trips to all these pits from the SYR's Hexthorpe mineral yard at Doncaster. There was also the Chapeltown Branch which contributed a further eight collieries:-

7 Wombwell Main
8 Barrow
9 Hoyland
10 Rockingham
11 Pilley
12 Tankersley
13 Smithy Wood
14 Dropping Well

Additionally, there was another short branch to Earl Fitzwilliam's collieries at 15 Lundhill and 16 Elsecar and later Cortonwood (of 1984 pit strike fame). These 16 collieries in the 1850s and 1860s were serviced by the 23 small, privately built 0-6-0 engines of the South Yorkshire Railway. The firms involved in the building of the SYR engine stock were:-

TYPE	BUILDER	No
0-4-2	Bury, Curtis and Kennedy of Liverpool	2
0-6-0	Gilkes, Wilson of Middlesborough.	4
0-6-0	E.B. Wilson of Leeds	7
0-6-0	Kitsons of Leeds	4
0-6-0	Beyer Peacock of Gorton	6
0-4-2	Thwaites of Bradford	1
0-4-2	Dodds of Rotherham	1
0-6-2	George England of London	1
0-6-0	Built at Mexborough Shops SYR	2
Total		28

This ragbag of small engines worked the traffic of the SYR until 1864 when the SYR was leased to the MS&LR, when they were supplemented by a number of MS&L types.

Because of the heavy nature of the gradients and the work involved, there were always difficulties maintaining the locomotives. The SYR was taken over fully in 1874 by the MS&L and in 1886 the new Locomotive Superintendent at Gorton, Thomas Parker, conducted a survey of the total MS&L engine stock. This survey reveals the Mexborough allocation at 79 engines, of which 20 (mostly old SYR and Sacre designs) were out of action in Gorton works - 25% unavailable! This situation took place at a time when South Yorkshire coal production was increasing, mainly because of its high quality. The allocation at Mexborough revealed in the survey in 1886 was as follows:-

TYPE	CLASS	NO IN CLASS MS&L	LOAD CLASS	
0-6-0	18	7	5	Class 1 was the highest load
0-6-0	22	12	4	
0-6-0	23	26	5	
0-6-0	6A	3	4	LNER J12
0-6-0	6C1	6	1	LNER J12
0-6-0	6C2	6	1	LNER J12
2-4-0	10	5	5	
0-6-0T	18T	14	5	
Total		79		

From these small beginnings sprang the great South Yorkshire coal trade, which developed into an enormous industry and one of the most lucrative coal fields in the country. In 1874 when the SYR had been fully integrated into the Manchester, Sheffield and Lincolnshire Railway, the output of coal had risen to over 3 million tons annually. A good proportion of this traffic was worked into the Hexthorpe (Doncaster) yard and sent forward to the ports of Hull and Grimsby for export; traffic also went on to the adjoining

Great Northern Railway for movement to eastern and southern England and to the LNWR.

Another route for traffic from the Wath area was that to Manchester and North Cheshire and the mills of Lancashire. It is mainly this westward movement with which we are concerned here. This west traffic was hindered in its passage by a number of factors:

(a) The rough nature of the land and consequently heavy gradients generally.
(b) The severe 1 in 40 gradient of the 2 mile Wentworth incline.
(c) The three mile block section of the Woodhead Tunnel.
(d) The inadequate size and construction of the locomotive fleet.
(e) The convergence at Penistone of the heavy traffic from the Sheffield district.

The classic method of improving the flow of loose coupled, unbraked coal trains was to double the number of tracks from two to four. This had already been done by the turn of the century by some of the major coal movers, the Midland, the LNWR, the North Eastern, Great Western and Great Northern. These were among the most prosperous lines in the country and could raise – or even provide – the necessary capital. However, the newly formed and impecunias MS&L, now the Great Central, having just financed the extension of their line from Annesley to London, could neither provide nor raise any further large sums for quadrupling. In the case of Woodhead Tunnel, it was out of the question in any event.

Around the turn of the century there were some important changes among the management. A financial expert, Alexander Henderson, became a Director in 1895 and on the resignation of the Earl of Wharncliffe, in 1899, Henderson became Chairman of the Company. This was the prelude to other appointments – Sam Fay became General Manager in 1902, coming from the London and South Western Railway where he had been Superintendent of the line.

This pair set about modernising the assets of the Company so as to improve the flow of traffic; particularly westward over Woodhead. With quadrupling denied to them, Henderson and Fay began other improvements to the running facilities. These consisted of running loops at such places as Penistone, Bullhouse and Dunford on the eastern side and also loops in both directions on the western side of the summit of the line and further down towards Guide Bridge. Derbyshire and Nottinghamshire were included as the Great Central Railway worked coal trains from all these areas of what, in essence, was a southern extension of the same coalfield.

In view of the expansion in coal output and the multitude of small 0-6-0s on the line, the MS&L/GC Directors, Chairman and General Manager looked around for a Locomotive Superintendent to replace Harry Pollit, who had tendered his resignation. The Directors and Henderson selected John G

Pom Pom Class J11. A Robinson GC design introduced 1901. This engine had a small firebox but it was very deep; the fireman only had to put coal at the back end and it would fall to the front. These engines were good steamers; and as Mexborough men would say, "they'd pull owt". No 64444 has probably just run onto the shed because it is still in steam; the tender is low on coal; and it is standing on No 10 road. Courtesy Great Central Railway Society.

Robinson from the Waterford, Limerick and Western Railway in Ireland, although most of his time had been spent on the Great Western Railway where he had family connections.

Robinson set about improving the engine stock, initially by continuing to build the Parker/Pollit class 9H 0-6-0, the final variant of the Parker Class 9, which all together by 1902, had numbered 161. The 9J (J11) was Robinson's first goods engine design in 1901 and it was excellent. I have personally fired and driven these engines for many miles and could recommend them for any job, mineral or express, so long as the speed did not exceed 60mph. They were universally liked by the footplate staff and eventually comprised 174 – they were class 3 for loading.

Further expansion of coal output posed a real problem for Henderson and Fay. Line improvements such as new loops and intermediate block signals on rising gradients brought some relief but there were still serious delays caused by line congestion. The only solution left was to build much bigger locomotives.

Following a high powered meeting, the decision was taken to approach the firm of Nielson & Co. of Glasgow who were already building six Class 8 4-6-0s, which had the same boiler as the projected 0-8-0 Class 8A. Neilson built only three examples of the Class 8A and the rest were produced by Kitsons (51) and the G.C. Gorton Shops (35) making a total of 89. The first example was No 1052 and it came to Mexborough. Mexborough had the

Class O4/3; this was the first modification to the 1911 design; introduced in 1917. Standing on the Cripple sidings at Mexborough on 16th September 1956.
Courtesy Great Central Railway Society

biggest allocation of Class 8A(Q4) before the First World War. Though excellent in every way, they were to be superceded in 1911 by the Robinson 8K 2-8-0. This was the ultimate mineral engine in 1911 and served the G.C.R., L.N.E.R. and B.R. right up to dieselisation in 1966. The following table illustrates Robinson's goods and heavy mineral designs built from 1901 to 1919 and the consequent increase in train loading from Wath to Manchester.

CLASS	BUILT	NO BUILT	LOAD CLASS
9J (J11)	1901-1910	174	3
8A(Q4)	1902-1911	89	6
8K/M (O4/5)	1911-1919	148	7

Another of Fay's ideas was to provide each coal train to the west with an additional engine, to be put at the rear of the train to the summit of the line at Dunford, with two thirds of the wagon brakes dropped beyond to assist in braking. This nearly doubled the load at a stroke and improved the operating statistics dramatically. The three factors affecting the increase in the throughput of wagons from the Wath area to Manchester were in place by 1922. They were:-

(a) improved running facilities; loops etc
(b) much larger locomotives
(c) double trains with banker assistance to Dunford and wagon brakes dropped beyond that point.

With these items in place, a limit was reached in what could be done, without recourse to building four tracks throughout. However, there were two more pieces to be put into the jigsaw before it could be said that all the problems aside from quadrupling were completely solved. These were major marshalling yards near each end of the Wath – Manchester route – the double hump yard at Wath, built in 1907 and the gravity yard at Mottram, built in 1932. The increase in train loading with the bigger engines and double trains is demonstrated in the following table:-

The table below gives the number of trains INTO Wath Yard on a daily basis.

	1902	1910	1914	1921	1928	1932	1943	1947
FROM THE WEST	0	24	24	30	38	35	34	16
FROM THE EAST	0	32	31	37	24	22	23	18
TOTALS	0	56	55	67	62	57	57	34

Most of the many colliery pilot trips into the yard each day were not entered into the working timetables. These pilots worked on an ad hoc basis and were arranged between Control and the yard inspectors. The system was also influenced by the varying practices at the pits. The figures are mainly coal empties. After 1941 many coal empties were kept out of Wath Yard and the trains went directly to the pits. This was brought about by the formation of a "National Coal Empties Poll", - effectively Government confiscation. Also in 1941, the night shift at the Yard was discontinued because the "chasers" refused to work when "Air Raid Purple" was declared; that is, "Enemy Aircraft approaching the area". The management therefore closed the Yard at 2200 except for departures. This system was helped by the aforementioned confiscation of the privately owned empties fleet. The majority of the Hull traffic was worked into Hexthorpe (Doncaster) Yard. It amounted to 13 trains daily in 1902; - all worked from Hexthorpe by the North Eastern Railway with Hull (Dairycoates) engines and men!

The twin centres of the South Yorkshire Coalfield, one of the richest in the Country before the Second World War, were the large towns of Barnsley and Doncaster. The portion of the coalfield around Barnsley was the older of the two, and by the time Wath Yard was opened in 1907, some of the smaller Barnsley area pits were reaching the end of their useful lives. Barnsley was for many years, the centre of this coalfield and the Headquarters of the Yorkshire Mineworkers was established in the town – and is still there despite the centre of the coalfield moving across to Doncaster. Evidence of this, is the presence in Doncaster of the Yorkshire Headquarters of British Coal, a more recent authority.

Wath Yard was placed midway between these two towns and to give some idea of the need in 1907 for such a large yard in such a large place, it must be said that within a radius of 10 miles of Wath, there were 46 collieries, and there were still 35 in 1940.

The yard was built on a piece of nearly level ground – there was a slight slope towards the east; the area was known locally as "Cunnigarth" and was very close to the Wath Main Colliery. It was the brainchild of the Great Central General Manager, Sir Sam Fay, following a visit to the United States. Its purpose was to concentrate the marshalling of coal wagons from the pits to the various destinations instead of it being done on a piecemeal basis in some of the smaller yards – and in many cases, the actual colliery yards. Logan & Hemmingway, a firm much used by the M.S.& L.R. and the G.C.R., was the builder of the yard for a sum of £60,879 and it was commissioned in August 1907.

The whole complex; it was really two yards, one for each direction, was one and threequarter miles long and contained 36 miles of track. It was the most modern hump yard in the country, and the first to use pneumatic power for both points and signals. The yard points operated by the two hump cabins, "A" and "B", were controlled by electro-pneumatic power and this later was used to control the main line points and signals. The total cost, taking into account rails, signals, air equipment and buildings was close to £200,000, a very large sum for those days.

Westbound, there were 9 reception roads and 31 sorting sidings: eastbound, there were 8 and 31. In each group of reception sidings, one line was kept clear as an engine run round line. The total capacity of the yard was 5000 wagons a day. In the days before 1940, all empty coal wagons passed through the yard as each privately owned vehicle had to be sent empty to the proper owning colliery.

There were two locomotive ash pits in the centre of the yard, together with water columns and a "push round" turntable. In addition there were various loops, engine lines and wagon cripple sidings. There were two humps, "A" and "B". "A" hump sorted wagons for the west, "B" for the east. Trains arriving on the reception lines seldom contained wagons which were all for one direction and hence there was a considerable number of vehicles that were "transfers". An example of this would be, that a train from a colliery to the west of the yard normally went onto "B" hump; however, if the train contained wagons for the west, then these had to go over "B" hump and into the transfer road. They would then be picked up by the "A" hump pilot and pushed over "A" hump into their correct road for a west departure. This was double humping – and there were many instances of it in a period of 24 hours.

The layouts in each direction were very similar: the two groups of 31 sorting sidings were laid out in the "gridiron" pattern with two long "ladders" and roads running off.The advantage of this arrangement was, that it allowed a straight, unobstacled run between the ladders so that the wagon "chasers" could run at the wagon side and control the speed of the vehicle by applying the brake. A good deal of agility was required on this job and advertised vacancies were usually suffixed "Must be a good runner".

The chasers were spaced out down each ladder and were equipped with short brake sticks: the top man dropped the wagon brakes as the vehicle passed him at moderate speed; the second and successive chasers ran at the side of the wagon and put pressure on the wagon brake to control it into the individual road. This reduced the impact with the wagons already in the road and avoided damage.

The system of chasing worked very well in the early days of the yard when all the wagons had axle boxes lubricated with fat. However, when oil fed axle boxes became more general after the Second World war, the wagons ran more freely. In this situation, if the top man missed the brake handle, the wagon was running too fast for any subsequent chaser to get at it and the result was a very heavy impact with the stationery wagons already in the road. The sudden and violent stop sometimes derailed the vehicle, but the more usual result was that part of the load of coal was shot over the wagon end and onto the ground; occasionally the end door burst open,with the loss of a few tons of coal. At Wath, the amount of such spillage in the fifties and sixties was considerable and led to a close investigation. The railway had, of course, to compensate the consignee for any loss of weight stated on the wagon label, which was put on by the weighman at the colliery. This spilt coal had to be picked up and was used at Mexborough shed- and other places- to fire the stationery boilers. It was poor stuff as there was a heavy mixture of ballast therein. However, its use ensured that the spillage was not a complete loss; it was always known as "pick up" coal.

There were no separate departure groups of roads at Wath where prepared trains could be parked awaiting the train engine; these were only found at more modern yards such as Whitemoor. Each light engine arriving had to prepare its own train; this usually involved attaching wagons, drawing them down and backing up onto the breakvan. Each guard was responsible for preparing his own train, assisted by the shunter, and knocking out any odd crippled wagon. This usually led to a late departure.

The modernisation of Wath Yard with retarding equipment was never possible because of the gridiron pattern of the roads resulting in very short space between the point blades on the "ladders". There was nowhere to put a retarder in this design of sidings.

Each hump had two specially designed 0-8-4 tank locomotives built by Beyer Peacock and Co of Gorton, and coming on the scene in December 1907 and January 1908

THE "DAISIES" AND THE "PUSH UP".
These three cylinder engines, 0-8-4 tank engines were built in 1907 for the very heavy humping duties in the new yard at Wath. Four were originally built, 1170-1173, to which numbers the LNER added 5000. They were

employed, two at each hump "A" and "B". This liberal provision of power was allowed so that humping, which could be almost continuous throughout the 24 hours, to cope with the planned throughput of 5000 wagons a day, could thereby be realised. This figure applied to a mixture of both loaded and empty wagons, as privately owned coal empties had to go to the owning collieries in those days and this applied right through to the early years of the Second World War. A break of only a few minutes was planned between the humping of trains – just sufficient time to allow the release of the humping engine after the last wagon had passed over the hump and before the next train moved up.

The physical characteristics of the two humps were radically different. A slight slope to the east determined that "A" hump (westbound) was steep (1 in 107) but that "B" hump (eastbound) was nearly level (1 in 2108). Therefore starting a 65 wagon train on "A" hump and slowly pushing it forward (the slower the better), was a stiff proposition.: so much so that, in wintertime, an additional engine was provided on "A" hump to assist the Daisy. This addition made it three engines at the east end of the yard. The extra engine was always called the "push up" pilot to distinguish it from the other four. The unfortunate feature for the "push up" crew was that they assisted every train on "A" hump whereas the Daisies pushed every other one.

In an attempt to obviate the use of the "push up" pilot, Gresley fitted No 6171 in 1929 with an American Booster engine on the trailing bogie.

Class S1 "Daisy" introduced 1907; a Robinson GC design. Four engines were built originally for the heavy humping duties in Wath Yard. Two were moved to March depot in 1932 to work on the new hump yard at Whitemoor. They were all phased out circa 1953 when the 350HP diesel shunters arrived. 6172 is probably at March MPD in this picture; a B16 "Walsingham" is standing in the background. Courtesy Great Central Railway Society.

This was a small two cylinder engine fitted inside the bogie frames with the bogie wheels coupled by means of side rods. The bogie wheel dimensions were so designed that the four exhaust beats per revolution occurred at exactly the same time intervals as the three main cylinders, giving six beats per turn of the driving wheels.

In 1932, 6172 and 6173 were transferred to March depot to work on the new hump yard at Whitemoor. However, Gresley built two new S1s, complete with boosters, as replacements for 6172 and 6173. Their numbers were 2798 and 2799. These two had side window cabs and cut down front corners to the side tanks so as to improve the outlook when going up behind a train. This, together with 6171, gave a total of three booster fitted Daisies, ensuring there would always be two booster fitted ones available for the steeper "A" hump.

The Daisies always worked with chimney leading towards the west thus giving added protection to the firebox roof plate when working on "A" hump. It also ensured that the engine would be going forward on the stiffest task – again "A" hump. This of course meant that the engines always worked bunker first on "B" hump, which was, as stated, nearly level, so the positioning of the engine didn't matter.

69904 was one of two new engines which Gresley introduced in 1932 for Wath to replace the two sent to March MPD. They were slightly modified, having side window cabs, the front corners to the side tanks were cut down so as to improve the look out when going up behind a train, and they were fitted with boosters. Now in BR livery and with its booster removed, it is seen standing on shed in September 53. Incidentally, when leaving the shed, this engine could not go round the curve from Mexborough No 3 to Mexborough No 1; it was too tight a curve for an engine with too rigid a wheelbase. Instead it had to leave the shed and go via Mexborough station where it was switched over to go to Wath.
Courtesy Great Central Railway Society.

The boosters were reversible but in practice, with the Daisies always chimney first on "A" hump, the back gear was never used. The fore gear booster was in use on "A" hump, but even with this, the tractive effort of 46,896lbs was insufficient to start a heavy train during frosty weather. However, on "B" hump, only a fraction of the power of the three main cylinders was ever used to push a train on the nearly level "B" hump – let alone needing a booster. The latter therefore was never used because it was never needed. How Gresley came to order reversible boosters for Wath will now never be known. The problem had obviously not been properly investigated before the decision was made. Volume 9B of the RCTS Locomotives of the LNER poses the question as to why the back gear operation of the booster was blanked off so soon after erection. The reason was that it was not needed – and this was no doubt very quickly discovered – and at some expense.

The Daisies had very long frames and consequently were barred from using the very acute curve between Mexborough No 1 and Mexborough No 3 when going to shed; instead they had to use the other two sides of the Mexborough triangle in each direction. The cabs were roomy, but because of the high floor, a tall man had to be careful to avoid hitting his head. The regulator was a long version of the normal Robinson design with the addition of a "foot" at the bottom end. This, together with the additional length, made for very sensitive handling as the load gradually reduced as the hump top approached. An unfortunate occurrence with this regulator was that a fireman once stood on the "foot" to close the roof ventilator. He slipped and

2799 was the second of two new engines which Gresley introduced in 1932 for Wath. Note the booster, side cab windows and the cut down front corner to the side tank. After nationalisation, this was renumbered 69905. Seen here at Mexborough shed; the building in the background is the old coal stage. Courtesy Great Central Railway Society.

injured himself in the process. On his claiming for compensation, all the "regulator "feet" were removed.

Steam reverse was fitted, but not to help the driver with constant reversal; the Daisies did not reverse as often as a normal shunting engine did, they merely went behind trains already placed on the reception lines, and pushed. It was always considered that the steam reverse was fitted so as to save space between the wide water tanks and the boiler.

All the Daisies were transferred away in 1953 when the standard 350 h.p. Diesel shunters arrived. Most of them went to Frodingham.

MOTTRAM YARD

After 1908, when Wath Yard really got into its stride, the despatch of double coal trains to the Manchester area was heavy and very efficient, so much so that the traffic tended to bunch beyond Woodhead. The cause of this was that there was no complimentary large yard at the Manchester end to receive and sort the traffic coming from Wath and Sheffield. There were a number of small yards in the Manchester district – all flat shunting yards – at Godley, Ashton Moss, Ordsall Lane, Asbury's, Ardwick, Phillips Park and so on. During winter months the traffic would back up in the loop lines west of Woodhead with trains head to tail for miles. This would mean train men from the east on overtime rates and relief crews being sent out from Gorton. The situation did not receive attention until the late 1920s – after Grouping, when, with Government assistance, it was decided to build a new yard at Gamesley near Dinting. The name was later changed to Mottram. The yard took some years to build as heavy excavation was necessary in order to get the proper levels.

[I have omitted the detailed notes about Mottram Yard as it is outside the scope of this book, but for any interested reader, a back copy of the publication could be obtained from Irwell Press Ltd on 01525 861888..]

The demise of Mottram in the early 1980s was for the same reasons as Wath Yard – natural gas replacing the industrial and domestic coal. In its later days Mottram was used as a locomotive changeover point, from electric to diesel for the Fiddlers Ferry power station trains to Warrington but it closed in 1982, after which this traffic was re-routed over the Calder Valley (L&Y) route.

After the slump years of the early 1930s, unemployment was very high. As some alleviation to this state of affairs, the Government offered the railways capital sums for certain works that were required, where these could be demonstrated to have positive effect on employment. The LNER share of these funds was used, among many other things, for two great projects. These were the electrification of the old GER suburban lines around London, and electrification of the lines between Manchester, Sheffield and Wath (always known as the MSW scheme). Looking west, these lines formed an inverted 'Y'. The reason for choosing the MSW route was the heavy expense of the operation generally – which electrification would reduce substantially, by dispensing with:

- Two engines per train to Dunford
- Light engines running back to shed
- Six brakesmen at Dunford and West Silkstone.
- Heavy overtime charges for the crews
- The nine or twelve enginemen at Wentworth Junction depending on the availability of the Garratt.
- Water Columns and Plant
- The cost of the heavy backlog at Wath Yard during winter months – usually cleared on a Sunday at time and three quarters

Erection of the supporting girders began in 1938-39, but ceased on the outbreak of war in 1939. The work restarted in 1946 and was completed in June 1954. The depots concerned were Gorton in Manchester, Darnall in Sheffield and Wath, manned by ex- Mexborough crews.

Enginemen were trained by six leading motormen at each place, where the techniques of notching and regenerative braking were taught. Regeneration was used on the long falling gradients and substantial amounts of electric current put back into the electric wires, to be used by electric locomotives moving uphill on the opposite lines.

Initially, electric bankers were used to Dunford and then gave braking assistance going back to Wath – mainly on the 1 in 40 of the Wentworth bank. This was eventually cut back to assistance to West Silkstone only on the rising gradients and also braking assistance from that point back to Wath – using many fewer men.

When the 1,500 ton air braked trains to the new power station at Fiddlers Ferry at Warrington were mooted in 1972, the locomotives were doubled to four – two at each end- worked by two crews, as before, with multiple working while at the same time, drivers would communicate by telephone, via the overhead traction wires!

In the late 1970s North Sea gas was eating into the coal traffic to the west and by 1981 it had almost finished. The final curtain came down in 1982, when Wath Yard, Mottram Yard and all the main lines between were closed and the tracks lifted as far as Hadfield. Beyond there, the Manchester suburban passenger trains continued to run.

CHAPTER 14

FIRST IMPRESSIONS – A PERSONAL VIEW OF THE THOMPSON B1s

BY RON FAREHAM.
FIRST PUBLISHED IN BRITISH RAILWAYS ILLUSTRATED
VOL 3 NO 4 JANUARY 1994.

A Personal View of the B1 4-6-0s from one who knows. The author, a railwayman of 44 years service on the LNER and BR, had extensive experience of Edward Thompson's B1 class, from 1947 until their demise twenty years later. During this period, he moved through four phases of the job- Fireman, Driver, Foreman at Mexborough shed, and finally, ten years as a Train Crew Manager at Leeds.

"Sir Nigel Gresley died in 1941 and his place was taken by Edward Thompson, a man who had worked on the Midland and North Eastern railways; he also spent some years on the LNER as Mechanical Engineer, Stratford, followed by similar positions at Darlington & Doncaster.

His ideas were very different from Gresley's and he soon set about planning a series of standard designs to cover the post war requirements of the LNER.

Lovely side view of 61060 at Cambridge on 31st August 1959. The B1s found particular favour on the G.E. section for much the same reasons as the Britanias which followed them - they were demonstrably superior in vital respects to the engines they replaced. The B1s on the G.E. went straight on to express duties and were preferred to the often run down B17s then in use. The B1s however did not stand up well to prolonged top notch duties. Photograph Peter Groom

165

The scope for quantity production of locomotives in 1941 was severely limited but this did not stop Thompson making the necessary preparations and formulating designs. He analysed the situation of the LNER locomotive stock and produced designs to match. The most important of these was for a medium weight, class 5 (loading) mixed traffic 4-6-0 with two cylinders. This was a type of engine the LNER had needed since Grouping but for some unexplained reason, Gresley had never provided; the only 4-6-0 built in his time was the B17 Sandringhams, but this was actually worked out by the North British Locomotive Co and something of a special design in that it was initially intended for the Great Eastern section, with its weak underline bridges.

The first Thompson B1 4-6-0 was originally numbered 8301, a number falling within the ex GNER number blocs – remember that Thompson was for some years at Stratford Works. The Railway Magazine for January 1943 gave the impression that the new B1 was an engine built up of spare parts from other locomotives – the boiler from the B17, wheels from the V2, cylinders from the K2 etc. What was really happening was that Thompson was putting into practice his ideas on standardisation by using the various parts from the other designs. What did impress one from the photograph of 8301 was the thoroughgoing LNER style about it; with perhaps a North Eastern smokebox door, reflecting Thompson's origins. E S Cox did it later on the BR engines with his L&Y chimney.

61327 at Darnall (Sheffield LNER) shed; it had just come off the wet pit and is having the tender tank filled. The signal box is Darnall West and the overhead supports for the MS&W electrification scheme are clearly visible. 61327 was an NBL built example, arriving in June 1948 and like most B1s from Glasgow, was equipped with the Stones electric lighting equipment. Photograph Peter Groom

At first, 8301 was stationed at Gorton, running trials to Sheffield, and it was at Sheffield Victoria station that I first saw it in late 1943. It was waiting on the middle road with its Gorton crew, to work forward a train from Marylebone to Manchester and I went onto the footplate to talk to the Gorton men. I was most impressed with the layout of the cab and the controls; one had become used over the years to equipment on GN engines placed in awkward positions and poor seats for the crews. (Gresley only put good seats on his really big engines). Here was a locomotive with a level, unobstructed cab floor, footstools provided in front of upholstered bucket seats, horizontal reversing shaft, GC style regulator, steam and vacuum brakes and steam and dry sanding. The Gorton crew were delighted with their machine and said that it had performed extremely well on the up journey and steamed very freely. The firebox was the usual NE and GN round topped style but, of course, GC men never expected anything else from Darlington & Doncaster.

I thought to myself, if it suits Gorton men to that extent, then it must be good, for Gortonians were very conservative and anti-Gresley to a man. When the train left Sheffield, 8301 took it out of the platform effortlessly and with a very positive sharp beat. It was an impressive start for Thompson with dyed in the wool GC men, and the footplate fraternity generally.

The first B1s, 8301-8310, came into being in the war years. There was then a twenty two month gap before production restarted at Darlington, where another 30 were built. 8301 to 8310 were renumbered 1000-1009 and the next thirty followed on from there (to 1039). At about the same time in April 1946, the North British Locomotive Co at Glasgow started on a series and I was somewhat surprised to read in the Railway Magazine that the total to be ordered would come to 400. In fact it was eventually 410.

Orders of this magnitude had never previously been placed by the LNER authorities, but it must be appreciated that hardly any engines had been built for six years and the demand reflected these arrears.

The B1s, it was originally intended, would be known as the "Antelope" class and, as is well known, 1000 to 1040, all built at Darlington, were given names of the Antelope family. – and pretty obscure some of them were. Nobody that I knew had ever heard of such animals as PUKU, SASSABY, ADDAX, and DIBATAG. At Stratford, they were collectively "Bongos", after one of the first ten stationed at Stratford for some years, but this general term never travelled north. "Antelope" never took on either; indeed, I never heard it mentioned by footplate men anywhere. They merely called them B1s, which was short, apt and accurate.

The numbers allocated under Thompson's scheme of 1946 were 1000 – 1409 and all the projected 410 locomotives were actually built. The manufacture of such a large group of engines was entrusted to four works as follows:- North British Locomotive Co (290), Darlington (LNER) (60), Vulcan Foundry (50), and Gorton (LNER) (10).

One of the Mexbough B1s (Note the shed plate 36B on the smokebox door) on an excursion to the Manchester area, possibly Belle Vue, on 6th April 1953.
Photo BKB Green. Courtesy of the Mike Hartley Collection.

Making a total of 410 – note that the GCR shops at Gorton were again building engines, for the first time in many years.

In the summer of 1947, five brand new B1s were delivered to Mexborough shed- 1164, 1165, 1166, 1167 and 1168. These machines were a joy to behold – resplendent in LNER apple green, fitted with electric lighting equipment, with a crisp beat and no Gresley knock – the men in the passenger link took to them immediately. Ernest Taylor became a Thompson fan overnight, a second generation dyed in the wool GC man. After the 'make do and mend ' years of the war, here was a passenger engine worthy of its name. I well remember Ernest, the senior passenger driver at the time, giving them a very good name. This was praise indeed as Ernest was a second generation railwayman and rabid, almost, in his following of Robinson. It should be realised that the Mexborough Passenger Link men had, for six years, been working expresses from Sheffield to Hull with nothing bigger than a Robinson B5, which, though good of their type, were 45 years old and only a class 2 for loading.

1164 to 1168 came from the Vulcan Foundry at Newton-le-Willows in Lancashire and were part of the series 1140-1189 and, in my opinion, they were the best group in the B1 series. The 'Vulcans' were very free at steaming, smooth riders and in my time on them, they had the Gresley drop grate. They had an orthodox smokebox which accounted for their good steaming properties. The later fitting of self cleaning smokeboxes to most of the class adversely affected the steaming and the blastpipes had to be altered.

After some months, no 1164 was transferred away to the Kings Cross district and was not seen again. In its place came 1194, one of the North British Loco Co series. This engine was less than two years old and it was a dud. The difference between 1194 and the Vulcan engines was dramatic – it wasn't free at steaming, it was rough riding at anything over 60mph and was quickly regarded at Mexborough as the black sheep of the B1 family. It was treated as something of a standby and kept off the Hull jobs in case of steaming trouble.

In my opinion, the trouble was twofold; - smokebox and firegrate. The grate was of the early rocker bar pattern; in this design, the bars and their frames were two thick and this cut down the free entry of primary air under the fire. The smokebox was of the self cleaning pattern. Both items were new to this country and were really in the early stages of development; some later work improved the situation and some sheds took to removing the smoke box screens to improve the gas flow. The same equipment was also fitted to the V2 class and they became similarly afflicted, but not to the same extent. If a locomotive acquired a bad name for steaming it was a disaster, for men would lose interest if they perceived their was no chance of winning. Such was the fate of 1194 in 1949 and it put all the staff at Mexborough against the NBL built B1s, perhaps unfairly.

There were two passenger turns worked by Mexborough men to Hull,

This had always been a Mexborough B1 although the shed plate on the smoke box door reads 41D which was Canklow. The reallocation must have taken place in the early 60s towards the twilight of steam. The engine is standing in one of the middle roads in Sheffield Victoria station. Courtesy Mike Hartley.

the first being the 0900 from Doncaster returning with the 1205 Hull – Kings Cross as far as Doncaster. This was a 10 coach train and a portion from York was added at Doncaster, the train going forward to Kings Cross with a Pacific and Doncaster men. This train was an easy proposition to work from Hull as it only had two stops, Brough and Goole. The second turn was the 1000 Sheffield to Hull arriving at 1145. Its return was the 1620 Hull – Liverpool via Sheffield and although a coach lighter than the Kings Cross one, it was a stiffer proposition as it stopped at the first three stations, Hessle, Ferriby and Brough.

The B1s were so good at steaming that, with both trains to Hull, one could, with careful management, arrive at Paragon station with the front portion of the fire all but dead. It was then an easy task to clear the rear half of the grate of clinker whilst standing in the station, and by the time you reached Botanic Gardens shed, (close by) the front half of the fire was dead and the back half clean. The clinker at the front then only needed pushing out through the drop grate with the long clinker shovel, just a few minutes work.

At Botanic Gardens, a passenger only shed, the coaling plant supplied first quality Brodsworth hard steam coal- beautiful stuff. Under the coaling plant there was always a quantity of good lump coal around which had fallen off other tenders during the coaling process. Harold Rutherford and I used to load all these lumps onto the footplate, to make up the fire for the return journey. Rutherford, whose nickname was "Rutt" was an excellent engineman, and something of a comedian to boot- my time with him included the marvellous summer of 1949. Excellent engines, very good driver and beautiful weather; what more could a 27 year old fireman wish for? The time passed all too quickly.

The injectors on the B1s were very good, so long as you kept the water adjustment handle and valve lubricated on the 'J' class steam injector. It should be explained here that these injectors did not function on exhaust steam only, but a mixture of exhaust and live steam, and when the regulator was closed, it was live steam only. The 'Monitor' injector on the left hand side of the cab had a screw down valve. I always had the 'J' class injector at minimum, the 'Monitor' at maximum and the water level at about two thirds of a glass, with the regulator open. This ensured that you always had room in the boiler, and, if the driver shut the regulator, you could quickly turn on the 'Monitor' at maximum and so kill off the tendency to blow off at the safety valves.

The five original B1s allocated to Mexborough were fitted with electric lighting by Metropolitan Vickers Ltd. It had a full switch panel in the cab roof above the fireman, controlling headlights, tail light, water gauges, steam and vacuum brake gauges, the reverse indicator and cab lights. There was a battery under the fireman's seat fed by an alternator fixed to the bogie left hand rear axle stub. It was a good system and worked very well;

unfortunately one of the alternators came loose and fell into the ballast at Broomfleet off engine 1166 and after that, the alternators were removed. 1194, one of the NBL series, was fitted with the Stones system of lighting; this had no battery and, if you wanted electric lighting, you simply opened the steam valves to the generator and the system started up. The main trouble with this equipment, which was otherwise reliable, was the high pitched whining noise all the time the generator was working. This was something of a nuisance particularly if you were standing during fog waiting for an audible signal to set back, and occasionally, one had to shut down the generator in order to hear the signal.

During the summer of 1949, no 1174 (another Vulcan) was sent to Mexborough and had of course at one time been fitted with the Metro Vick system. This had been removed together with all the others, but with 1174 the original equipment had been removed and a small turbine generator provided in place of the axle mounted alternator. This equipment was similar in principle to the vacuum brake ejector in that a jet of steam induced a strong current of air to drive the small turbine, and thus the generator, which supplied the current. It was at least, not as noisy as the Stones generator. This isolated example was removed two years later without comment, though it was the better system of the two.

1174 itself was also removed from Mexborough in 1950 and sent to Kings Cross shed. This was the best B1 I ever worked and always had a slight edge on the other four Vulcans; at Mexborough it was something of a flyer. One could

A Mexborough B1 No 61165 standing in Sheffield Victoria station on 4th May 1963 probably heading a local stopping train to Doncaster or Hull.
Photo R J Buckley. Courtesy Mike Hartley Collection.

often see it passing through Doncaster on the Kings Cross to Hull fish train empties, or its return with the loaded vans, a lodging turn for the Kings Cross men. They knew what they were doing when sending it to Kings Cross.

During 1951, there were a number of special trains from the Newcastle area to Marylebone for the Festival of Britain. These trains were re-engined at Mexborough West Junction and worked through to London by Mexborough men, with a conductor from Leicester. My driver at the time was Bill Thompson who signed most of the roads on the GC section and we had a total of six trips to Marylebone during that year, mostly with Mexborough B1s. They played with the job and ran like sewing machines.

I must say that the Mexborough B1s were well looked after by the fitting staff and problems thereby were rare- though I recall one instance at least, with no 1168. "Rutt" and I relieved Jim Phillipson and Cyril Morley on this engine, on a Barnsley to Doncaster train, tender first as there was no table at Barnsley. Jim declared that a knock was developing when the right hand big end was passing through the back quarter – engine or tender first, running made no difference. Off we went, and sure enough there was the knock- it was more of a heavy click- at the right hand side. Rutt knew that I was interested in things mechanical and he asked my opinion; the symptoms I thought, indicated a loose piston head, a diagnosis with which he agreed. The problem here was that the piston heads and rod were supposed to be welded together, not nutted, so in theory, they could not come loose. We had both seen the pistons, after all, on the fitting shop floor during repairs. Harold thought quite rightly, that we would look rather silly (bloody fools was the actual prediction) booking a loose piston head if they couldn't come loose, and my response was to suggest we book it as a sympton, then have a word with Joe Crossley, the chargeman fitter. This he did and Joe, who was a very good type, but possessed of a short fuse, fair went up in the air, amid wince inducing language. It couldn't be a loose piston head as – they were all welded. However, to satisfy all concerned, he would arrange for the right hand front cylinder cover to be removed, to see immediately whether the piston arrangement had been altered. Rutt and I booked on next morning and went straight round to Crossley's office together. He saw us coming and came out to meet us. "Don't look so bloody smug – you've won", was the comment which greeted us and he went on to recount the removal of 1168's relevant cylinder cover, finding that the piston head was after all, nutted onto the rod, and not welded. It was loose but only marginally so, enough to cause the click. He also announced that a stiff letter was now on its way to Doncaster Plant as to why Mexborough shed had not been appraised of the alteration. This said, Rutt and I went about our business somewhat self satisfied. It was one of those occasions when Mutual Improvement Class training had paid off. It had also revealed that the highly instructed staff of the Chief Mechanical Engineer at Doncaster had a chink in their armour.

The B1 tender front was well designed with two good lockers, one for clothing, the other for tools and oil bottles, and there was a fire iron tunnel at the right hand side, obviously copied from the LMS class 8F tender, some of which had been built at Doncaster and Darlington. There were two good coal grates and two well placed water feed handles, altogether a carefully thought out arrangement. The driving controls could all be operated from a sitting position and wooden foot platforms were correctly positioned for comfort. There was no need for any loose footstool. The bucket seats, which were smaller than those on the V2, protected the driver's back from draughts. The operating handle for the drop grate could be operated by one hand, if kept properly oiled, the handle being secured by a chain. This was an important item on a steam engine- if a thing wasn't secured, it went missing.

Many lines have been written comparing the B1 with Stanier's Black Five and indeed there is some logic to this, for they were very similar in dimensions. They were however, very different in design and construction. Here there is some echo of previous pairs of engineers – take Webb and Stroudley or Whale and Churchward.Webb and the LNWR generally, went for cheapness of construction, standard parts and Spartan footplates. Stroudley, in a similar period, went for perfection of construction, performance, finish and a very good cab for the time. The difference in policy of these two men can be clearly seen at the National Railway Museum. Churchward went in for design perfection, especially in the development of boiler shape, valve gears and cylinders; Whale continued Webbs general policy except for compounding, demanding simplicity and cheapness.

Another of the Mexborough B1s passing Great Coates on its way to Cleethorpes on a summer excursion. This would have been after the Divisional reorganisation as can be seen by the new shed code 41F. Courtesy Mike Hartley Collection.

Stanier's Black Five passed through 25 years of development on the LMS with improvements to Superheaters, top feed, roller bearings and valve gears. In these circumstances the Black Five should have been head and shoulders above the B1, but was it? I always equated Thompson's B1 with Whales' Precursor class – round top firebox designed and built in a hurry on the cheap, soon getting run down through flimsy construction. The Black Five was a more solid job. In my experience, when they were both new, or new from the shops, there was very little in them except that the B1 had a better cab. Get on the same engine after 80,000 miles and you could tell the difference! The B1 would be more run down; the Black Five stood up to heavy work better because of its robust construction and all the development work put into it.

My experience with both types differed. With B1s it was as a Fireman and a Driver. With the Black Five it was as a Locomotive Inspector, although I fired and drove them quite often. Of course, I had by that time, a more practical eye and ear and knew what to look for and record. My worst ride on a B1 was from Leicester to Loughborough (GC) start to stop. This had always been a very tight timing on this line, ten miles, three uphill and seven down. And speed could rise into the 80s. At this sort of progress the fore and aft motion was considerable, the cab was shaking violently and the noise was indescribable. It was like riding on a racehorse. The coal was being fed forward by "jigger" action all over the cab floor, falling down the steps. We did time, but at a cost. I have never had a similar ride on a Black Five despite some of them being rough and run down. One of the hardest jobs at the ex-LMS shed at Sheffield Millhouses was the 1833 from St Pancras, first stop Nottingham (125 miles). This was a heavy train, the men were out of lodge and you had to run hard to keep time. But even on this job with high speeds on the downhill 17 mile stretch from Leagrave to Bedford, I never experienced a really rough ride on a Black Five. The job was diagrammed to a three cylinder 5x but you didn't always get one.

In 1958 the ex LMS Midland Division sheds came into the Eastern Region. These were Grimesthorpe, Canklow, Barrow Hill and Millhouses; the latter being a passenger only shed, the others freight. For some years after 1958 the LMS engine allocations and diagramming remained as before but when the power situation got tight, as on a summer Saturday, the Midland passenger services had to resort to borrowing B1s from the now parent shed at Darnall (ex LNER). This meant that for the first time, the LMS men came up against B1s on their passenger work; in accordance with time honoured practice, Darnall did not send its best examples across the city, and Millhouses inevitably got the ones that were run down and rattling in every joint. They were 11 years old and Darnall had more than 40 on the books at the time. To add insult to injury, the LMS firemen couldn't get on with the LNER trap firedoor; for years they had been used to having a fully opened door to fire through. Trap firing, although a much superior method, was something they simply didn't want, the trap being only half the depth of an LMS firedoor, and oval instead of round – it meant that the coal had to be broken up; which was extra labour. Some of the firemen were not much bothered about the principles of combustion- it meant cracking the coal and the consequence was that the B1s got a bad name on the Midland side of Sheffield, and all things Eastern Region were as mud. This attitude lasted at Millhouses until the advent of diesel traction in 1960.

There is no doubt that the B1 class filled a yawning gap in LNER locomotive evolution, for they were such a downright useful type – they could be put on any sort of train. Their comparatively short life was of course curtailed by the introduction of diesels in the early 1960s. At the end, in 1967, there would normally have been another ten or more years life left in them. They were Edward Thompson's main contribution to British locomotive design.

At the end of the war, there were still only ten B1s at work; the following year a start was made to enlarge the class when Darlington built six and NBL 72. 1947 was the bumper year with Darlington building another 30, Vulcan Foundry 50 and NBL 106. At the end of the LNER in 1947, there were 274 of them at work. After that, there were small batches each year until the final 7 brought out in 1952, completed the grand total of 410.

The last three to be withdrawn from train work were 61030, 61307 and 61337, all in September 1967. No 61168 (a Vulcan) survived until October 1967 in departmental service as a stationery boiler – it had gone from train work in 1965. Leaving aside preservation, this was the end of the class".

CHAPTER 15

LOCOMOTIVE NOTES BY RON FAREHAM

As explained in my introduction to Ron Fareham, he wrote so much about all nature of technical and handling aspects of the various types of locomotives. Drawing on his experiences as Fireman, Driver, Running Foreman, Instructor, Locomotive Inspector and Assistant Area Manager, Ron has given written accounts of numerous classes of locomotive, although I have only included in this book, those classes which were allocated to Mexborough and thus known to Mexborough men. My book was not intended to become technical at the risk of boring readers and I have abridged just a few of his accounts where it would be difficult for the non railwayman to understand his points. The majority of his writings are indeed fascinating even to the non railwayman.

I have selected Ron's account of the O4 to start with. This was the main freight loco at Mexborough depot until the WD Austerities arrived after the war. He first of all describes the Chief Mechanical Engineer of the Great Central Railway who was responsible for designing the O4, that is John G Robinson. He gives an interesting account of how this locomotive was developed and became deployed in several parts of the world.

"John G Robinson was born in 1856. He served his apprenticeship on the GWR with which his family was closely associated; his father was District Locomotive Superintendent at Bristol. His son was later to occupy a similar position at Neasden LNER during the second world war.

J.G. left the GWR in 1884 and went to Ireland, as many budding CMEs did prior to Irish independence. He worked there for the Waterford and Limerick railway which, by any standards was a small concern, becoming Locomotive Superintendent in 1888.

Robinson became Locomotive Superintendent, later to be known as Chief Mechanical Engineer, of the GCR in 1900, and thus became responsible for all the locomotives, rolling stock and outdoor machinery of the Company. He came to Gorton at a critical time for the Great Central; this expanded, re-titled company was experiencing something of a boom in traffic. The GC was only three years old and its new routes to London and the Great Western were attracting new traffic; also the new collieries being sunk in South Yorkshire were adding to the export trade via the new Clee coaling facilities at Grimsby. The locomotive situation was critical, with nothing bigger than 0-6-0 types to work the necessarily small trains. All the British locomotive builders were busy and therefore unable to help. During this period, the G.C., in company with the G.N. and Midland Railways, placed orders for new locomotives in America. The G.C. ordered their 20 examples from Burnham Williams and Co of the Baldwin Locomotive works, Philadelphia, USA.

Robinson's name will always be associated with the Great Central Railway. To say that he was revered by the enginemen of that railway would be an understatement and the reasons for this are not far to seek. The "Churchillian" saying "Give us the tools and we'll finish the job" was certainly true of Robinson's 23 years with the GCR.

I suppose that the main public attraction of Robinson engines was their neat and graceful appearance, with the lavish use of well balanced curves- without anything that could be regarded as fancy or out of place. They do not look old fashioned even now, 75 years or more after being built. However, if looks were all that mattered then they would not have commanded the respect of the footplatemen for so long. As well as good looks, it was their performance, capacity and comfort in the cab, which made them all such firm favourites.

G.C.R. CLASS 8K (LNER CLASS O4) (LOAD CLASS 7)

These locomotives, Robinson's lasting memorial, were very solidly built, with main frames 1¼ inch thick, surely the real reason for their longevity. Sure footed, and with a very reliable and effective dry sanding gear – usable either for traction or to assist in braking a heavy coal train: good injectors and, most of all, a free steaming Belpair firebox (this is a square flat top firebox which ensures a large quantity of water above the top of the inner firebox, where the heat is most intense), - and a comfortable cab. With all these advantages, a driver's words were few, what else could a footplate crew want?

The two most exacting tasks for a locomotive on the Great Central Line, ie Sheffield Victoria to Dunsford westbound, and Ardwick Low Yard to Dunford eastbound; two almost identical lengths of nearly 20 miles of rising gradients, necessitating continuous heavy steaming for at least an hour on a goods train. Those trips could be accomplished with the ease of an O4.

All the equipment on the footplate; ie injector steam and water valves, regulator, reverser and brakes, could be operated by the crew from a sitting position. The long seats were made of good wood with deep wooden footstools which were well positioned and relieved the pressure on the underside of the thighs – an important feature when sitting on wood. A hinged shield restrained the heat of the fire in summer and the glare at night. There were three good lockers; two smaller ones under the seats for oil and tools and a larger one on the tender front with sliding lockable doors for clothing, food or lodging boxes, detonators and spare water glasses. A good view forward from a sitting position, either by looking over the side, or through the double windows in the cab front completed the picture of a well designed footplate. The first 8K (O4) engine was 966, later 5966. It appeared in September 1911 and created something of a sensation. It was equipped from new with a superheater, as were the rest of the class, and when the first allocation arrived at Mexborough shed, they were promptly named "superheaters", and this name stuck until the end in 1966. Other sheds had other names and "Tiny" was a popular one. At Mexborough, "Tiny" was a Robinson 0-8-0, and remained so called.

666 of this class 8K (O4) were built in all. 128 were held by the GCR at grouping in 1923; 17 were built with larger boilers (class 8M (O5)) but were later given the standard size. The Government recognising the value of rail transport for the mass movement of troops, arms and military equipment, adopted the Robinson design and 521 were built by numerous firms for the Railway Operating Division (ROD) of the Royal Engineers between Dec 1917 and Dec 1919 – thirteen months after the end of the war! 218 were built after the Armistice and this was done to ease the employment situation until more normal times arrived. These 218 locomotives were something of an embarrassment and were stored in dumps at various points of the compass. In time, they were joined by the other 303, most of which came from service in France. The disposal of 521 large 2-8-0 locomotives became a serious problem for the Government, because they were in the dumps for all to see.

Small batches were purchased by the various companies; the GW bought 20, G.C. 3, L.N.W. 30 during 1919-20.

Eventually, the sales came to an end. Following this the Government loaned out most of the rest to the major railway companies which were still under Government control. When this control was ended in 1921, all the engines on loan were called back into the pool, the intention being to try and sell them overseas. Despite great efforts to sell the engines, success was hard to come by. One of the problems in 1921 was that the railways were facing the "grouping" scheme, and of course, the Directors were very cautious. Another drawback was the asking price, which was £12,000 per locomotive. The LNW paid £10,500 for their 30, GW paid £10,000 each for 20 and the GC £6,064. After January 1923, things became easier and the LNER started to buy large numbers. However, the price fell dramatically. LNER bought 237 engines in three batches between 1923 and 1927 at prices which ranged from £2000 each for the first batch, £1,500 for the second lot and the give away £340 each for the final 100. This must have been the best bargain any railway ever had.

Of the remaining locomotives in the various dumps, 13 went to Australia to a mining company and some of these were still at work in 1973.

26 engines were sold to China in 1925 but their whereabouts was difficult to follow because of political difficulties in that country in the 1930s and 40s.

The following table gives the complete picture of the final distribution of the 521 8Ks (O4) built for the war department.

COMPANY	NO PURCHASED
G.W.R	100
L.N.W.R.	30
G.C.R.	3

L.N.E.R.	273
L.M.S.	75
Australia	13
China	26
Scrapped	1

Total	521

The locomotives purchased from the Government by the LNER which we can now refer to as class 04, and many of which came to Mexborough, were initially fitted with the Westinghouse air brake and steel fireboxes in place of the normal copper ones. These two unfamiliar features were disliked by the footplate crews – especially the steel fireboxes, as they were prone to leak badly at the tube plate end. These two problems were later solved by Gorton works fitting copper fireboxes and steam brakes, thereby bringing them into line with the rest of the class – and more to the men's liking.

The fire grate had a slight downward slope towards the front but this did not affect the style of firing, ie the fire did not feed itself towards the front unless the engine was being worked exceptionally hard, then the position had to be watched. The firebox was a very deep one, about 3 feet under the firedoor. The practice was, when preparing for heavy continuous steaming, to build up a big fire under the door, made up of large lumps, then after it had slowly burnt through with the damper nearly shut, to push some of the fire forward to the front. This would give a sloping fire about 2 feet thick at the back down to about 10" thick at the front. This type of fire when burnt through, would give you all the steam required for any duty and for any length of time until the firegrate clinkered – or a stop was made for water or signals, or the summit of the gradient was reached. Subsequent firing required four shovelfuls down each side and one under the door.

The firedoor on all Robinson engines was circular and hinged vertically at the right hand side for a full opening of the door. This gave access to clean the fire, or the entry of a boilermaker or barlayer. After the fire was built up and the train on the way, then it was the practice to fire through the "trap": this was a sort of half door let into the main one; it was hinged horizontally and fitted with a small handle. The latter was really superfluous as the trap was operated with the aid of the firing shovel.

On a long rising gradient such as the 20 mile climb to Dunford, the best and most efficient way to feed the boiler with water was to "set" the injector to keep the water level at just under a full glass, so that the level could be actually seen. This was accomplished by adjusting the water regulating handles towards the minimum position.

When the main regulator was opened by the driver, it had the effect of drawing the water up the gauge glass so this had to be borne in mind when checking the water level when the engine was working hard. Gradients, of course, also had an effect on water levels, especially with locomotives with long boilers. There was therefore the actual level – the important one, the level caused by the action of the regulator and the effect of the gradients. An example of the latter was when working over the Chapeltown Branch from either side of the summit at Wharncliffe Silkstone. The gradient here changed abruptly from a 1 in 62 rising to the same degree falling. A fireman could have 7/8 of a glass approaching the summit, but when the driver closed the regulator just after the summit, the level would fall to about ½ inch of water in the glass. The prime consideration here, of course, was the firebox crown sheet which, if the water level was low on the rising gradient, could become uncovered after passing the summit- with disastrous results – fusible plugs melting and possible collapse of the crown sheet – a boiler explosion!

Another useful feature of the O4 class was the smokebox ash hopper, an item I have never seen mentioned in any technical description of these engines. It consisted of a small 8" square opening in the floor of the smokebox; a 24" deep hopper, tapering down to a 6" square hole at the bottom; this was closed by a heavy hinged door with a large counterweight at the back. It was operated by a small foot treadle immediately behind the left hand pony wheel. When the treadle was kicked open it did two things:–

(a) it opened the hopper door, and
(b) the heavy counterweight struck the side of the hopper and released any ash that was stuck in the bottom.

The fireman then opened the smokebox door and raked the smokebox ash into the hopper and down into the ash pit.

There was very little side protection in the cabs – only a handful had side windows and, when working in the Pennines, with its north and west winds, it could be uncomfortable in winter. Some of the lodging drivers carried small, folded hessian sheets which could be carried in their tin boxes. Horace Shephard also carried a hessian back sheet in addition. This man was a rabid DIY fan and was always regarded as the "Chief Mechanical engineer" of the Gorton lodge link. He had a variety of gadgets for making footplate life more comfortable.

Many C.M.E.s in the past tried to ease the fireman's work by positioning the tender shovelling plate at the same level as the firedoor: Johnson, Ivatt, Gresley and Stanier come into this category, aided by the fact that their engines had shallow fireboxes. On many of Robinson's engines, the fireboxes were deep – the O4 firedoor was 3 feet above cab floor level – and the tender shovelling plate was on the floor; there was therefore, an element of lifting in the fireman's movements which needed extra energy. The necessary action was locally called "getting your back hand up", because of the high firedoor. However, I never heard a G.C. man complain about this, but if the engine was steaming well, he would be prepared to put up with it.

There were also a few awkward items during the preparation of these engines. The eccentrics for the link motion were, of course, inside the frames and low down, so that only a man with a very long arm could reach them for oiling purposes. This meant that most drivers had to get inside between the frames and stand on the brake stretchers. There were many corpulent drivers at Mexborough, especially in the Gorton Lodge link – it was said that it was the effect of the Manchester beer. These chaps just could not manage to get "inside" from the top, so the fireman had to do it. The manoeuvre involved squeezing in between the top of the framing and the boiler, a space of about 18", and there was a knack of doing it without rupturing oneself.

Another drawback was the oiling of the eight axle boxes. These had the oil receptacles in the crown of the box and were fitted with spring loaded lids behind the wheels. To raise the lids to feed in the oil, one needed a "lidlifter"; this instrument was an 18" long ¼" steel spindle with a loop at one end and flattened at the other. The fact that oil could be poured in meant that in stormy weather, water could do likewise, and this had to be removed during preparation. This involved fetching a syphon pump from the stores to pump out the water. The fact that this was a very awkward and dirty job – and could also involve a ¼ mile hike to and from the stores, and another to take the pump back – meant that it tended to be neglected by the type of man who is of that bent. Because of this factor, it was always said that the 20 or so colliery pilots, all class O4, ran on "watter", instead of oil, and as they hardly ever broke into a gallop, none of them ever seemed to run hot!

The first G.C.R. 8K (later O4) to be built was no 966 in September 1911. It was one of a batch of 30 constructed at the G.C. works at Gorton. The numbering of this group was haphazard and seemed to fill in a series of blanks existing in the system. The group was distributed to the various "coal train" sheds, Mexborough getting about 10. The next batch of 20 built by Kitson's of Leeds in mid 1912 and numbered consecutively, all came to Mexborough.: the numbers ran from 1183 to 1202 (later 6183-6202) and were all allocated personally to the drivers in the Gorton Lodge Link., which at that time had 30 sets of men in it; so that each man had his "own engine". These men worked the heavy coal trains from the new Wath Yard, mainly to Manchester, but also to Immingham and Annesley. Driver Herbert White had engine no 1194 allocated to him from 1912 to the abolition of lodging in 1916. This man's son George was the Roster Clerk at Mexborough in my early years and later went on to Divisional Headquarters – he was always interested in matters Great Central. The personal allocation of locomotives ceased in 1916 but was reinstated in 1920. In this later period, the driver did not always have his own engine as the working day had been reduced from 10 hours to one of 8 hours in 1919. This method of allocating engines to men lasted for a few years but it was doomed at a place such as Mexborough

Class O4/3 introduced 1917. Standing at Mexborough Shed on No 4 road in front of the fitting shop in BR days. This loco was purchased by LNER in March 1924 and was withdrawn in May 1959. Courtesy Great Central Railway Society.

where engines didn't always work to schedule, and certainly not to time, mainly because of the uncertain nature of coal train working. A further item militating against it was that the locomotives could not be allowed to languish in the shed for 16 out of every 24 hours. With engines on passenger work, with regular punctual diagrams, it was possible to run such a scheme – and many passenger sheds did, nearly to the end of steam traction; with two sets of men to an engine.

Just before grouping in 1923, there were 148 engines of class 8K/8M (O4/O5), and of these, 64 were at Mexborough, reflecting it's pre-eminence among the "coal sheds". The 8K/8M class were always classed together, as they were the same engine with a bigger boiler.

The position at the outbreak of war in 1939 was similar, with 60 O4s at Mexborough. The total number in this class was now 421, the increase coming from the purchase of 273 from the War Department surplus fleet in the 1920s.

The O4 was designed for heavy duty freight work, principally coal trains, and would run without discomfort upto 40mph and this speed accounted for 98% of their work. Anything over this figure usually brought problems. They were not properly balanced for any work in the middle speed range. If pressed above 40mph, the usual reaction was for them to develop a hefty "fore and aft" motion. This was alright if the coal was at the back of the tender, as the "jigger" action soon brought it to the front. The problem was that, once started, it could not be controlled; it came forward onto the footplate faster than the fireman could move it, resulting in a cab floor full

Robinson Class O4/5, modified in 1932 and rebuilt with shortened O2 type boiler and separate smokebox saddle. Seen here at Mexborough on the Cripple sidings on the 15th June 1958, coaled up and ready for Monday morning duty". Courtesy Great Central Railway Society.

of coal and falling down the steps onto the ballast. As far as Mexborough was concerned, the run from Thorne Jcn To Hull was about the only one where these problems occurred. On this line of the ex North Eastern Railway, still regarded as somewhat foreign, the operating authorities were always keen on timekeeping and letters were received by drivers if any, even small amounts of time were lost. The upshot of this tradition was that speeds in excess of comfort were the order of the day, and coal went over the side by the hundredweight on an O4 engine.

Sir Nigel Gresley who died in 1941, had a high regard for Robinson and his locomotives. His place was taken by Edward Thompson. This man had been on the Midland and North eastern Railways in his time and had somewhat different ideas to Gresley. One of these was that, except for the largest passenger engines, all his engines would be of 2 cylinders. His ideas and subsequent designs were no doubt influenced by austere conditions of wartime Britain in 1941, and also the material and manpower shortages. It is said that he went for simplicity in advocating 2 cylinders; another view was that he had a very strong dislike of Gresley's ideas, particularly the "two to one and equal lever" arrangement of valve gear. Certainly Thompson never built an engine with any such equipment.

In the previous 12 years, Gresley had made 3 attempts to rebuild Robinson O4 engines, and each time produced something a good deal worse than the original. Each one had the round top firebox, always regarded as a retrograde step by G.C. men, as they had abandoned it 30 years before. Why Doncaster always avoided the Belpair firebox is a mystery, because, when forced by

Robinson Class O4/6 standing on the Cripple Sidings 15th June 1958. To the right of the chimney, on the engine behind, is the home signal at Mexborough No 2 coming off the Sheffield branch to enter Mexborough Station. Courtesy Great Central Railway Society.

the Government to build Stanier 8F engines in 1943, the plant produced a very good belpair boiler, and Stanier's was a far more complex task, with its curves and coned barrel than Robinsons Belpairs.

The first of Gresley's 04 rebuilds emerged in 1929 and as O4/4. This machine was a real affront to Great Central eyes, with its lengthened frames, pseudo North British Cab, a round topped firebox and G.N. chimney. The horror was compounded inside the cab with the high stirling pull out regulator, a small square piece of wood for a seat – no footstools – and a smelly hydrostatic lubricator under the fireman's nose. The cab was shorter than before, with therefore, less room to swing a shovel into the lower firedoor. It would appear that these two engines 6287 and 6371 were the victims of an experiment with the GN class O2 boiler, with a view to standardising it. What was the hurry in 1929 to find a replacement boiler for the 04 class? When one looks through the records, one finds that 5133-one of the original batch, built in 1912, went through to 1965 with a Belpair boiler! It is also interesting here to note that, of the 13 engines going to Australia in 1923, two went through to 1973 with the same Belpair boilers complete with War Department 1919 steel fireboxes.

Gresley's next attempt was class 04/5, out in 1932. This one had shorter O2 boilers, still round topped, with most of the Robinson cab intact but still with the GN pull out regulator, which the GC men loathed mainly because it was difficult to regulate and so belied its name; it also had a tendency to fly open unexpectedly. 9 engines were rebuilt to 04/5. The last Gresley rebuild was class

04/7. The difference to 04/5 was minimal and concerned mainly the smokebox which was a GC type. This was the best rebuild of the three Gresley attempts. The steam brake was always regarded as weak, the steam supply pipe being much narrower. All three were looked upon with contempt by GC staff as they considered them the ruination of an excellent basic design.

Edward Thompson's attempts at rebuilding the class 04 engines were tackled more logically and in two ways:-

1   To replace an ageing boiler – again the new one was round topped. - but this time the successful 100A design which Thompson had standardised, was used. A proper side window cab with bucket seats for the crew; a Robinson style regulator, with the right hand drive position retained. This design was considered by the men to be the best of all the various rebuilds of the class O4, however, it must be said that the original design, the 419 engines of class 04/1, was the best all round performer of the entire class.

2   Thompson's second plans were for a completely redesigned concept of a 2-8-0 mineral engine with increased capacity, (loading class 8), using parts of other classes – B1 boiler, K2 cylinders etc. The main frames, wheels and tender remained. The reason for such a thoroughgoing rebuild was if the boiler, cylinders and valve gear needed replacement. It was a note of confidence in Robinson's original (1911) frame design that another engine should be redesigned around it 30 years later.

Class O4/8 No 63882 at Mexborough shed on 30th July 1962. This was a Thompson rebuild in 1947 using the 100A (B1) boiler but retaining the original cylinders. Note the round boiler top as opposed to the Robinson boilers which had a Belpair (square) firebox top. It was fitted with a standard LNER double side windowed cab. The loco was withdrawn in May 1965.
Courtesy Great Central Railway Society.

CLASS 01 (LOAD CLASS 8)

The result of the foregoing was Thompson's 01 class introduced in 1944. The 100A boiler, pressed at 225 psi was a very efficient steam raiser and, with a bigger grate and more heating surface was, if anything, sharper at steaming than the original 04 Belpairs. The new cab with side windows solved the side protection problem. Bucket seats and a GC regulator, as with 04/8, and the drop grate, made fire cleaning much easier.

The cylinders were an inch less in diameter than the 04, however, with some 45 psi more boiler pressure. The result was 4192 pounds of extra tractive effort resulting in a class 8 for loading. The class was well regarded on the GC section, even by the dyed- in-the wool Robinson fans. The reliable dry sanding gear was retained. It was always regarded as a new design and given a separate classification 01.

My first experience with an 01 was in August 1945 with a train from Wath yard to Cudworth (H&B). The engine concerned was 6220 (later 3803) and was one of the 50 built by N.B.L. in 1912. My regular driver at the time was one Hedley Turpin, a member of an old Mexborough railway family and a firm Robinson supporter. He detested the various Gresley rebuilds of class 04 and when we approached the newly rebuilt 6220, which was the first one Hedley had seen, he said "Aye Aye, another attempt to ruin a superheater (04)" However, as he prepared 6220, he seemed gradually to be changing his opinion about it. I think this came about because of the ease of preparation – there was now no need to go in between the frames to oil the eccentrics because there weren't any. All this plus a spanking new engine seemed to put Hedley in a good mood.

As we went the 3 ½ miles, light engine, to Elsecar Jcn; it was obvious to me, and to Hedley, that with the smooth running and sharp positive exhaust beat of 6220, here was a machine that had every appearance of being master of the job.

The 8 mile trip from Wath yard to Cudworth was a short sharp experience with steep gradients for most of the way. The load was 60 wagons of mineral unassisted. With this load, 6220 simply played with the job and Hedley's enthusiasm mounted as time went by. He said on arrival at Cudworth that 6220 was the finest mineral engine he had ever handled and I was somewhat of the same opinion myself as the maintenance of 225 lbs of steam had been "child's play".

The upshot of this experience occurred when we were in Cudworth yard waiting to start the return working. The Guard came up to the cab and said "Well Hedley, we shall have to reduce this lot as there is equal to 10 wagons above a load in this road. We shall have to put the excess into the next road". It was at this point that Hedley's enthusiasm got the better of him for he said to the Guard "No, don't bother reducing nine wagons. We'll tek 'em – this engine'll eat 'em". I was surprised at this statement, as Hedley could not be considered an over confidant type of man, rather the reverse. In the event, we took the whole lot, equal to 70 of mineral, 10 above a load. We were assisted at the rear end for the first ¾ mile up to the bridge over the LMS Midland main line.

The road back to Stairfoot from Cudworth was something of a switchback, and the approach to Stairfoot North was preceded by 2 miles of falling gradient, followed by ½ mile rising steeply at 1 in 75 over the bridge for the Grimethorpe colliery branch, with the last ¼ mile falling at 1 in 100. This meant that any rushing of the 1 in 75 had to be expertly managed, as too high a speed would result in one being unable to stop at the home signal in the short falling section. Hedley kept steam on down the falling gradient and into the "dip", but he was not going fast enough to take 10 above a load through the 1 in 75 up to the bridge. His caution was conditioned by the ultimate task of stopping at the home signal and the result was we stalled on the 1 in 75 section.

After conferring with the Guard- a typical Rule Book statement – we decided to divide the train and take the front portion to Stairfoot and then return for the rest. At that time, this procedure meant that Hedley would need a "Guard's Pink "Wrong Line Order", Form A, for the signalman to allow us to return for the rear portion in the "wrong "direction. This was the only occasion in my firing career that I was involved in the use of the said Pink Wrong Line Order. So ended a day on which over confidence – so unlike the man- resulted in failure. My only other outstanding memory of Hedley was that I was with him at Milford (NER) yard when Victory in Europe was declared and the Shunter came out of his cabin having just been told on the phone, shouting the news and waiving his hat in the air.

The 01 class were better riders than the 04 at speeds approaching 40 mph. The 04 "fore and aft" was absent, resulting no doubt from a rebalancing exercise by Thompson's staff.

An old driver once said to me, "Thar knows a good steaming engine can cover up a lotter faults". There is some truth in this statement, and faults there certainly were in the 04 and 01 classes. One shortcoming with the latter was, as with most Thompson engines, they soon got run down, with knocking big ends and axle boxes. However, as the man said, they were covered by a fine steaming boiler.

Before closing on these remarkable locomotives, it must be said that Robinson himself, made various attempts at improvements. In the early 20s, he produced a number with large boilers (later class 05) but with no increase in grate area or tractive effort. It is hard to imagine what the purpose of these experiments was. These large boilers were all removed by 1943. I fired the 05 class on many occasions but never detected any difference in either steaming capacity or coal and water consumption. There were three of them at Mexborough in my young days.

Finally, some three weeks after war broke out in 1939, there was a government scheme for 300 of the 04s to be handed over for service in France and the Middle East. Not content with that, Gresley offered the whole

421 to the Government, if he could be given the material to replace them with GN 3 cylinder 02s. What a moan there would have been at Mexborough and Gorton etc if this had come about. The 300 request was cancelled but, in the event, 92 actually were sent to the Middle East in 1941. This group contained a few old Mexborough engines, 6183, 6185, 6197 and 6202. After the First World War the drivers in the Gorton Link were again allocated their own engines and 6202, which belonged to John Willis Jackson, is rumoured to be reposing at the bottom of the Mediterranean – it is certainly recorded as being lost at sea.

CLASS V2 (LOAD CLASS 7) RA.9
The first locomotive of Gresley's class V2 was named "Green Arrow". This was in June 1936, and the name persisted until December 1966 when the last of the class, 60831 was withdrawn. The origin of the name came from the LNER Express Freight Service, which guaranteed a next day delivery to the customer – the "Green Arrow Service". The flagship of this service was the 1540 Kings Cross to Glasgow, which for many years was always worked by either a V2 or a Pacific. This was always a heavy train, with a fast timing, and was worked with ease by a V2.

The V2s were ideal for this class of work, having a good large boiler, large grate, a 6'2" wheel and very good riding qualities. It had the Gresley chassis with a carrying axle under the cab and none of the tail-wagging buoyancy of the G.N.Atlantic – you always had a good ride.

The boiler was similar to the A1 Pacifics, but two feet shorter in the barrel. This boiler was of excellent proportions and initially was very free at steaming. The secret of this, apart from a large combined heating service, grates and adequate free gas area, was a special type of firebar which resulted in a grate with a 56% air space through the bars – a good deal higher than normal. To give such a high percentage of air space, the bars would normally have to be either:-

1   the ordinary thickness of bar – but at 56%, this would have given too wide an air space and the "fall through" of ash and fire would have been excessive, or
2   thin bars to attain 56% air space but limit the fall through. An individual bar at this thickness would not have maintained the strength and stability of the grate and would have been easily broken by the action of darts and clinker shovels.

Gresley's solution to this problem was to have thin bars but cast in multiples of four and joined at the middle and ends. These were certainly in vogue during the early 1940s. However, there must have been some weaknesses with the multiple bars as they were all removed and conventional bars put in place. This, and the advent of self cleaning smokeboxes, adversely affected the free steaming qualities of the class, and they never seemed to steam so well again. They were certainly made to steam, but the sparkle seemed to have gone.

My earliest experience with V2s was during 1940 and 1941. This was a period when many troop trains were running on the G.C. section, to and from Southampton, it was assumed; and the passed firemen and passed cleaners at Mexborough got their chance to have a go at long distance express work. My first trip was to Leicester one night (70) miles with Tom Piper. In this case, we relieved York men at Mexborough West Junction with V2 No 4782. This engine performed beautifully and we were relieved by Leicester men. The next night we took 4867 off Mexborough shed and changed engines at West Junction. In this instance, we took the train through to Woodford and lodged. It was a night trip and a distance of 105 miles. Of course, I knew nothing of the road, even in daylight, and I thought we were never going to reach Woodford. We went into the barracks and after some tea and toast, I went to bed and slept heavily for nine hours. If I thought that this was tiring work, I didn't know what was facing me on the return trip. We took 4867 off Woodford shed during the afternoon of the second day and went the twelve miles light engine to Banbury station (G.W.R.), there to await the arrival of the special train for the north. Train crews were never

On a summer Saturday in those days, fast freights continued to be scheduled but their departure times were delayed until things quietened down. At 7.14 p.m. V2 60928 of Doncaster heads north near Brookhams Park with a class D freight for the West Riding. We don't know whether or not this is the photographer's last shot, but my diary shows that A1 60122 CURLEW was hard on the heels of this goods with the down Aberdonian. The next Saturday it was not allowed out until both the 7 p.m. and 7.15 p.m. had left King's Cross.
Photograph J. C. Flemons, The Transport Treasury.

told the destination of troop trains. There were Great Western engines moving about around the station and I had never seen one before, though of course I had read about them. This was the furthest I had ever been from home and I was fascinated by the place. One thing struck me forcibly, as I was used to the big end knock on Gresley's engines, and to a less extent on Robinsons, the G.W. big ends went round with never a whisper – I was most impressed. I was even more impressed when our train ran in as it consisted of 17 Southern Railway coaches and ten luggage vans. It was hauled by two G.W. 4-6-0 engines, but I cannot now recall what class they were. The train weighed over 500 tons and there was some discussion as to whether we needed assistance to go forward.

After attaching to the train and before creating a brake, the release chords had to be pulled on every vehicle throughout the train. The reason for this was that, at that time, the G.W.R. worked on 25 inches of vacuum when all other companies used 21" – hence the need for complete release of all vacuum in the brake system, with trains from the G.W. to the L.N.E.R. before a fresh start was made. We must have stood 20 minutes in Banbury station before we received the "right away" from the guard.

The first six miles out of Banbury were uphill and 4867 took some hammering on this stretch. We were stopped at Culworth Junction to allow a London- Manchester express to precede us and another stop was made at Woodford to drop off the conductor. After that it was water on Charwelton troughs and next stop Leicester – 35 miles. Here we got more water and my driver went to enquire again about an assisting engine. After some argument, it was agreed that we should get assistance at Nottingham, where the real hill climbing started. The road from Leicester to Nottingham was not difficult and no problems ensued.

On arrival at Nottingham Victoria station we again got water and whilst we were doing so, a G.N. Atlantic backed on to us and coupled up. They were Doncaster men – Jack Lamming with no 4428. This man was a member of the Doncaster-Banbury link and was ex Mexborough. From Nottingham, things were a good deal easier with the two engines. However, when we reached Killamarsh troughs, the Atlantic took most of the water and we got hardly any. The question then was – would our engine be going through to York – if so we would need water at Tinsley. This we did and on reaching Mexborough West Junction, we found that York men were waiting with a fresh engine, another V2. We went to shed with 4867 and signed off duty about midnight – I was glad to get into bed.

At the end of 1940, Mexborough was allocated two Green Arrows, nos 4812 and 4877. Prior to this date, whenever Mexborough required a V2 for a heavy troop train, or other such work, it had to borrow them from Doncaster. This acquisition avoided any borrowing, unless three or more were needed.

In April 1941, I had two rather interesting trips with V2s. I booked on at

1040 for the 1200 Manvers to Mottram, and lodge. Manvers Main was one of the larger collieries of South Yorkshire and generated enough westbound traffic to demand a service direct to the Manchester District yard at Mottram. The latter was a comparatively new yard and worked on the gravitation system; with no pilots. The majority of the wagons on Manvers – Mottram belonged to Stephenson Clark & Co., a large coal agency. However, for some reason, that day it was cancelled.

My driver on this trip was one Peter Woosey, the senior driver in the Gorton lodging link. This man, then aged 62, was the last man to be engaged as an engine cleaner by the Manchester, Sheffield and Lincolnshire Railway at Mexborough in 1897, as the name changed in August of that year to the Great Central Railway. Peter Woosey was always very conscious of this, and was of a very proud nature. He was always a staunch J G Robinson man, and a typical Victorian in his habits. Nigel Gresley and all his works were a complete anathema to Peter. He said "What has he ever done for the coal train driver except to give them inferior tools to work with". Of course, he was referring to the G.N. O1 and O2 class 2-8-0s, and also the various Gresley rebuilds of Class O4: such were his views.

Manvers to Mottram was apparently cancelled and we were ordered to go to Wath Junction and relieve a special York to Mottram train with engine 4806. Whether Peter realised that this was a V2, I don't know, as he never made any comment. However, when the train came into view, he could see that it was a Green Arrow. "Why do they put these damn things on a heavy train to Manchester? Don't they know what the gradients are/" he said. I doubt whether the running foreman at York Shed knew, or even cared, about the gradients: possibly at this stage of the war, 4806 was the only engine available. When we got into the cab, Peter started to have a go at the York crew about the engine, but they were having none of it. The York driver said "She's nooan a bad 'un" and promptly got off. Apart from the awkwardness of a large wheeled, vacuum braked engine on a heavy loose coupled train, the trip was uneventful.

We were relieved at Mottram yard by a set of Gorton men and made our way to Gorton Barracks. This was not a purpose built hostel for enginemen – it had originally been a school. It was built by the M.S.&L. Railway in 1855 for the children of the staff at Gorton Works and Shed. In 1863 it was extended with a library and reading room. In 1894 it was transferred to Manchester School Board and the library etc was closed. Some years later it was handed back to the Railway Co. and converted into an enginemen's lodging hostel. It stood on the corner of Ogden Lane and Cornwall Street, opposite the offices of the C.M.E. of the G.C.R. In the next street, Wellington Street, was the Gorton engine shed office block where one signed on for the return working – it was quite near to the hostel.

The "Barracks", as it was always known, had the look of a chapel from the outside. It had pointed Gothic windows and was single storied. It contained a large dining room with a big open Yorkshire range with an open fire. There were 42 bedrooms – they were really open topped cubicles. As this was my first trip involving lodging, I was shown round the premises by Peter Woosey. At one point he opened a large linen cupboard and on the top shelf was an old bowler hat – it was so old that it had a green tinge to it. Peter explained that, although most lodging men went about Manchester in their overalls and uniform coat, he, Peter, always wore a blue serge suit under his overalls, when going into town or to a local pub – he always went out with a blue suit and the bowler.

At about half past nine, when we had settled in, he asked me if I took a drink. I said yes, in moderation, and he suggested we go out to the "Wellington", a pub further up Cornwall Street. Off we set, bowler hat and all, and in a few minutes we were in the pub. There were other Mexborough men in at the time, but what amazed me, was that most of the local people in the pub, including the landlord, addressed him as Peter. Peter was a gregarious man, well read generally and particularly about railways – and articulate with it. However, he did tend to embroider things somewhat.

In previous years he had given talks to the local improvement classes for footplatemen. He had once given a talk to the class at Longsight (Manchester) L.N.W.Ry, and as a result of this, had been invited to give a lecture to the class at Crewe – the L.N.W. holy of holies. The hall was full, he said, and after he had finished, a man stood up at the back and said he was surprised at the level of Peter's knowledge – he didn't realise that enginemen took such an interest in the theory of the steam locomotive. The man in question said Peter, was none other than the great Francis William Webb, the redoubtable chief Mechanical Engineer at Crewe. Some time later, I checked the dates involved in this statement. Peter started on the railway in 1897, Webb retired in 1903 - I thought it unlikely!

For the return trip from Gorton, we signed on at 0700 and, on reporting to the timekeeper, he told us that our engine was 4877, a Mexborough engine returning home. "Good Lord", said Peter. "Another long legged prancer". It was a foggy morning, a real Manchester "pea souper," and Godley, the starting point, was 6 ½ miles up the line. We left Gorton shed and in no time at all, I was completely lost. Peter, however, exuded the confidence born of years of experience, and if he asked me about a signal, it came up at my side in a matter of yards – he was a born railwayman.

At Godley we backed up onto a long string of coal empties for Wath yard and off we went, up the bank towards Woodhead. 4877 steamed quite well but the right hand injector, which was an "H" class exhaust steam type, kept flying off and wasting water. However, it came right again after some adjustment, but it needed constant attention. We went into the loop at Valehouse and continued therein for the 6 miles up to Woodhead. The normal stop was made at Crowden for water and eventually, we arrived at Woodhead, there to await the passing of a Manchester to London express. This was hauled by two Directors, which seemed to be in cracking form as they passed us. "Now, there *is* an engine", said Peter."If they'd have built more of them instead of these damned things, they'd have done some good". He of course, overlooked the fact that a V2 was a Class 7 for loading and a Director was only a Class 3!

I had been keeping the fire well banked up at the back end, with the damper shut, whilst we were standing at Woodhead, it being a sensible tradition that you arranged the fire so as to avoid firing up in the tunnel and making smoke. At Woodhead, there were two single track tunnels and a locomotive just fitted inside with very little headroom to spare. This, together with a following wind – and this was nearly always – meant that you travelled in your own exhaust as far as the second air shaft, so smoke from the chimney had to be at a minimum. The signals came off and into the tunnel we went (3miles 15 yards).

The conditions were quite reasonable on this occasion, though steam and some smoke were always present from the previous trains. About three quarters of the way through, the exhaust injector started to "click clack" and, of course, I couldn't stick my head out in the tunnel to check the overflow pipe, so I decided to shut it off and work the left hand one. I went across the footplate to do this and had just got it to work when Peter shouted "Get that distant signal". I leant across to my side but I had missed it. There were two distant signals, one each side for either main line (RH) or goods line (LH) at Dunford No 1. They were fixed to the tunnel walls. Peter had to slow the train down as the Dunford home signal was just outside the tunnel mouth.

When we emerged at the Dunford end, all the signals were clear for main line and Peter shouted at me for missing the tunnel distant. "I'll get a letter about this now", he said. However, I never heard anything further about it, but it was a bit of good experience.

It was twenty miles downhill from Dunford to Wath, so I was able to enjoy the rugged scenery and the bucket seat. We were relieved on arrival at Wath Yard and so ended my first lodging job to Manchester. Perhaps it would not be thought necessary for men to lodge only 40 miles from home, but the slow progress along the Worsborough Branch, obtaining water, train engine and banker at Wentworth, also delays there waiting for the two extra bankers or the Garratt, and the general congestion on this route, meant that on arrival at the Manchester end, it was not unusual for crews to have 3 or 4 hours overtime in. Lodging in these circumstances was inevitable. However, in 1941, lodging at Manchester was abolished, mainly because of the wartime food situation. A relief cabin was set up at Barnsley Junction (Penistone) and after that, men from both ends were relieved instead of having to lodge. There were also sighs of relief in the domestic situation, as wives had to prepare and pack three or four meals for a lodge turn.

LNER CLASS 07 (AUSTERITY) (LOAD CLASS 8)

Early in 1943 there appeared at certain LNER sheds a locomotive built for the War Department via the Ministry of Supply. I first saw one in the Carr sheds at Doncaster one night – on first examination they looked to be a sound solid job.

935 engines were built in all and they were intended for service in continental Europe after D-Day, which was more than 12 months into the future in 1943. In the interim, many were loaned to the Railway Companies; the LNER received over 300 by this arrangement. The class was known as the "Austerity", reflecting the grim period of their first appearance and also their angular looks. This name stuck until their eventual demise in 1966.

The ex GC men took to these machines immediately, having worked on Gresley's three cylinder 2-8-0s with their pull out regulators and uncomfortable cabs. They liked the Austerity's roomy footplates, two cylinders, Robinson style regulators and steam brakes. The latter was a new design by Gresham and Craven and was a first class job – a truly graduable steam brake capable of being worked manually on either vacuum or compressed air, both of which were fitted, with of course, European braking systems in mind. The engines were painted a sandy colour with a small W.D. on the tender.

The Austerity footplate was a reasonable one, if very draughty. There were single square openings at each side of the cab, but no sliding windows. Instead, there were a number of hooks and two small tarpaulin sheets to fit on the hooks and stowed in the tender lockers. These sheets had to act as draught stoppers or black out sheets. There were no side doors, so when the small tarpaulins disappeared, as they did in weeks, then no side protection existed. There were no roof ventilators, so in summer, one roasted, and in a winter cross wind, one was frozen. These two omissions were later put right

Ex WD 2-8-0 No. 90587 in clean condition circa 1956.
This engine was allocated to Mexborough at the time. Photo M. Whitehouse.

by the LNER after the war. One good point was a comfortable padded seat for each member of the crew.

Later in 1944, the whole class started to disappear into Europe and were not again seen in Britain for some two years. When they, or most of them, started to return to this country, they were put to work immediately, and a sorry mess they were in. Many had Belgian style numerals painted on the smoke box doors, they also had an oval tube inserted into the coal space and opening onto the tender front. The use of this contraption was something of a mystery and its presence was never explained. It was always assumed that it was for a long fire iron, but of course, there was a special rack for that purpose on the right hand side of the tender. When returning from Europe, they were poor steamers and very run down. However, when they had all received a general overhaul, mainly at Newcastle, and fitted with side doors and roof ventilators, side windows and longer water gauges, they became a good general service heavy goods engine. In its final form the Austerity did some good work, most being allocated to the "heavy coal" sheds in 1947; Mexborough had 57, Colwick 44, but the largest allocation was at Wakefield (ex L&Y) with 61.

Initially, the Austerity had a drop grate section in the middle of the grate. This was operated by a detachable four foot lever which slotted onto a spigot in the cab floor. The drop grate was hinged at the front and so dropped backwards!!! This of course, was useless as the clinker could not be cleared out of the ashpan, as there was only one damper at the front. I should imagine that the person responsible for this item received a real "rocket" for such a useless fitting. The drop grate was very quickly removed and all the later engines were built without it.

BR Austerity 2-8-0 No 90582 of Mexborough seen hauling freight on the Great Central mainline, probably to Annesley or Woodford. This class of loco, more than any other, always looked grimy and neglected and any trainspotter of that era would remember them for their metallic clank, which could be heard from a great distance.

An example of the drop grate: - one day in late 1943, Alf Llewellyn and I received a train from York for Banbury (GWR) with austerity engine 7068. This engine was fairly new but didn't seem to steam properly. When we arrived at Tinsley loop, I examined the fire and it was full of clinker although the tender was well coaled. What had occurred was that the train had come from Newcastle and it had then gone into the then new yard at York Skelton for loco duties. There were good new facilities at this place – ash pit, coal supply etc. The York crew had obtained coal but had not either cleaned the fire or raked out the ashes.

I said to Alf "I'll clean the fire, it won't take long as these engines have drop bars". I had read about these in the railway magazine of which I was a regular reader. I put the extension handle onto the spigot in the cab floor and pulled it backwards as far as I could, which was not to its limit. The drop grate went down partly, and I could see that it had dropped backwards and was of no use whatsoever. "Put it back up", said Alf "and we'll throw some clinker out through the firedoor". I tried to put the drop grate back up, but couldn't. What happened was that the grate, instead of dropping fully, had pivoted on a large heap of ashes in the ashpan, and the hinge had come out of its sockets and could not be replaced by the operating handle. Worse was to follow – because the long handle could not be pushed to its forward extremity, so it would not clear the slot in the cab floor, and so could not be removed. Alf decided that we were not going to fail the engine so we removed some of the clinker and put some of the pieces over the gap in the grate. The engine certainly steamed better but I had to fire up with the extension handle sticking up through the cab floor; not an easy proposition. So much for Mr Riddles' drop grates.

We were changed over with a Staveley crew at Woodhouse Junction and they gave us a knowing look when we explained the situation.

Another defect with Austerities was that at speeds above 35mph, there was a violent fore and aft motion set up: this, besides being most uncomfortable, resulted in the coal in the tender being deposited in the cab by the "jigger" action of the tender. I have experienced footplates 18" deep in coal and with it rolling off at both sides onto the ballast. I understand that the cause was due to a balancing defect in the general design – it was never really cured.

Mr Bradshaw, another driver and foreman at Mexborough said that in his opinion the WDs (Austerities) were not as good as the Robinson O4s on the Worsborough Bank because the WDs sanders would only work on odd occasions; never when they were needed most, whereas the O4s with a good dry steam sander, worked by a simple lever, made all the difference. The steam sanders required a lot of maintenance and were liable to freeze up in the winter, when they were most needed.

D10/D11 GC DIRECTOR CLASS

There were none of this class at Mexborough in January 1940. However, during February, when the K2s departed, two Directors arrived at the shed and remained there for some five or six years. The two engines were 5429 and 5431. The class was always known as Directors, and originally all carried names of GCR Directors. However, two of the ten later, were named after Royalty, 5429 being one of them. These engines really belong to what could be called Robinson's third period. In his first period, he designed the two Pom Poms – goods and passenger with inside cylinders: the second period 1902-1911, seven classes of engine were built with two outside cylinders – these I consider were Robinson's most fruitful years, when such handsome examples as the B1, B4, B5, C4 and O4 were created. His third period after 1913 was, with one exception an unhappy one when such engines as the B2, and its freight counterpart, both with inside cylinders came on the scene. Finally, in his fourth period, 1917-1922, he went mainly for four cylinders with the B3 and B7 for passenger and freight plus the gem that got away – the B6! These of course were all tender engines.

The exception of the third period was the D10 Director: this engine, for its size, was a remarkable piece of machinery, and once again, Robinson seemed to get all the proportions right – a very good steaming boiler with a good deep firebox; short tubes and a very roomy cab, this time with corner quadrant wooden seats and footstools.

The tenders of the original Directors were of the standard Gorton type with a U-shaped coal hole at the front. This tender was effective for medium length runs but, if put on a through Manchester to Marylebone express,

LNER Class C4 No 6084, leaving Marylebone around 1931. Courtesy G Coltas.

coal became a problem after Nottingham.; the reason being that, as soon as the coal hole became empty, the coal would not fall to the shovelling plate. This necessitated the fireman climbing onto the tender to get coal forward. This was a dangerous practice when running at speed as overline bridges became a lethal hazard. Robinson cured this problem by designing a new type of tender with a hopper at the front so that the coal would fall forward as the journey progressed. The same tender was later fitted to the two four cylinder classes B3 and B7. There were very few of these hopper tenders and they were always reserved for the London workings.

I think it can be said that the Directors, after various experiments, represented the cream of the passenger power on the old G.C. railway. This being so meant that Mexborough, because of its small passenger complement, was well down the list for an allocation. The first ten came out in 1913 and Mexborough received two in 1940, when they were 27 years old. The numbers were 5429 and 5431, the former being the first of the class to be built. In 1940 they were still in good form and did excellent work on the Hull trains until the advent of the B1s.

The two engines carried the names of Prince Henry and Edwin A Beasley. 5429 was originally named Sir Alexander Henderson after the Company Chairman. However, when Henderson was made Lord Faringdon in 1916, that name was given to the first of the class B3 – 6169. 5429 was then named Sir Douglas Haigh, but again there was a move up for Haigh in the aristocracy and his name, now Earl Haig was also transferred to a class B3 – 6166. 5429 then acquired its final name Prince Henry.

It would seem that engine naming on the G.C. railway and the early

GCR 4-4-0 Director Class No 506 "Butler Henderson". This locomotive is part of the York N.R.M. collection and is on long term loan to Barrow Hill Engine Shed; - it in itself a locomotive preservation site. On the day of my visit in May 2008, Chesterfield Camra branch were having a beer festival; - now how co-incidental is that?

years of the L.N.E.R. had something of a political content about it. 6167 was named Lloyd George when it was built in 1920: this engine was transferred to King's Cross shed in 1923 to work the Leeds and Harrogate services. David Lloyd George suffered his political demise in 1922 and it appears that he had enemies on the railway as well as the House of Commons because the higher management of the L.N.E.R. ordered the removal of the name plates at Kings Cross. It is rumoured that the plates were found behind a cupboard at Kings Cross shed when it was being pulled down in 1963; this was 38 years after the removal of the plates.

I attended a Railway exhibition whilst on holiday in Bournemouth in the summer of 1985 and was surprised to see one of the Lloyd George name plates exhibited on the wall. Knowing the history of the plates, I sought out the owner and asked him how he had acquired the name plate, and he said, "with money": he would not expand on that. It is my opinion that the name plates were removed at the request of an aristocrat Director in the L.N.E.R.

My experience with Directors was somewhat limited, as I did not reach the passenger link as a fireman until May 1949, and by then, the new B1s were in command. 5429 and 5431 were fitted with "T.A.B." piston valves and a notice to driver was displayed in the cab. The effect of the valves was to act as a by-pass, as when steam was shut off, the valve heads moved to the middle of the valve spindle leaving the steam ports wide open, thereby preventing compression in the cylinders. The overall effect of this arrangement was that the engine ran very sweetly when coasting.

I had an amusing experience during the summer of 1941 with D11 No 5510

BR Class D11 62667 "Somme" at Sheffield Victoria Station. Courtesy Great Central Railway Society.

– "Princess Mary". This was at a time in the war when anything on wheels was pressed into service – on any sort of train. I had worked with Driver Harry Williams, on a Worksop to Hull train which normally went via Braithwell Junction and the ex Hull and Barnsley line, but because of flooding at Bentley, had been diverted via the G.C. line and Goole. On arrival at Dairycoates shed at Hull, we were informed that we should be working a train back to Doncaster with engine No 5510. We took this engine into the Outward Yard and coupled onto some wagons of pit props. The guard, a Hull man, informed us that the train consisted of 60 wagons of pit props for Doncaster Mineral Bank. Harry Williams, a bachelor, and something of a joker, but a thoroughly practical railwayman, said, "How many wagons did you say?" The guard repeated the number – 60, whereupon Williams exploded, "How do you think I am going to stop 60 wagons of props with this engine"? The guard was nonplussed – he had probably never seen a D11 before, and, if he had, he had no conception of its traction and braking capacity.

This whole comic episode was further complicated by the different loading arrangements of the L.N.E.R. with the North Eastern area (Hull) and the Southern area (Doncaster). The latter also contained the ex G.N. loads tables. The G.C. section tables stated that the class D11 was to convey 6 wagons of mineral less than a class 1 freight engine and one wagon of mineral was the equal of 1 ½ wagons of goods (pit props). Another complication was that the North Eastern area did not calculate train loads in wagons of mineral or goods – they used weight, expressed in tons! This was in fact, the old North Eastern Railway system of loading, still in use 18 years after the demise of the N.E. Railway. A further point of contention was that the G.C. loading book did not contain a column for a Class 1 loco – it started at class 2. Furthermore 60 wagons was actually the length limit for Doncaster Mineral Bank and the train had obviously been prepared with a class 6 or 7 engine in mind. Was there any wonder that the guard was so confused? On Harry Williams' insistence, the train was reduced by 25 wagons, so we left Hull Outward Yard with 35 wagons of pit props, and old Prince Mary simply played with the load. We were relieved at Bentley Junction on the outskirts of Doncaster by some Carr Loco men, with a few acid comments about horses for courses.

CLASS N2 (LOAD 2)

In these notes, Ron refers to Superheaters. This is an arrangement which dries the steam and heats it up to a much higher temperature to give it extra working power. A superheater consists of a number of small tubes enclosed in large flue tubes through which the flames pass. Steam only enters the superheater when the driver opens the regulator.

"As the second world war progressed, very few new locomotives were built, as steel was needed for war purposes – shells, guns, tanks etc. By 1941 the Kings Cross suburban service had been reduced and some of the locomotives used thereon were thrown spare. In May 1942, therefore, ten class N2 suburban tank engines arrived at Mexborough shed from the Kings Cross area to be used as bankers on the westbound trains.

These engines, designed by Nigel Gresley in the early 20s, were provided for slow passenger work, principally in the Kings Cross suburban area, although a few were stationed in the West Riding, Scotland and around the Liverpool Street district. They had the same boiler as the older Ivatt N1 class but had an inch bigger cylinder – and here was part of the weakness. The numbers were 896, 2586, 2588, 2594, 2684,4611,4726,4740, 4744 and 4769.

Designed for the intermittent steam demands of an all stations passenger service, they were seriously over cylindered for the heavy and continuous steaming required on Dunford banking work. They failed completely on this work, mainly for the following reasons:-

1)   The men were unfamiliar with the design and didn't want them: there was a very strong anti GN tradition at all GC sheds.
2)   Mexborough water didn't suit them. There was a lot of priming with the small boiler.
3)   Mexborough coal was of too low a grade for such a small grate.
4)   The cylinders overpowered the capacity of the boiler on the continuous steaming requirements.
5)   They were never good steamers even on their own ground mostly due to Gresley "twin tube" superheater elements leaking at the smokebox end. This was apparently cured later by the fitting of Robinson superheaters at Doncaster.
6)   As with all inter-depot engine transfers, if the actual engine

BR Class N2 0-6-2T No 69498 introduced in 1925. These locos were used quite a bit for bringing and withdrawing carriage stock out of Kings Cross station. 10 of this class were transferred to Mexborough for a four year period during the Second World War.

Going no further. Gresley Class N2 0-6-2T Nos 69557 and 69566 on the scrap line at Doncaster Plant. Built in 1925, they were withdrawn in 1957.

numbers are not specified in the official letters, the despatching depot always sent their worst performers. This was the oldest trick in the book with engine loans and transfers.

Out of the ten engines sent to Mexborough, only one could be said to be upto the work: this was no 2588 which, with orthodox treatment was a good steamer. The inference was, therefore, that if one could be made to steam, there was nothing wrong with the design as a whole. That being said, there were never any alterations or amendments to the design during the four years that the engines were at Mexborough. It was later learned that there was difficulty in keeping the superheater header joints steam tight in the smokebox. This of course, would be fatal to good steaming as it would partially destroy the smokebox vacuum.

I cannot accept that the superheater trouble affected every locomotive in the group as, except 2588, they had on and off days depending on the treatment used. I personally always kept a very thin fire and the "little and often" style of firing: this suited some of them – but not all. No 2684 was beyond redemption as, whichever style of firing and driving was adopted, it never responded normally.

Some of the ten were fitted with condensing gear for use on the London Underground lines and this proved useful at one location. The three tunnels on the route were always troublesome for the men on the bankers because the rear engine had to contend also with the smoke and steam of the train engine at the front, as well as its own. This was doubly so in the 560 yard tunnel at Oxspring as it was a single bore in each direction and the fumes could not get away so readily – the products of combustion and steam were present from three or four previous trains: it was a really awful atmosphere. On this situation, some drivers operated the condensing gear. I never detected much advantage in doing this as it ruined the steaming of the boiler, which was always on a knife edge anyhow; this was because the majority of the steam was directed into the water tanks and its effect on the fire was thereby reduced.

During the four years that they were at Mexborough, there were various "cures" applied by the men themselves, including "cutting their throats", ie applying a "jimmy" across the blast pipe: removing one or two fire bars by pushing them up via the ashpan damper and spreading the remainder, thereby increasing the air gaps between the bars and admitting more primary air under the fire. There was little else the crews could do to improve things. The men soldiered on during the war years – as did everybody else – and there was a unanimous sigh of relief by the whole of the depot staff when they went back to Kings Cross in 1946. On their arrival in 1941, Hitler's Stukas were doing tremendous damage in Europe – so the N2s were immediately christened "Dive Bombers".

'ROBINSON B5 AND B4 (LOAD CLASS 2)

In 1940-47 the South Yorkshire to Hull services, of which Mexborough had two, were worked by Robinson B5s. The trains concerned were the 0910 Doncaster – Hull, and the 1000 Sheffield ditto, with heavy return workings, KX (King's Cross) 1210 and LL (Liverpool) 1610.

The B5 class, good mixed traffic engines, were originally allocated to Grimsby and Neasden sheds and because of their associations with the fish trains from Grimsby to Manchester, London and Banbury, they were known all their lives as Fish engines. In my time, the B5s had the same superheated boiler as the Q4 0-8-0, and were very free at steaming. They were a class 2 for loading, and could take 54 of "goods" from Sheffield to Woodford, a fair load for a mostly rising road.

At the grouping of the railways in 1923, there were six Fish engines at Mexborough, all of which were allocated to the six drivers in the Banbury link. Their numbers were 186, 1067, 1068, 1069, 1071 and 1072. At that time, Mexborough worked fish trains from Marshgate Yard at Doncaster, to Banbury and Manchester. These trains were formed of fish vans from both Grimsby and Hull (N.E. Ry) which were made up into trains at the G.C.R. Marshgate yard at Doncaster, of which more later.

These engines, together with a number of O4 and Q4 classes, were transferred to Doncaster shed in 1924 when the work in and from the Hexthorpe and Marshgate yards were so transferred.

This transfer of footplate staff to Doncaster in 1924 caused a considerable upheaval at the large ex G.N. establishment at Carr Loco. There were 33 drivers and 20 firemen moved, with the locomotives from Mexborough to Doncaster. At the same time, the Great Eastern shed at Doncaster (it was actually on loan from the L.N.W. railway) was closed and most of the staff were also moved into the G.N. shed, in this case 30 drivers and 21 firemen. The total intake of "foreign" men to Doncaster Carr was therefore 63 drivers and 41 firemen – 104 men!. The effect of this on staff morale with the G.N. men was enormous and took some years before it settled down.

The B5 and B4 classes were, in my opinion, the best looking engines

LNER Class B4 No 6104 built by Beyer Peacock in 1906.
Courtesy Great Central Railway Society.

produced by Robinson when they were built; they then had saturated boilers and, for the G.C.R., a very shallow firebox. In this form, they were difficult to fire. My father-in-law, who fired them then, told me that with the shallow box, saturated boiler and Mexborough water – which was poor – the fireman had to be careful how he performed. It was certainly a case of little and often with the water kept at about half a glass.

When the class was superheated between 1926 and 1933, the true Q4 boiler was provided with a deeper firebox. This made a considerable difference to the performance of the class and they were thereafter a first class mixed traffic engine, wonderful for seaside specials. Of course, the higher pitch of the superheated boiler, spoiled their looks somewhat, but the footplate crews wouldn't worry too much about that. For them it was "handsome is as handsome does".

The cab was the usual Robinson pattern with a cut out cab side, long wooden seats and good footstools. The one thing that spoiled the cab at the fireman's side was the presence of a hydrostatic cylinder lubricator straight in front of him. These "Detroit" lubricators were smelly things and that corner of his cab could never be kept as clean as one could have wished. The oil spillage had seeped into the seat boards and it could not be removed.

With the advent of the B1 class in 1947, all the B5s were relegated to banking work between Wath and Dunford and such like duties. All 13 were at Mexborough in 1947. All had gone by 1950 – 1686 (5183) was the last.

In a similar group to the B5s were Robinson B4s. These engines had a 6" bigger wheel and the larger O4 type boiler. They were very similar in looks to the B5, but the larger splashes and a slightly smaller chimney gave a better impression of power.

Five of these locomotives were sent to Mexborough in 1914, specially to work the heavy troop trains which ran through Mexborough for the next four years and they were allocated to five of the six drivers in the Banbury Link, as follows:-

Driver	Fireman	Eng No	GC Class	LNE Class
Ernest Hague	Jack Hurst	1071	8	B5
Jack Costello	Horace Ardron	1095	8F	B4
Jim Richards	Bill Sawyers	1097	8F	B4
George Sadler	Tom Walker	1098	8F	B4
Jack Ford	Fred Holmes	1099	8F	B4
Bill Towers	Fred Royle	1104	8F	B4

As will be seen, the odd man out was Ernest Hague who had a B5 with six inch smaller driving wheels and a less boiler. Hague was an excellent engineman and I wouldn't think the difference in wheel size would worry him too much.

To quote George White, a one time roster clerk at Mexborough Shed – "These men were selected for the Banbury link by Mr W.G.P.McClure, the all powerful Locomotive Running Superintendent for the whole of the Great Central Railway". White paid tribute to the Banbury link crews for the work they did during the First World War, as they were responsible for the working of troop trains between Mexborogh West Jcn or Doncaster, and Banbury during the whole of that period, lodging at Woodford and returning with ambulance trains. He said "many a young soldier from such military camps as Catterick, must have made part of their last journey on British soil behind these men"." I am reminded of them every time I visit Leicester and see the broken arches of the former Great Central Railway striding across the city". The men were later to work trains through to the Wembley Exhibition in 1924.

CLASS Q4 "OLD TINIES" (GC CLASS 8A) (LOAD CLASS 6)
This locomotive was Robinson's first essay in an eight wheels coupled design, and was first built in 1902. The boiler and firebox were slightly smaller than the 04 and the firedoor was not so high. All the boilers were saturated when built, but a plan to fit them all with superheaters was started in 1914 but for some reason, it was never finished, as nine engines remained saturated to the end (1951). The boiler was standard with LNER B5 but with a deeper firebox made possible by the smaller wheels.

There were slide valve and piston valve versions, mostly the former. The slide valves were of the balanced type and so no difficulty was experienced when notching up under steam. The balance of cylinders, heating surface and grate area was well matched and the steaming qualities were excellent.

There were 41 of these engines at Mexborough in 1923 out of a total of 89, so that Mexborough, as the main "coal shed" again had the lion's share.

There were only 8 left in 1940 and they were used turn and turn about with the class 04, as the difference in loading was only 5 or 6 wagons. (The Q4 was a class 6 for loading). The one exception to this arrangement was the Elsecar Branch which served both Cortonwood (fateful name in the 84 pit strike) and Elsecar Collieries. On this branch the 04 was barred because of weight restriction. This limiting feature was an old lifting bridge across the old Dearne & Dove canal and it was raised by a windlass and chains whenever a barge was to pass. The cast iron beams across the top of the winding gantry had the words "South Yorkshire" cast into them. This was the only surviving article I knew of with this device upon it, and it denoted the original railway company operating the branch. It was worthy of preservation but it never survived.

The canal was disused in my time and I never knew the lifting bridge to be operated. The canal was filled in after the second world war, the lifting bridge dismantled, and the larger 04 class worked the branch thereafter. The Q4 had all the reliable Robinson features of the 04 class; free steaming boiler, good dry sanding gear, good injectors, surefooted and the same semi circular fire door and trap.

The one thing to be watched with the saturated engines, especially with Mexborough water, was priming: the water level had therefore to be kept low, particularly when the engine was nearing a boiler washout.

There was a development with this class in the early 1940s when 13 of them were converted to tank engines. This was done in order, so it was said, to:–

(a)   create a new class of heavy shunting engine, and

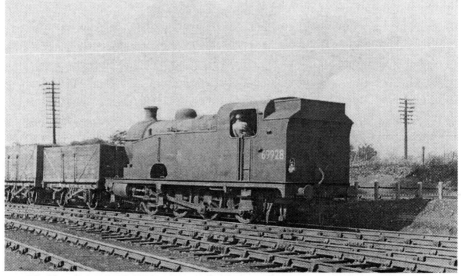

BR Class Q1 0-8-0T 69928. This engine was a Thompson rebuild of the Robinson GC Q4 0-8-0. Courtesy Great Central Railway Society.

Class Q4 nicknamed by Mexborough men as "Old Tinies", was Robinson's first essay in an eight wheels coupled design. It was first built in 1902 and was the forerunner to the O4 2-8-0. Out of a total of 89 in this class, Mexborough, as the main coal shed, had the lions share; 41 of these engines were allocated to Mexborough in 1923. Courtesy Great Central Railway Society.

   (b)   to release a number of tenders (steel was in short supply at this time) for use on some new class 03 gn type 2-8-0s then being built. Such was the statement released to the railway press.

It may be said here that none of this batch of 03s ever appeared with a GC tender, as in any case the brake systems were incompatible (GN Vacuum; GC steam). I understand that an 03 and a GC tender were placed together in Doncaster works for photographic purposes – they were not coupled together.

However, soon afterwards GC tenders started to appear, painted green, behind one or two of the Hunt Class D49s, working from Botanic Gardens shed at Hull. In the latter days of steam traction, the authorities would never have got away with such a cosmetic statement about the disposition of locomotive tenders, as the lynx eyed spotters would have rumbled them.

The rebuilds from Q4 tender engines to Q1 tanks could never be regarded as a success by any stretch of the imagination and Edward Thompson lost quite a few Brownie points with Mexborough men over this scheme.

Eight Q1s were sent to Mexborough in 1944 and were put onto the Wath – Annesley coal trains. The Q1s only worked as far as Rotherwood up exchange sidings, 16 miles; from that point the trains were worked forward to Annesley by Darnall men with a fresh engine. The Q1s then worked back to Wath from the Rotherwood down yard. They came to Mexborough at a time when Hitler's V1 flying bombs were tormenting southern England and naturally, the men promptly labelled them "Doodlebugs", the Cockney name for the flying bombs. This name became permanent, at least at Mexborough.

The LNER 1944 loading book lists the Q1s as class 6 for loading, the same as the Q4 tender engines. Now whoever was responsible for this Q1 loading classification could not have had much idea of unbraked train working, as they had obviously based the load on the tractive effort only, which remained the same as the tender engines. The following tables will illustrate the case:-

	Q4	Q1	Difference
Water Capacity	3250 galls	1500 galls	1760 galls
Heating Surface	1805 sq ft	1209 sq ft	596 sq ft
Braking	14 wheels	8 wheels	6 wheels

All the superheaters were removed from the converted engines, which exacerbated the water problem still further. The position was, that whatever their capacity as a heavy shunting loco, as a train engine they were a complete failure.

The route from Wath yard to Rotherwood, although short (16 miles) was replete with heavy gradients. In the 1940s, it was also a very busy line, heavily occupied with coal and general freight traffic in addition to a frequent passenger service running over the entire route. This meant that progress was slow and intermittent. The order of the day was usually – into every loop line – backed into blocked sidings – run onto branch ends etc etc. so as to clear the way for more important trains.

In practice, it meant that a driver with 1760 gallons of water less in the tank and a saturated boiler, was ultra cautious about the water situation: the presence of lifting injectors made the position even worse, as they sometimes refused to work when the water level in the tanks became low. The upshot of all this was that some drivers would not pass a water column. What this did for train regulation on a busy line can best be left to the imagination

The most serious let-down was braking with nearly half the braking effort (the tender) removed. On the return journey from Rotherwood, the 1 in 72 gradient approaching Attercliffe Jcn was the main trap, and many were the run-byes with a full class 6 load.

This disastrous episode was finally concluded in 1946 when all eight locos were bundled off to Frodingham to do trip work between the various yards there, and where they were always in sight of a water column. Here they remained until 1958 when the whole class became extinct..

CLASS N5 0-6-2 TANK (LOAD CLASS 2)
Thomas Parker who came from Scotland, succeeded Charles Sacre as Locomotive Engineer of the M.S. & L. Ry, in 1886. He had been Carriage and Wagon Superintendent sine 1858, so he had waited 28 years for promotion to the top job. His engines were, in the Gorton tradition, very solidly built. In the seven short years in the Locomotive Engineer's chair, he constructed 480 engines for the M.S.&L. Ry., most surviving into LNER days and some into BR times.

The only Parker engines at Mexborough in 1940 were nine of the 0-6-2 tank class N5. Built in the 1890s, they were sturdy and comfortable machines, ideal for shunting and short trip work. The driver could perform all his driving functions from a sitting position and at the same time watch the shunter for hand signals. Being an 0-6-2 design, and therefore longer than a conventional 0-6-0 tank, they had a roomy cab with plenty of space to wield a clinker shovel when cleaning the fire; they had the best cab of any steam shunting engine that I knew.

Although used primarily as a shunting engine, in my time the N5 had other work to do at Mexborough. One was always provided for Wath Main Colliery pilot. This pit was on the very door step of Wath Yard and had a severely curved entrance into the sidings – hence the use of a six coupled engine instead of the usual eight coupled one normally used for colliery work. The use of a small six coupled engine in this instance, was no detriment, as it was always within sight of a water column and the distance from Wath colliery to Wath yard with the loaded wagons was less than 400 yards. This pilot was always known as "Wath Anna", though I have never discovered the reason for this; it was always shown as "Wath A" in the timetables of 1910 onwards.

Another job for an N5 was Bentley Banker. This name was something of a misnomer as the engine was always operated from Sprotborough Junction, the next box to Bentley. It was used here for assisting heavy trains up the ¾ mile short steep gradient to Hexthorpe Junction. An interesting part of this job was the assisting of coal train trips from Yorkshire Main Colliery to the Mineral Bank at Doncaster. In this case the Bentley Banker acted as the train engine for the short trip to Hexthorpe Junction. In this arrangement the

Class N4 Loco Pilot No 9231 used for supplying and servicing the coal stage at Mexborough MPD. This photo would have been taken sometime after July 1946 when it was renumbered under BR to 69231. This loco was withdrawn in October 1954.
Courtesy J Raybould collection.

train did a "z" movement: when it arrived at Sprotborough, the train drew past the signal box and Bentley Banker coupled onto the brake van at the rear of the train. The train then reversed upto Hexthorpe Junction with the train engine acting now as the banker, and the banker as train engine. On arrival at the top of the gradient, Bentley Banker was uncoupled from the train by the guard detaching a coupling, whilst leaning from the verandah of the brake van with a shunting pole, while the train was still in motion. The train then reversed for the second time, the train engine resumed its proper role and took the wagons down to Doncaster.There were three or four such movements during each day.

After 1900 hrs the engine abandoned its banking role and went light engine to Doncaster South yard to work a pick up goods train to Mexborough; always called "scuffter" because of the heavy shunting work involved.

N5 tanks also worked the "Flying Flea". This was a local, general purpose pick up train which serviced the local works such as Queens Foundry, the glass works of Dale Brown & Co. It also shunted the wagon works of Burnett & Co which now occupied the site of the Old Plant, the original Mexborough Shed of the erstwhile South Yorkshire Railway. Its last job was to bring the locomotive coal from Wath Yard to Mexborough Shed. The turn was a considerate work job for the engine crew, but for different reasons. For the driver it was for medical reasons, ill health etc, but for the fireman it was a job one could have if the wife was about to give birth to a child, so that the fireman could be easily reached if an emergency arose at home. It was therefore usually easy to spot who was about to become a father.

In 1923 there were 40 engines of class N5 at Mexborough and they were used on all sorts of trip work, usually colliery pilots, but also some longer turns. They were used, for instance, on trips between Wath Yard and

Class N5 awaiting repair at Mexborough. Behind can be seen the leading wheel of a WD Austerity.
Photo H.C.Casserley printed in British Railways Illustrated Vol. 10 No 4 January 2001.

Frodingham. This was a distance of 37 miles each way, with water columns only at Mexborough and Crowle, 22 miles apart. The capacity of the tanks was only 1360 gallons and with lifting injectors, left little leeway for emergencies. An old driver of mine, Fred Fisher, put the situation to me this way; "if tha looked in't tank at Mexborough, tha wanted watter; if tha didn't look tha awlus got through to Wath (3 miles).

The one thing that had to be watched with an N5 was the level of water in the boiler. It is recorded that a few N5s were equipped with superheaters, but I never came across one.

Sheffield and Barnsley could always work wonders with these little tank engines; in fact at Barnsley, they formed the bulk of the allocation. The main reason for the good work performed by these two depots was, of course, water – they were both in soft water areas and priming was rare. At Mexborough, the water came from a large well on the premises but it was poor stuff for a saturated engine. The well was just 50 yards from the river Don, which was an open sewer. Incidentally, at Crowle, the column water was taken directly from the canal and, after taking water there, one could occasionally get small fish swimming about in the tender tank.

CLASS J11

The best of Robinson's small mixed traffic engines was the J11 "Pom Pom". These locomotives were built in the very early part of the Robinson era, 1901 to 1910, and were his first good design. The nickname reflected the sharp staccato exhaust, said to be reminiscent of the pom pom gun in the South African war.

This Pom Pom Class J11 No 64377 was allocated to Mexborough. Seen standing on the shed road, probably between roads 1 and 4. Three roads behind can be seen a Class K3 from March depot. Courtesy Great Central Railway Society.

This Pom Pom Class J11/3 was rebuilt in 1942 with long travel piston valves (see under smoke box door) and a higher pitched boiler. These valves facilitated a much easier motion when freewheeling with the regulator off as the steam would be diverted from the cylinders thus reducing steam friction. Seen here at Mexborough on 15th June 1958.
Courtesy Great Central Railway Society.

One of the rebuilt Pom Pom class J11/3 standing on the back road of the Cripple sidings on 7th October 1962. The wagons seen behind the tender would be in Goods Yard No 2 and in the background to the right, can be glimpsed a coach which would be in the carriage sidings.
Courtesy Great Central Railway Society.

They were distributed throughout the old Great Central system and were capable of working any type of train up to a speed of 60mph; they were therefore used a great deal on summer special trains to the Yorkshire and Lincolnshire coasts. I clearly remember taking a Pom Pom to Bridlington in the summer of 1950. It was new from Gorton shops and in cracking condition. When we examined the engine on Bridlington shed, the right hand small end was hot, and the shed fitter failed it. Alongside Bridlington shed on a summer Saturday was the most run down K3 from Dairycoates shed at Hull, standing as a pilot for failures, and this was the one we brought back. Now K3s were generally rough riding but this was the worst. Everything about it rattled; the cab roof, which had some missing bolts, sagged in unison with each turn of the wheel – the noise at speed was indescribable. K3s were always good at steaming and could always "get there". I was pleased when we got relieved at Mexborough station; relieved was the right word that day.

Although the Pom Pom was a very free steamer, it had a small firebox and grate. A fireman had to be careful not to get a heavy fire at the front of the grate or he was sunk. The best way to fire them was – a shovelful in each back corner and another under the door, one down each side and one thrown at the tube plate. Because of the sharp blast, one had to smartly turn the shovel with the first five shovelfuls, or the blast would pull the coal off the blade and pull it to the front of the grate. The result would then be a thick fire at the front and the steam gauge finger moving backwards.

In 1942 Edward Thompson rebuilt a Pom Pom, No 6009 with new cylinders and piston valves. To make room for the new valves mounted on top of the cylinders, Thompson had to raise the position of the boiler; this resulted in a shorter chimney and a new look to the design. This rebuild made a good engine even better. The exhaust sound was different and one had not to be so choosy about the shape of the fire – they were certainly an improvement. It also cured the kick back from the valve gear.

The rebuilt Pom Pom was selected by Thompson to be one of his ten standard classes, and he intended to build more after the war. What a standard Pom Pom would have looked like was never divulged, as Edward Thompson had gone before he had chance to produce any – they were never built. Presumably it would have had a side window cab and standard tender; a Belpaire firebox? – an interesting question with no answer.

CLASS D9 "PASSENGER POM POM"
Robinson's first engine built for the GC Railway was the 0-6-0 Pom Pom as described previously – they first appeared in September 1901. In the next four weeks there appeared Robinson's first passenger tender locomotive and, as this example had a similar explosive exhaust as the goods Pom Pom, it was straight away labelled a "Passenger Pom Pom". These names applied throughout the lives of both engines.

The D9 was built to the normal Gorton "Battleship" construction standard:

it had all the normal Robinson equipment including a short, and very deep firebox. The steaming was exemplary provided that one did not get too thick a fire at the front of the box, as with the J11. The Achilles Heel of this class was the Gresham and Craven faceplate lifting injector. With this apparatus the first operation was to open the water valve, then the steam valve, to create a vacuum in the water pipe, and thereby draw up the water and pass it into the body of the injector. If you succeeded in doing this, they were trouble free and capable of very fine adjustment. The latter feature was because the water regulating handle was immediately under the steam valve. There were no spindles, rodding or lost motion to affect the water adjustment, as on the under footplate flood type injector. The main problem of this injector was that, being attached directly to the boiler, it was always rather warm. However, if you didn't strike water at the first attempt, as when the water level was low in the tank and therefore had to be lifted from a lower level, the thing tended to get hot: this was caused by the action of the steam of course. In this situation, the more you tried to lift water, the hotter it became, and had to be cooled by applications of cold water from the bucket.

Meanwhile the boiler would no doubt be blowing off because of the non operation of the injector, and this would further deplete the water level in the boiler. If this went on for more than a few minutes, you were in trouble. I only remember this happening to me once. In this instance, I was with Cliff Porter on 5108 working a Cleethorpes to Penistone passenger train. We had a heavy load and took the pilot on the front from Stairfoot to Penistone. Approaching West Silkstone Junction, about 2 miles from Penistone, I tried to put the left hand injector on, but failed. The tank water

Class D9 "Passenger Pom Pom" on Mexborough shed circa 1930.
Courtesy Mexborough Heritage

level was getting low and neither injector would respond. Cliff Porter signalled our situation to the pilot driver and closed the regulator. I, in turn, closed the damper to save blowing off. We had about 2" of water in the gauge glass and the pilot meanwhile was pulling the heavy train plus the 104 tons of our engine. I managed to get the driver's side injector on passing Barnsley Junction signal box and the day was thereby saved, but it was a very close run thing.

During the early years of the war when troop trains were frequent, and often heavy, Mexborough had to provide assisting engines as far south as Pilsley, which is the summit of the line south of Sheffield. My driver was one Charlie Harrison who was, at that time, a young passed fireman, and we were given the task of so assisting for a number of nights one week with Class D9 engine 5108.

These trains came from the North of England and were re-engined at York and relieved by Mexborough men at Mexborough West Junction, the crew going through to Woodford and lodging. The assisting engine attached while the engine crews were being relieved. The train engines were Class V2s "Green Arrows", so the weight of the trains would be excessive if a V2 needed assistance. The train engine crew on the first night was Driver Charlie Wilkinson, with Eric Smith as his fireman: the second night it was Driver Ernest Liversedge with Reg James firing. After giving assistance to Pilsley, the pilot detached and returned to Staveley shed to turn then light engine to Mexborough. This was my first experience of fast running, and, between bouts of firing, I hung on for dear life. 5108 steamed very well and the experience was a useful one for a 19 year old spare fireman.

CHAPTER 16

THE SHEFFIELD DIVISION OF BRITISH RAILWAYS

BY R FAREHAM

In January 1958, a new division of British Railways was formed at Sheffield: this area included some ex LNER sheds and also a number from the erstwhile LMS. This was a radical change for the Mexborough and Barnsley sheds as they had been, for the previous 35 years, part of the Doncaster District.(District was by now, an outdated term). Prior to the grouping in 1923, Mexborough had been a District Headquarters in its own right, with a number of outstations (Barnsley, Wakefield, Barnsley Junction and Keadby).

Sheffield was a big division so far as footplate staff were concerned; there were nearly 1300 enginemen, spread over the following ten depots:-

			PREVIOUS DISTRICT
Ex LNE	Darnall	41A	Manchester
Ex LMS	Grimesthorpe	41B	Sheffield (LM)
Ex LMS	Millhouses	41C	Sheffield (LM)
Ex LMS	Canklow	41D	Sheffield (LM)
Ex LMS	Barrow Hill	41E	Toton
Ex LNE	Mexborough	41F	Doncaster
Ex LNE	Barnsley	41G	Doncaster
Ex LNE	Staveley	41H	Colwick
Ex LNE	Langwith	41J	Lincoln
Ex LNE	Tuxford	41K	Lincoln

The Divisional Motive Power Superintendent appointed to oversee the new organisation, was a John Blundell, an ex Great Central man, whose father had been a Chief Civil Engineer prior to the grouping. John Blundell was very straight; an ex Colonel in the Operating Division of the Army in World War 2, and a much respected man. He initially had a very difficult job in trying to combine ex Midland and Great Cental locomotive interests in Sheffield.

In August of 1958, I was asked to become an acting Locomotive Inspector at Sheffield and I accepted with enthusiasm. The work of the Sheffield Inspectors was extremely varied and the area of operation was wide. The function of the group was basically – Inspection, Training, Examination, Investigation and maintenance of standards. A good proportion of the work involved riding with, and reporting upon, the standard of driving and firing the locomotive (steam in 1958). The main routes involved from October 1958 were:-

From	Sheffield (Victoria and Midland Stations) –
To:	KINGS CROSS
	St PANCRAS (3 Routes)
	BIRMINGHAM
	MANCHESTER (3 Routes)
	LIVERPOOL (2 Routes)
	CARLISLE
	CLEETHORPES
	LINCOLN
	BANBURY
	NOTTINGHAM
	LEICESTER
	YORK AND HULL

I tried to concentrate my efforts on learning the ex LMS lines, as I knew and signed for as a driver, many of the LNER lines.'

In October 1958, the MASTER CUTLER service from Sheffield Victoria to Marylebone was re-routed to run via Retford to King's Cross, and diesel hauled by an English Electric Type 4 (old classification, later class 40). This was the first train in the Sheffield Division to be hauled by a main line locomotive. (Diesel Multiple Unit trains and Diesel shunting locomotives had been in the area for some years).

A special link of 10 drivers was formed at Darnall and the men were sent, in turn, to the Ilford Diesel School to be trained for 3 weeks on the type 4 locomotives. The inspectors had also to be trained and an inspector's favourite riding diagram in those early diesel days was – from Sheffield Midland station to St Pancras (steam) with the 0705 train; (the Millhouses crew on this train lodged at Kentish Town Hostel): and return from Kings Cross with the 1120 pullman to Sheffield (the return of the Master Cutler) with Darnall men.

The Darnall drivers in the "Cutler" link took to the diesel locomotives very well – bearing in mind their ages – they were all senior men and the success of the running of the "Master Cutler" was a credit to them all. The English Electric Locomotives were well regarded and reliable machines. Later on, when faster and more powerful locos became available, the EE 4s became downgraded.

The training side of the Inspector's work was the one I liked, as it fitted in well with my previous work in the M.I.C. movement. Groups of upto a dozen engine cleaners were given two weeks classroom training, including a few days practical work on a steam engine, shunting yard and signal box visits. They were then passed out as Firemen. I did many of these courses which were very rewarding, if somewhat of a strain on the voice.

After some two years of this interesting work, I was informed that, commencing on October 3rd 1960, the intention was to dieselise the whole of the Sheffield Division. Six men were selected to be the first of the Sheffield team of Diesel Instructors and were to attend the Ilford school for a period of four weeks. Training was to be on what was at that time the basic locomotive for the Eastern Region, the 1365 hp Brush Type 2, now class 31. During this time, we were to live in the Ilford Hostel, which was part of the same premises. The first team consisted of:-

KEN STOKES of GRIMESTHORPE
COLIN TRIPPETT of GRIMESTHORPE
ROWLAND JONES of CANKLOW
CROMPTON LUND of CANKLOW
JACK STACEY of DARNALL
and MYSELF of MEXBOROUGH

It was a most strenuous mental period for us all, and some of the older men found it hard going. Added to this was the fact that some of them found it hard to sleep; mainly because of the close proximity of the old Great Eastern Main Line; from 0430 the trains seemed to be coming through "the middle of the house".

The instructor allotted to us was an old friend of mine, Dick Hunt, an endearing old character from Kings Cross, and a holder of the British Empire medal for service to the M.I.C. movement; he had been conference chairman for 10 years.

The course consisted, firstly, of two weeks theoretical training in a classroom; during this time we did very little but write notes. I filled two hefty note books, and this was before we ever saw a diesel locomotive other than the ones running outside our bedroom windows on the main line.

The second and third weeks were spent at the new diesel depot at Finsbury Park on the Kings Cross line. Here we were put through all that we had learnt in the classroom, and also some actual driving experience on the Hitchin to Cambridge line. Faults and Failures were particularly sticky subjects, and we were not allowed to consult our notebooks unless everyone in the group was stuck.

During the classroom work, one particular item kept cropping up. This was the engine governor with a button with a red band on it.This latter was the fault indicator. If you could see the red band there was a fault; if not, the fault lay elsewhere This appeared so many times in our written notes that we thought it must be at least a foot long. When we got to the locomotive, we were all anxious to know where this button was and Dick Hunt set two of us off to find it. We had to come back and admit defeat – we couldn't find it. When it was pointed out to us positioned in a dark corner at the side of the engine; it turned out to be a little grey coloured thing about half an inch long and ¾" when out and showing the red band. On the final day at Finsbury Park, we all assembled in the classroom and each one had to give a 20 minute talk on a given subject; I was given the fuel system, which was fairly easy.

On returning to Sheffield, we were told that the Grimesthorpe (ex LMS) depot was to be the first one to be converted, and as Darnall was to be the first diesel depot, that was where the training was to be carried out. The ex D.M.U. shed was given over to Diesel locomotive maintenance and the depot had a very good classroom. Each instructor had a team of 3 trainees, and we started with the men in the Grimesthorpe top London link (freight). All the men in this link were over 60. Ken Stokes and I always worked together with the trainees, three at each end of the loco.

The training of men of 60 years of age was real hard work and a good deal of repetition had to be done to get such things as knowledge of faults and failures understood and retained. The training trips had to include the handling of freight and passenger trains. The freight trips were the two AM/PM Barnsley pick up trains from engine shed sidings at Brightside. The first one left E.S sidings at 0430 and, for me, living ten miles away at Mexborough, this meant getting out of bed at 0200 hours to catch the Leeds – Sheffield mail train at 0310 from Mexborough. There was also the lunch time relief to this turn which was also used for training. The work involved on both turns was therefore equal – running and shunting. Two more turns used were the pick up trains traversing the Hope Valley line. Passenger work was the 0750 to Manchester Central and the 1145 return.; each man had to be given his turn of handling the train. The Manchester train was all stations to Chinley, followed by a 20 mile gallop, non stop, to Manchester. The afternoon turn was the 1430 Sheffield – Leeds with a 1730 return all stations to Sheffield.

In early December 1960, a new type of diesel locomotive appeared at Sheffield. This was the English electric 1000 h.p. type 1 (later class 20) and the Instructors were given a weeks conversion course on it. When an instructor or a driver had been through the basic three weeks (drivers) course on the 1365H.P. Brush loco, all subsequent diesel locomotives were classed as conversion courses. They were dealt with at local level, the Ilford instructors training the local instructors, who then trained the drivers. With 1280 drivers and five types of diesel locomotives, D.M.Us and some on Electric locomotives, the size of the training problem in the 1960 was enormous and it went on for years.

In the original Eastern region (before the merger with the North Eastern Region in 1969), the local training was done by Driving Instructors. These were drivers who were given a small supplement to their rate of pay, men who were actually pleased to do the work because of the experience gained In a matter of weeks, mainly because of constant repetition, these men became real experts at diesel operation.

In the North Eastern region, the diesel instructors were given a salaried grade which was permanent. I always thought that this was a better scheme, as it made for a more settled group of men. In the Eastern Region, if for some reason the work load reduced temporarily, the Instructors were sent back to driving work – this caused some disappointment from time to time. It was in this situation that I realised I was at a crossroads in my railway life. It was obvious to me that because of dieselisation, in a short time, many steam depots would close all over the country; consequently, many salaried Running Foremen's positions would disappear. In the Sheffield Division alone, out of 35 Foremen, 20 would become redundant. The question was, where would higher management put 20 redundant foremen? Some, of course, would take early retirement but I could see that the position of Locomotive Inspector – my ultimate goal – would be a closed book for years, until all the redundant men were placed or retired.

I liked the diesel instruction work: it was very interesting and a rewarding position to be in. However, what was the future to hold, how long would the instruction work last, and what would the result be? There were another 26 years to serve on the railway and I pondered the situation for some weeks. The decision that was taken was that, while plenty of Foremen's positions existed – and I gave this two years – I would try to obtain a permanent salaried position at the March Motive Power Depot in Cambridgeshire. I was called for interview in April and a week later I was informed I had been appointed.

CHAPTER 17

L.N.E.R. CLUB

There had been rumblings for some time that the Company should provide recreational facilities for its staff. With the ending of the 2nd World War, an ideal site becoming available on Rowms Lane; just a short walk from the station and the depot; approaches were made to the Company for financial assistance. The project was to purchase land and build a clubhouse; to be known as the L.N.E.R. Athletic Club

A foundation meeting was held on the 9th April 1946, and the minutes read as follows:-

PRESENT

Mr B Atkinson	Chairman	District Loco Superintendent, Doncaster
Mr J Hodgson		District Surveyor, Manchester
Mr C S Glenesk		District Engineer, Guide Bridge
Mr A Rose		Asst. District Engineer, Sheffield
Mr A E Beer		Asst to District Superintendent, Doncaster
Mr R L Vereker		Loco Shed Master, Mexborough
Mr G Hurd		Asst District Goods Manager, Sheffield
Mr A P Roberts		for Chief Mechanical Engineer, Doncaster
Mr A Redpath		Station Master, Mexborough
Mr G Hobson		Chairman, Athletic Club, Mexborough
Mr H Pursehouse		Secretary, Athletic Club, Mexborough
Mr J Clarkson		Treasurer, Athletic Club, Mexborough
Mr J Bannister		Trustee, Athletic Club, Mexborough.
Mr T Risley		Dist. Loco. Supt's. Office, Doncaster.

1 The Chairman explained that the meeting was called to consider questions raised in a joint letter, dated 3rd April 1946, from the Estate Surveyor, and the Locomotive Running Superintendent (Western Section), addressed to the District Loco Superintendent, Doncaster, and the District Surveyor, Manchester, which reads as follows:-

"The Divisional General Manager informs us that the Chairman requests that this matter shall be dealt with as expeditiously as possible. Sir Ronald, as you know, has accepted the Presidency of the Mexborough Club and he feels that the committee would be very much disturbed if they thought he was losing interest in their affairs. Would you be good enough to give the question your special attention and, let us have a full report containing the District Engineer's comments on the estimates given for levelling, turfing and fencing on the sports ground, and also the latest information obtainable respecting the temporary headquarters required by the Club. We also attach a copy of the draft rules of the Club which appear to be based on rules already in existence for similar Clubs elsewhere, and to which we do not think the Company can take exception. Your report should reach us, at the latest, by Tuesday 9th April."

The Club have decided to ask the Company for a loan of £6,000; £4,000 of this to be available at the present time, with the option of a further call on the other £2,000 as and when needed. They estimate the £4,000 will be expended as follows:-

Purchase of Land from Wentworth Estates	£1,200
Fencing	£800
Building of Clubhouse	£2,000

2 It was stated that only one estimate had been received, viz, from Messrs E. Sutcliffe & Co Ltd., Contractors, Rotherham, for the levelling of the site, erection of unclimbable fencing, building lavatories with necessary drainage, and Groundsman's hut at an inclusive price of £7,650. This estimate does not include the laying down of two hard tennis courts, two bowling greens, turfing the cricket pitch, and laying out of the running track, which are to be included in the amenities of the grounds. Neither does it include anything for the pavilion or other buildings which it is hoped to erect at a later stage.

3 In the opinion of the District Engineer, Guide Bridge, the estimate submitted is apparently on the high side, and he was therefore asked to obtain competitive prices and to furnish his own estimate for all the work shown on the plan which was given to him; this plan included two hard tennis courts, two bowling greens, running track, cricket square, groundman's hut and lavatories with drainage for the latter.

Until these estimates are provided, it is impossible to give any approximate cost of what the expenditure is likely to be, but as it is likely to exceed what was originally in the minds of the Club Committee, it was decided that the estimates should be sent direct to the Club for consideration, and they would then be in a position to decide how far the loan they originally decided to ask for would meet their requirements.

4 It was stated that it would be impossible to carry out the whole of the work shown on the plan at the present time, owing to the fact that certain portions of the land were not available for this purpose, and it may be some months before the land would be available.

5 In connection with the levelling of the land, the Club asked whether the Company would provide the necessary ashes free of cost.

6 The Club Committee are of the opinion that the rent of £10 per annum suggested for the Company's portion of the land adjoining the Wentworth estates, is somewhat on the high side and asked if it could be modified, although they are anxious that this should not prejudice their request for a loan.

7 The District Officers concerned have already reported that in their opinion they see no objection to the land being leased to the Club for a period of 21 years without the short determination clause.

8 The Club's representatives would like to know whether the Company's Chief Legal advisor would undertake the conveyancing of the land they intend to purchase from the Wentworth Estates Ltd and suggest that this might be done free of cost to the Club.

9 For the purpose of temporary Headquarters, the Club have already purchased from Messrs Earles Cement Co. a wooden building situated on land belonging to the L.N.E.Railway Co. adjoining Rowms Lane, Swinton. This land was, until recently, let to Mr E.V.Waddington at a rent of £10 per annum, exclusive of rates. The Club Committee asked, if in this case also, some modification could be made in the rent. In the meantime, they are proposing to make the building habitable for their immediate requirements out of their funds.

10 The proposed rules of the Club were read and the Company's representatives have no comment to make regarding same, so far as the Company is concerned.

The L.N.E.R. confirmed by letter to Driver H Pursehouse, Secretary of the Club on 25th July 1946 that a loan of £6,000 would be made available. The terms were that no interest would be charged during the first two years and thereafter, the rate of interest would be charged and reviewed annually. There would also be no requirement for repayment of the loan during the first five years of the Club's existence and thereafter the question of the repayment of

LNER Sports & Social Venue. The event was attended by senior managers of the BR Board NE Division & Officers of the BR Staff Association many of whom were railway workers at nearby Mexboro Loco Depot & Yards. The original building was breeze (concrete) block & corrugated sheeting. Courtesy Swinton Heritage

the loan would be reviewed annually in the light of the financial position of the Club. The legal charges for the conveyancy of the land from Wentworth Estates Ltd would also be done for free.

It was to be another almost four years however, before the Club finally opened. Further competitive estimates were sought and the first contract let was for the levelling, soiling and seeding of the site. In 1947, attention was turned to the provision of the Clubhouse. After inspecting several types, they opted for a building from the Ministry of Supply, in March, but

Mr K. L. Bird, General Manager NE Region British Rail hands over the Clubhouse keys to Mr H Pursehouse, the Club Secretary, while Mr George Hobson, the Club Chairman looks on. He was an engine driver at Mexboro.Courtesy Swinton Heritage.

unfortunately they could not get a license to erect it. Only permits and licences were being granted for work of National importance. This was repeatedly pursued; several applications were turned down and it was not until late 1949 that it was eventually granted and construction could commence. In this interim period, some splendid work was done by the Committee, men and women, who by their ceaseless efforts raised more than £1,000 as their contribution towards the liabilities of the Club.

The official opening of the Club was a very grand affair with a full afternoon and evening of events. The programme, dated 18th April 1950 was sent out to members by the General Secretary Mr H Pursehouse. It is reproduced here:-

FELLOW MEMBERS,
OFFICIAL OPENING OF THE CLUBHOUSE,
THURSDAY 4TH MAY 1950

The undermentioned British Railway Officials will be present to assist with the opening ceremony of the Club.

C. K. Bird Esq., Chief Regional Officer
E.W.Rostern Esq., Chief Operating Superintendent
H.H.Halliday Esq., Regional Staff Officer
W.S.Barnes Esq., Estate & Rating Surveyor
L.P.Parker Esq., Motive Power Superintendent
J.E.Jackson Esq., District Surveyor
F.R.L.Barnwell; Esq Assist. District Engineer
A.Rose Esq., District Engineer
W.Young Esq., Head of Welfare Section
M.B.Thomas Esq., Public Relations & Publicity Officer
H.C.Johnson Esq., Divisional Operating Superintendent
J.I.Campbell Esq., Civil Engineer
J.F.Harrison Esq., Mechanical & Electrical Engineer
M.S.Pallett Esq., District Welfare Representative
A.Taylor Esq., C&W Superintendent
F.W.Wheddon Esq., District Passenger Manager
E.J.Stephens Esq., District Operating Superintendent
A.R.Ewer Esq., District Motive Power Superintendent
O.C.Stuart Esq., Motive Power Superintendent
H.H.Beastall Esq., Motive Power Superintendent
C.M.Booth Esq., Motive Power Superintendent
H.Parker Esq., Station Master
G.Cranfield Esq., Station Master
L.Thomas Esq., Station Master
R.Redpath Esq., Station Master
R.L.Vereker Esq., District Motive Power Superintendent
J.Cartledge Esq., Goods Agent

R.B.Temple Esq., District Goods Manager
A.E.Reesbeck Esq., Motive Power Depot
J.Carr Esq., Retired Engine Driver
J.Bannister Esq., Retired Station Master

PROGRAMME

2-30pm Grand Football Match
5-00pm The Opening of the Clubhouse by C.K.Bird Esq.,
5-15pm Knife & Fork Tea.. Price 3/- each by ticket.
6-00pm Chaiman's remarks, introducing
        C.K.Bird Esq.,
        E.W.Rostern Esq.,
        W.Young Esq.,
        R.L.Vereker Esq., Mover of the Vote of Thanks
        R.Redpath Esq., Seconder of the Vote of Thamks
7-00pm Concert
        "Margarita" Soprano B.B.C.
        "Cliff Hurst" Comedian.
        "W.Dunn" Tenor
        Pianist: A.Seddons Esq., Compere: F.S.Pedley Esq.,
The above is subject to alteration.
Yours Faithfully
H Pursehouse.

George White was living in Foundry Lane, Swinton when the Club was being built. There were always wagons of ashes (from the ash pits) left at the top of the embankment. These were to be emptied onto the L.N.E.R. site as foundation material for raising the ground and whilst the ashes were provided free of charge for the benefit of the Club, no official time was given for emptying. Enthusiasts like George would finish a night shift, go home for breakfast and then return to Mexborough No 1 box to empty a wagon of ash. Some relief men would also take the opportunity to empty a wagon

TELEPHONE No. 2195

L.N.E.R. ATHLETIC CLUB
MEXBOROUGH

CHAIRMAN:
G. HOBSON,
35 SLADE ROAD,
SWINTON, MEXBOROUGH.

GENERAL SECRETARY:
H. PURSHOUSE,
11 WHITE LEE GROVE,
MEXBOROUGH, YORKS.

TREASURER:
J. CLARKSON,
5 POPLAR GROVE,
SWINTON, MEXBOROUGH.

PRESIDENT:
SIR RONALD W. MATTHEWS
CHAIRMAN L.N.E.R.

The Club House,
L.N.E.R. Athletic Club,
Rowms Lane,
SWINTON,
Mexborough, Yorks.

The club's letterhead. Note Sir Ronald Mathews, Chairman of LNER was the club's president. An A4 streamlined pacific was named after him. Class A4 No 60001.

rather than stand around waiting for the train on which they were relieving, to arrive. The ash would be shovelled down the embankment and the Club would then use a small bulldozer to spread and level it. Certain sections of the site were lifted nearly a yard with foundation ash.

The Club brought about happy days for those that used it. It was really good fun as George put it. On a Sunday, all the young families would go down with their sandwiches and picnic outside the Club. The men would play cricket or football, whilst the young children would have plenty of space for running about or pushing their dolls in the pram. Across the road from the Club were two large gasometers. When full, these were very high. It was possible to hit a six from the Athletic Club wicket and sometimes the ball could soar over the fence onto the road. It took a very good hit however to land the ball on the top of the gasometer. Only two people were known to have done this; that was George White and Frankie Davies.

CHAPTER 18

THE RAILWAY MUTUAL IMPROVEMENT CLASS MOVEMENT (M.I.C.)

BY RON FAREHAM

In the early years of this century, the Railway Companies, possibly with some prodding from the Government via the Board of Trade, decided that a more stringent examination was becoming necessary for locomotive drivers; for some Companies this included a written paper based on a number of questions embracing the Rule Book, the General Appendix and the knowledge of the working of a steam locomotive.

No special training was given, as it would be today, so it was now up to the men themselves to acquire the necessary level of knowledge to satisfy the examining Inspector. The examinations, written, verbal and practical, were conducted by specially appointed Locomotive Inspectors, who were themselves ex footplatemen.

In order to acquire and develop the necessary knowledge, the men decided to form their own voluntary training organisation, to be known as "The Mutual Improvement Class", a typically Victorian description. Lectures were organised, the Railway Companies usually providing a suitable room. The speakers were usually men of experience – Drivers, Inspectors – but the young men also lent a hand.

The secretary of the Mexborough class in my early days was Harry Pursehouse. He was very enterprising and worked hard to provide a varied selection of talks each week during the Autumn and Winter months There were many good lectures among the younger drivers and I well remember two particularly entertaining men – Bernard Mawson who was a vacuum brake expert and George Lee who had mastered all the various types of working single lines. Mexborough was also fortunate in having a man who was a real expert on steam locomotives, one Charlie Hepworth who had actually built two miniature working steam engines himself. This man was a gentle sort of person, infinitely patient, and, of course, was listened to with great respect and concentration. He had originally been a fireman at the Midland and Great Central joint shed at Wakefield. This place was closed after grouping in 1923 and Charlie Hepworth, along with the others, then transferred to Mexborough. On his going to pass as a driver in the early 1930s, he failed the eyesight test and was removed from the footplate grade. This, of course, was a tragedy for such an able man. He was given the position of Oil Controller and later was a Timekeeper, jobs he always did with great distinction. The last time I saw him was at the Blackgates Small Locomotive Society at Wakefield where he used to run his small steam engines. His eyesight failure was a loss to the railway as he would have made an absolutely first class Locomotive Inspector, as he had just the right sort of helpful personality and excellent knowledge. Typically, despite his affliction, he continued to give lectures to the M.I. Class and for a period, wrote the LNER technical notes in the ASLEF monthly journal.

In the early 1940s, Harry Pursehouse was trying to produce a set of lantern slides on Colour Light Signalling, which was a comparatively new concept at the time. What he wanted was a series of photographs and some drawings. Harry got in touch with the Westinghouse Brake and Signal Co. and obtained a good selection of photographs. Westinghouse promised him they would have the slides produced if he could supply the necessary drawings, and they would stand half the cost because of the publicity. As I had done various items of drawing work at the depot, Harry asked me if I could help: I said that I would and he outlined what he wanted. The drawings were sent up to Westinghouse, and eventually a set of 60 slides arrived and, as the cost had worked out cheaper than expected, the Westinghouse Company said that they would be pleased to present them to the class free of charge. Another identical set was produed in 1943 for the use of all the classes in the LNER Southern Area, but of course this set had to be paid for. I have the first set at home and they are now of historical value. One cannot now obtain projectors for 3"x 3" glass slides, so I had a set made in 45mm – the now normal standard. Another such set also resides in the National Railway Museum at York.

As a result of the work with the signalling lantern slides, I became better known among the LNER Mutual Improvement Classes, and in 1946 I attended the MIC Conference at King's Cross with Harry Pursehouse, and this was repeated in 1947, this time with Bernard Mawson. On this occasion, I was elected to the position of Conference Secretary on the retirement of Tom Sands of Hornsey. This organisation was formed in 1906 for the classes of the Great Northern Railway and was extended in 1923 to take in the classes on the ex GC and GE Railways. There were 44 classes affiliated and the conference was held annually. Items arising from the conference were put before the Regional Motive Power Superintendent at Liverpool Street Station offices, following which an interview was granted to the Secretary and a Conference Delegate to discuss the conference items with the M.P.S.

I am not likely to forget one of the annual interviews – it was with the redoubtable L.P.Parker, always regarded as the most effective trainer of Motive Power Managers in the country. It occurred at the time that Regional Boundaries were being chopped and changed. Parker's opening gambit was "Now Fareham, what is the proper title of your organisation?" The conversation developing as follows:-

R.F. "The title sir, is "British Railways Eastern Region Locomotivemen's Mutual Improvement Classes" (Quite a mouthful, but I dutifully spelt It out in full).

L.P.P. "Um, is the class at Ardsley a member?"

R.F. "Yes Sir"

L.P.P. "Is Ardsley in the Eastern Region?"

R.F. "No Sir"

L.P.P. "Is the class at Woodford a member?"

R.F. "Yes Sir"

L.P.P. "Is Woodford in the Eastern Region?"

R.F. "No Sir, not now". (In the recent boundary amendments, Ardsley had gone to the North Eastern region and Woodford to the London Midland.)

L.P.P. "Do you then think your organisation is correctly named?"

R.F. "Well Sir; on your letterheads, your title states "Motive Power Superintendent Eastern Region" and I understand that you still retain control of Woodford and Ardsley, is that not so?"

L.P.P. "Well done, yes, I still administer the two depots concerned even though they are technically in other regions. My area is to be called "The Eastern Motive Power Area" and that should also relate to your organisation."

R.F. "Well sir, I take all the Railway Journals including the Railway Gazette and I have not heard of this before".

L.P.P. "You will do – as it is to be published next week. I am sorry to lead you up the garden path but at least you are now fully informed.!"

Class O4/1 No 63593 on the Cripple Sidings at Mexborough, circa 1961.
The coach behind this engine was one of the three "Loco Instruction Trains". One was in Scotland, another on the LMS. It appeared at Mexborough at roughly 18 month intervals and served as an instruction classroom. This was after the days of the Mutual Improvement Class, when all training had to be done in voluntary time; all training was now done in official time. Courtesy Great Central Railway Society.

The title of the organisation was duly altered, but of course, it did not last long as we lost the out depots the following year and went back to the "Eastern Region" title.

The above conversation taught me an abiding lesson – don't see L.P. Parker unless you know all the facts – this is of course, exactly what L.P. had intended. However, he chose a subject, the answer to which he was certain I couldn't possibly know. He was a remarkable teacher and a formidable man.

I did the job of M.I.C. Conference Secretary for 14 years (1947-1961) and I must say that that experience broadened my outlook considerably.

In 1951, the then Railway executive organised a national M.I.C. competition, and a special committee was set up to formulate the framework and I served on this body for 9 years. The competition itself ran for a total of 11 years. The team from Mexborough were the National winners in 1958 and again in 1962. The national competition didn't run again after 1962 so the competition shield was kept at Mexborough (and later, Wath, after Mexborough closed). With the ending of the National competition, the Eastern region Authorities decided to run their own version, and this has run continuously ever since, and long may it continue.

In 1958, the winning prize was a week's trip to Western Germany, based on Cologne. Germany at this time, was busy rebuilding after the war, and the scars were everywhere to be seen, especially around Cologne. This was the first trip abroad for all concerned, and the experience was unforgettable.

Ron Fareham (on the left) with a BR Official holding the nameplate prior to naming a BR Type 56 loco No 56101 at York station "Mutual Improvement", in recognition of it's contribution to footplate excellence. Courtesy Mrs M Fareham

A model presented to Ron Fareham to commemorate the occasion of the naming ceremony on 26th April 1990. Courtesy Mrs M Fareham.

The week had been well planned by the BR Agent's office in Cologne, and there were a few unplanned episodes as well. For instance, on our way in, we stopped at the border station of Aachen and it was known that a German engine would be coming on to haul the train forward. The engine actually backed onto our train, propelling two sleeping cars, so a colleague, Raymond law and myself had to move further along to see the engine at close quarters. As we stood looking up into the cab, the driver motioned for us to go up onto the footplate – of course we didn't need a second invitation and up we went.

There were language difficulties, and I indicated that Ray and I were also footplatemen. The driver indicated his understanding and hands were shaken all round. Ray and I were trying to sort out all the equipment when the driver popped the whistle, opened the regulator and away we went – first stop Cologne 70 miles away. This was an unexpected, but delightful event for the two of us. The engine, a German Class 01, two cylinder Pacific, was in very good form; firing was fairly easy with the wide firebox and each of us had a go. One thing puzzled us both – the water in the boiler gauge glass was maintained at a constant three quarters of a glass, and yet no injector seemed to be used. Eventually, it was decided that there must be a pump in use somewhere, though there was no evidence of one. This turned out to be true as we later found out. The injector was used however, when the driver shut the regulator and braked for a speed restiction. This was to prevent the safety valves from blowing.

The riding quality of the engine was excellent, and there was no knocking from the big ends. This was something of a revelation to the two of us, used as we were to banging about on old Austerities at Mexborough. The secret of this silent running was the presence of adjusting cotters on the large and small ends of the connecting rod – and also on the side rod crank pins – something new to us.

When we reached Cologne, we shook hands with the crew and went down the platform to rejoin the party, one of whom, when sighting us, shouted "Hey they're here"; they thought that we had been left behind at Aachen as we did not tell them where we were going. The BR Agent at Cologne expressed surprise at the jaunt on the footplate. He said he had been in Germany seven years and had yet to obtain a footplate pass. The rest of the week was spent visiting railway installations at such places as Frankfurt, Wuppertal, Cologne, and rack railway at Konigswinter; a most edifying week, if rather tiring.

BACK TO MIKE BREARLEY

Nearly all of the Mexborough engine drivers I spoke to would make a mention of the Mutual Improvement Class. Attendance was voluntary, the annual subscription was 1/- and one would be encouraged by the older drivers to attend. It was, of course, something you knew you should do if you wanted to be a passed driver but as one driver put it, "in the war years long hours were worked and in trying to enjoy yourself, you didn't really want to spoil life and attend". With low wage levels, there was always a tendency for the young men to put overtime before attendance. Nevertheless, Mexborough did have over 300 members whereas Kings Cross, which was a main line depot only had 30 or so. One reason for this would be that when one had passed for driver, they would not see a need to continue attendance but at Mexborough, they were good classes, and they tended to carry on; the really keen ones, like Ron Fareham and Cedric Lockwood would become

MIC evening, 1964, New Mason's Arms, Mexborough. Left to Right – Cedric Lockwood, Ron Fareham, Len Hall, Ron Mansell. Len like Ron was an Inspector after progressing from driver at Mexborough. Courtesy Cedric Lockwood.

instructors. I gather that after one had done 8 lectures in the class, they received a badge (this was designed by Ron Fareham and depicted a book, a signal and a loco – the three things you had to have knowledge of.)

Quizzes were held, locally, regionally and nationally and Mexborough MIC had quite a reputation; it was one of the most successful in the country. As the Stratford Quiz team captain Bert Pell once put it to Cedric "we'll have to shoot them "buggers" in Mexborough before we win awt". Interestingly, I happened to be in the York National Rail Museum browsing through some Eastern editions of the British Railways Magazines. These are internal publications for staff, containing just about everything and anything concerning staff and news. I came across two mentions of the Mexborough MIC Quiz team. They read as follows:-

Volume 6 No1 January 1955. It was headed, MIC Competition at Doncaster.

On November 10th, the first round of a "quiz" contest took place in the Ambulance Room at Doncaster Central Station, between teams representing Mexborough and Retford Mutual Improvement Classes before an appreciative audience of railway staff from the Doncaster Motive Power District.The competing teams were: (Mexborough) W Parkin, Captain; R Fareham, F Law, R Mansell, R Hepworth and R Law. (Retford) H Herrick, Captain; E Self, H Millicon, E Crute, K Downes and E Tyson.

The Questionmaster was Mr A.R. Ewer, District Motive Power Superintendent, Doncaster. Adjudicators were District Inspectors E.W.Betts, Motive Power Department Sheffield and H.A.F.Tether, Motive Power Department Ardsley. District Inspector G Tasker acted as timekeeper. The contest was won by the Mexborough team with 37½ points against 31½ points awarded to the Retford team

Volume 6 No 3 March 1955. It was headed Motive Power MIC Competition.

The final tie to decide the winners of the Eastern Region Quiz Competition and also the team to go forward to the Inter Regional Finals, was held at Liverpool Street gymnasium on February 9th when the chair was taken by Mr J.S.Jones, Assistant Motive Power Superintendent Eastern Region.

Adjudicators for the event were; Mr C.N.Morris, District Motive Power Superintendent Kings Cross and Mr R.L. Verther, District Motive Power Superintendent Norwich, the Questionmaster being Mr T.C.B.Miller, District Motive Power Superintendent, Stratford and the Umpire, Mr J.F.Jenkins, Chief Inspector MPSO.

A most lively and interesting contest concluded with Mexborough team being the winners, gaining 57 points against 49 to March and 46 to New England. In a short commentary made by the Chairman Mr J.S.Jones, he congratulated the teams but also paid a tribute to members of many other teams in the Eastern Region who had taken part in the competition but had not proved successful on this occasion.

Onto the diesel days, and I make a short reference to Ken Wyatt, who was a Secondman at Tinsley Depot in 1975. He used to attend the Mutual Improvement Classes held there. British Rail would provide a room free of charge but the structure was still the same as in the steam days, in that the tutors were all volunteers and attendance was undertaken in one's own time. One to one coaching was available to Secondmen who were preparing for their driving exams. The rule book was always the Bible and Koran for the aspiring drivers, guards, signalmen and others, in supervisory grades. Most would become familiar with the structure of the rule book; it was never a problem to equate with it. As Ken said, "The book gave discipline; if you knew the content of it, understood it, and stuck to it, you would not go far wrong". There was one MIC class on the 3rd July 1975 which he will never forget, having set out to attend but never arriving there. Whilst waiting on the platform for his train at Mexborough; he was caught up in an incident, which is documented in this letter he received from British Railways Eastern Region. His good deeds made it too late to attend.

 British Railways Eastern Region

P.O. Box No. 159
Sheaf House
Leadmill Road, Sheffield 1 S1. 2BQ.
Sheffield 20002 (STD 0742)
Telex 54443 **Ext. 2261.**   G. MYERS Divisional Manager

Mr. K.J. Wyatt,
Secondman,
TINSLEY.

y/r
o/r OA17/184/15.   29th July, 1975.

Dear Mr. Wyatt,

INCIDENT AT MEXBOROUGH 3.7.75.

I understand that whilst at Mexborough at about 18.00 hours on the above date, you heard a woman screaming near to the river opposite the Railway Station and that you ran across and found the woman in the water. She said that her boyfriend had disappeared beneath the surface and I believe you intended to go into the river, but was persuaded not to do so by the woman.

As you know the police were called and the Chief Constable, South Yorkshire Police, has expressed his gratitude and appreciation of the excellent co-operation and assistance his staff received from you and from Leading Railwoman Mrs. A. Salmons at Mexborough Station. It was most unfortunate that the young man's life could not be saved, but this in no way detracts from your efforts.

I am very pleased to add my own appreciation to that of the Chief Constable.

Yours sincerely,

G. Myers

BR 14300/1

CHAPTER 19

DIESELISATION AND THEN CLOSURE

Prior to the advent of diesels and well before the twilight of steam, there came about the Manchester – Sheffield – Wath electrification scheme for which the LNER had given approval in September 1947. It was implemented in three stages, the first being the Wath to Dunford section where huge amounts of coal were hauled up a steeply graded section of line (the Worsboro Bank) and this was completed in February 1952. The other sections were from Manchester London Road to Woodhead and Woodhead to Sheffield Victoria. In total 65 electric locomotives were built by Metropolitan Vickers, 7 Co-Cos for passenger work and 58 for freight, and these were serviced at three depots, Reddish, Darnall and Wath. Reddish was the main depot for heavy repairs, Darnall only remained open for a short time before becoming a DMU Depot and Wath did light repairs. The site chosen at Wath was slightly north of Wath Yard towards Moor Road When the electric depot opened in 1952, 24 drivers from Mexborough volunteered to train on electric traction and after training, they were transferred permanently to Wath. A further 24 drivers were then trained and were put in a "Dual Link" at Mexborough so that they could be used as temporary replacements for any vacancies which arose at Wath and ultimately they would fill any permanent vacancies. In addition, 48 firemen were electric

Driver Alf Hughes and Inspector George Potts on an Electric Bo-Bo outside Wath depot.
Courtesy Alf Hughes

A cab view of Alf Hughes and Inspector George Potts on the same Electric Bo-Bo 76012. Courtesy Alf Hughes.

trained and they rotated on a six monthly basis between the dual link and Wath, spending six months on each.

Diesel traction arrived at Mexborough in the early sixties. The intention was to dieselise the whole of the Sheffield division commencing October 3rd 1960. Six men were selected to be the first of the Sheffield team of Diesel Instructors and they attended a school in Ilford for a period of four weeks. Training was to be on what was at that time the basic locomotive for the Eastern Region, the 1365hp Brush Type 2, the later class 31. There was one representative from Mexborough on this first training team, Ron Fareham. Grimesthorpe was the first depot to convert . Each driver and fireman had to undergo a 3 week conversion course, whereby they had to learn how diesel engines worked, and how to cope with faults and failures. Dennis Porter recalls there were 6 at a time in the classroom. The tutor was a London cockney; some thought a 'bit clever'. Dennis sat on the front row in his conversion class and the tutor enquired of him if he was a Driver; because he looked a bit too young compared to his classmates; all who were over 50. For the older driver in the twilight of his career, it was not an easy task to assimilate the training to adapt from steam to diesel and a good deal of repetition was necessary to get things understood and retained. Most would have preferred to stay with steam but there was no denying that diesels were a different ball game; so clean to work on and so much less physically demanding. In this class of 6, there was only one pass, two failed altogether and 3 had to be retrained on another course. Mexborough being a steam depot, was unsuitable for diesel locomotives and apart from a very brief period when the first Brush 2s arrived and they were kept at Mexborough, all the diesels went to Wath. It was a very big learning curve and Dennis recalls the Brush 2s standing over the Christmas period. There had been a particularly cold snap, and not one of the engines would start up after the holidays. What had happened was that it had been so frosty, the engine coolant had frozen up. From finding that out, whenever there was a cold snap, management decided they would have one or two men on frosting duties which involved starting engines up every hour or starting up and leaving them to idle all night if it was very frosty.

His very first Diesel booking came about one Sunday evening when he recalled Shedmaster Jones looking on the list and telling Dennis that he was

Class O4/3 2-8-0 No 63659 at Mexborough Shed on 9th November 1963 standing between a WD Austerity and another class O4/3. Note the 350 HP diesel shunter; which had taken over on shed pilot duties. By this time, many of the steam locomotives were disappearing and being withdrawn for scrap. Courtesy Great Central Railway Society.

O4 2-8-0 departing rather noisily from Mexborough shed in 1963. The picture is unique in showing the first Brush Type 4 to enter the shed. A new era was certainly dawning and it is astonishing to contemplate now how swift the diesel take-over was - in two years steam would have gone completely". Printed in British Railways Illustrated Vol. 10 No 4 January 2001.

BR Standard Class 9F 2-10-0 N0 92113 introduced in 1954, locally named "spaceships" is coupled to an 0-6-0 class J15 introduced in 1893. The whereabouts and date of this photograph are unknown.

booked on a freight train from Scotland destined for the South. The train was already waiting at Mexborough No 3 for its relief crew, the engine was not a steamer however, but a brand new Brush Class 31 diesel. The shedmaster directing him towards the train, said "here y'are Dennis, look after it and bring it back; nobody knows owt abart em darn there". He came back light engine from Banbury.

Diesels were obviously much easier to drive than steam, but they were prone to minor technical breakdowns and they could make you look an awful fool. Again Dennis recalls he was once returning to Mexborough light engine when he was stopped at Rotherham Masborough station. The signalman told him there was an express passenger at Aldwarke heading for Sheffield; broken down and the driver unable to locate the problem. The signalman asked Dennis that if he dropped him down on the line adjacent to the passenger train; would he have a look at it? He agreed and the signalman routed him so. The passenger driver was an old experienced hand (on steam); he was sweating profusely and irritated at not being able to release the brakes. There was a fault on the system, but through the training, they had learnt that it could be temporarily rectified with an emergency key; which Dennis showed him how to operate. Dennis' advice was that the loco should make it to Sheffield, but there, he should declare it a failure.

So this is how it was in those very early days of diesel. Simple little problems which could knock a large engine out whereas with steam, more often than not, a good driver could always limp home. There were three warning lights in the cab; red, yellow and blue which were the starting points for locating faults. If all the lights were dimmed; the engine was running normally. If any of them brightened; there was a problem. Red meant the engine had stopped; amber was for auxiliaries and blue was an engine fault. Only one engine ever failed Dennis, and this was outside the GEC at Swinton. The air supply was lost and so the brakes could not be taken off. The engine had to be hooked off and taken to Wath. Had he known it was simply a fuse on the compressor which needed changing, it could have been quickly rectified by the driver, but the footplate handbooks were so big and complicated, that a driver was often overwhelmed before he had started to identify the problem. An extraction from the Brush Book: on Wheelslip is an example of this. –

"Bearing in mind that the higher the generator current the more likelihood there is of wheelslip, good driving constitutes applying power at the correct rate to give a high value of current and pulling power without wheelslip. It is possible to apply very heavy tractive efforts without wheelslip if power is applied smoothly and not erratically or jerkily. If wheelslip occurs, the amber warning light will become bright. Reduce power until the light becomes dim and then notch up again more slowly. If slipping persists due to bad rail conditions; reduce power; apply sand when the amber light is dimmed and reapply power again slowly".

On steam locomotives, all drivers were issued with a Bardic Lamp; they were used a lot to check water gauge levels. Not all footplates had electric lighting and there were some longish tunnels in the area; not least Woodhead and Dore and Totley tunnels; both over 3 miles long. They were a general purpose lamp; they could be turned to red and used as a train light in an emergency or to green, but at the demise of steam; they were not recovered by BR and many drivers realised their handiness and wouldn't dare to go to work on diesels without them for they were

operating manual

British Railways locomotives D 1500 - D 1519

BRUSH SULZER

This was the 1ˢᵗ edition Driver's handbook for the Brush Class 47 locomotive. It had 89 pages covering a General Description, Diesel Engine, Electrical equipment, Air System, Driving Compartment, Steam heating boiler, Fire fighting equipment and Fault finding. Courtesy D Porter always having to probe about in the engine compartment and electrical cupboards which were too dark.

On satisfactory completion of a Diesel Conversion course, the Mexborough men were gradually moved over to Wath depot. There they went onto diesels but they also had to learn the electrics as there was an Electric Link there. The last locomotive to leave Mexborough was a WD Austerity 90265 on 1st May 1964.

Although the engines had gone, there was still one link left, comprising of 12 sets of men to mop up the steam operation at Mexborough. They relieved engine crews from distant places, as it had always been. They could of course, be relieving on steam or diesel because the transition from steam to diesel was not simultaneous at every depot. Vic recalls his last steam trip in August 1965. He'd signed on duty at midday, his fireman was John Myford and they were to relieve the crew of a freight train coming down from York. It happened to be one of the new Standard Class 9F 2-10-0 locos; locally known as "spaceships". The trip was fairly uneventful; they hooked off at Annesley near Nottingham and their orders were to leave the engine at Annesley as Mexborough MPD had closed. Disposing of the engine however, became a problem. Annesley were due to close the following week and they didn't want it either. It seemed on frantic ringing around that nobody did.

THE LAST LOCOMOTIVE TO LEAVE MEXBOROUGH DEPÔT
MAY 1ST 1964
LOCO CREW

| D.SMITH | R.SIDEBOTTOM | | | | | | | | W.SMITH | D.TRASH |
| (Labourer) | (Telephone Attendant) | | | | | | | | (Fireman) | (Fireman) |

| D.TONGE | G.HOBSON | R.F.HAGUE | G.FISHER | G.LINLEY | A.SKIRROW | M.COOPER | J.TINGLE | G.SPENCER | ? | E.FOSTER | W.SKINNS |
| (Fireman) | (Driver) | (Driver) | (Fireman) | (Fireman) | (Driver) | (Frm Cleaner) | (Firedropper) | (Driver) | (?) | (Toolman) | (Shunter) |

My Grandad Vic and my Mum in 1972 in the Flying Scotsman.

A rare sight indeed at Wath depot. The locomotive was in South Yorkshire on a 3 day visit and Wath was it's servicing point. Courtesy V Parkes.

Finally, Vic was told to take it to Staveley and return home on the bus. This he did, and I presume that this would have been the very last home for that engine after just 11 years of working life. Had it not been for the diesels, these Standard 9Fs would have had a long and successful life; they were certainly winners with their large haulage capacity.

Vic Parkes was in this relieving link. He also recalls a time in 1972 when the Flying Scotsman, then in preservation and owned by Alan Peglar was visiting South Yorkshire for 3 days. Wath depot was chosen as the stabling point because it had a good watering column and access to quality coal supplies. From Wath, the engine was to travel light to Sheffield, where it would hook onto a rake of coaches in the carriage sidings and run them into Sheffield Victoria station. It was exhibitional and the engine stood in the station all day, and then made the return trip to Wath in the evening. Vic drove the engine from Wath to Sheffield, and although he did feel priviledged, it was down to chance that he had the opportunity; it was just that his name was on the duty roster at the time the Flying Scotsman job was required. His fireman was Pete Good and the travelling inspector, Len Hall. Vic recalls when cleaning Flying Scotsman at Doncaster, as with all the Pacifics, their tenders would be brimming with coal; whereas at Wath, he recalls there not being more than a few barrowfuls of coal in the tender. Of course, by then the locomotive was in private ownership.

Another very different turn came up for Dennis Porter in the 70s when he was offered a more special duty; that was to take the pope's train from

Manchester to York; he was visiting York racecourse. This became possible because he had been in the Gorton link for about 4 years which thus completed his route knowledge for Manchester. He was already passed for York whereas the Manchester men only had route knowledge to Sheffield. Security precautions however, determined that the train would take a meandering route round the "back alleys" of Castleford and to prepare for this, Dennis was given a week off to refresh the route. He would ride on trains or on footplates. Finally, the day arrived and Dennis climbed onto the loco at Manchester. It was a Peak Class 45 No 45064. The journey went according to plan but strangely enough, Dennis never caught a glimpse of the pope.

Whether it be steam, diesel or electric, every fireman or driver can recall an unpleasant experience or incident and I have inserted a few of these in previous chapters. I will include here a couple more incidents recalled by Alf Hughes, this time on diesel and electric locomotives. The first was in the early days at Wath at the time of the changeover. Alf was driving an English Electric Diesel Type 3 and pulling two 'dead' diesel locomotives to Wath Depot. Thereafter he was to go onto Barnsley to collect a wagon from the newspaper train which was running from Manchester to Sheffield to Cleethorpes. It was really a black night; he was travelling through Wath station at approximately 0130 and all he could see was the home green light on Elsecar Junction some way in the distance. Suddenly, there was a loud bang followed by the sound of the engine's jumper cables rattling about on the track. He immediately thought the engine had come off the rails but soon found out that he'd hit an empty 20 ton hopper wagon. How had that got there? The theory was that the wagon had been mischievously released from Cortonwood Colliery (the wagon had a Cortonwood empty wagon label on it), whereupon it rolled through Tingle Bridge, smashed through two sets of crossing gates and onto Elsecar Junction. The wagon should have been derailed there by a "jack catch" left open for this purpose. It wasn't. Again the theory was that the "jack catch" was located just before a concrete roadway section and whilst the wagon's front wheels were derailed; it ran along the concrete road and managed to jump back onto the rails again before the back wheels could be derailed. The signal box at Elsecar Junction was closed from Saturday noon until Monday morning and thus there wasn't a signalman to take avoiding action. The diesel engine wasn't travelling fast but in hitting a 20 ton deadweight, for the wagon had come to a rest; it was too heavy a load for the buffers and the engine's nose buckled. There was £50,000 of damage. Alf escaped serious injury due mainly to the fact he was on a Type 3, which had a nose. Had it been a Sulzer or Brush locomotive which have flat noses; he could have been very badly injured. Alf promptly arranged for the train to be protected by the guard and then he set off to walk into the Wath Depot where he told the foreman Ron Mansell that he needed another loco because he'd hit a wagon. He was badly shaken and bruised and he would have been justified in taking time off work, but he thought he might lose his nerve and thus decided to take another locomotive and get straight back onto the job. On he went to Barnsley to meet the newspaper train. The damaged loco was recovered and brought into the depot using one of the diesels it was towing, and thereafter, it was sent to Tinsley for repair.

The second one was a braking incident on a Bo-Bo electric. Alf was driver, having been newly trained; he had hooked onto a laden coal train at Wath and he was heading for Mottram. By the time he'd got to Woodhead, he had three inspectors and three trainee drivers in the cab who were being taught how to brake these trains. (Midway through Woodhead tunnel is the start of a severe down gradient into Lancashire). There were two electric Bo-Bos coupled together and with the jumper cable, both could be controlled by the leading loco. Going through the tunnel, the locos were "regen braking". (In layman's terms; this is like cruise control on a car. It is only used when going downhill. The motorman would set a lever at say 30mph and irrespective of the steepness of the decline or the weight of the train pushing the engine, the loco speed would be a constant 30 mph enabled by the control of the current taken from the wires by the engine. It was an engine brake rather than a mechanical brake. In "regen", the loco would also return electricity generated by the engine back to the wires to be used by locos travelling uphill in the other direction). However on emerging from the tunnel the instructor told Alf that the rear loco was not "regenning". By now the train was picking up speed quickly. There was another braking system at his disposal whereby he could put both locos into "rheostat" that is to cut the supply to the electric motors. Things didn't improve. It was heavy rain and Alf had learnt that this was a trial train, put together specifically for this test. The train load was 1650 tons, slack coupled, meaning that the only brakes were on the locos, each of which weighed about 65 tons or 130 tons in total. Still the train gathered speed, it didn't help when both locos started to "pick their wheels up" (skidding on the wet rails). They had not enough brake when "regenning" because one loco was faulty, they had enough brake with rheostat provided the locos didn't "pick up their wheels". They got into Mottram without mishap but the locos did slide for a good way; they made it a very hair raising experience which Alf would not want to repeat. Losing control, he said, can turn you "barmy".

On the 8th May 1961, Ron Fareham moved on from Mexborough; all the Diesel Conversion training had been completed and he took up a post as Running Foreman in March, Cambridgeshire. This was a much bigger depot than Mexborough. By December 1962, Ron had accepted a similar position at his old shed, Mexborough. He made notes about his return and they are relevant to be inserted here:-

"After 18 months at March, which was a very rewarding experience, I returned as a Running Foreman to my original home station at Mexborough.

A weekend shot of Wath depot, probably in the late sixties. A bank of 15 (or maybe more) electric Bo-Bos are stabled in the sidings, ready for Monday morning work.

In the two years since I left, this place had become only a ghost of its former self; most of the work – and men – had transferred to the new Mixed Traction Depot (Diesel & Electric) stationed at the former small electric shed at Wath, at the side of the Wath marshalling yard. Mexborough had lost most of its work, but it had gone three miles down the line to Wath.

The rump of the men left at the Mexborough Depot were mainly for relieving purposes – at that time, it was a major relieving point. There was also a steam allocation of some 36 engines, mainly Austerity 2-8-0s for working trains to Frodingham, York, Hull and Toton (L.M.). These latter depots were, at that time, still "steam" areas. In the new position, I had to work at either Mexborough or Wath as required and, of course, the Wath situation was new to me. Wath Depot dealt with diesel and electric traction but there were only two roads wired for the electrics, as against four roads originally. This arrangement, which was rank bad designing, led to all sorts of shunting problems, as there was nowhere to put an electric loco when the wired inlet road was full, in the evening, with diesel locos, from all the colliery pilots, awaiting fuel. The arrangement was very cramped, with much unnecessary movement being made. Of course, as at March, during this transitory period, it was an adapted situation, but it could have worked fairly easily if the two roads had not been de-wired.

245

In the middle of Wath Yard, there was also a diesel servicing shed for locomotives turning round in the yard area. This was a new building, but it also had faults. The fuel pumps were inside the shed, but were so near to the buffer stops that only one loco could obtain fuel; if two locos in "multiple" came into the shed; and there were many instances of this, then they had to be uncoupled. If only someone had had the foresight to have included an experienced running foreman on the shed layout committee to advise the designers, he could have saved his salary many times over by avoiding shed delays".

As steam was coming to an end, there were those firemen; many starting out as Cleaners in the early to mid fifties, who never passed to be a steam driver. They were transferred to Wath . Initially, all the diesels were double manned and so as a fireman, there were very few duties to do other than sit in the right hand seat known in jargon as the "union chair". Eventually, firemen would also be trained on the electrics (drivers were known as "motormen", firemen were "second man"); their main task being to keep the pantographs pumped up; of which each loco had two. Double manning did not last very long and career progression became very slow.

Richard Case was one so affected. With the passing of steam, his progression was to Driver and not to Passed Fireman. This wasn't offered to him however, as many depots had qualified Passed Firemen; albeit with

The inside of the shed was airy and well lit; it was kept very clean and the side of the pits were white with good artificial lighting. Six electric locomotives were provided initially; one for each of the instructors, all in pristine condition in 1951 as the photograph shows. The locomotives were out on the line for very long periods; only coming into the depot for sand, brakes or relief. Ron Fareham

This group were in the course of training. Here they are in Bridlington circa 1985/6, having come from Doncaster. At the controls was Doug Barrett. On the platform from left to right: Frank Grice, Ken Sharpe and Richard Case. Courtesy R Case

much less railway experience than Richard, but these were selected in seniority for driving vacancies. His breakthrough didn't come until 1974 and that was when an application for a driving vacancy at Tinsley was accepted; - at last 18 years of past experience, had been recognised. There he was trained on a whole range of diesels locomotives; the English electric Type 3s & 4s, Class 45 &46 (Peaks), Class 20 (single cab Bo-Bo) and shunters. His duties were mainly on freight diagrams but he also did the odd passenger from Sheffield Midland to York, Derby, Lincoln or Manchester.

Wath Motive Power Depot finally closed in 1983. This was still Richard's home depot to which he could have returned as a driver, at any time, but now as "officially" a redundant driver he could be relocated almost anywhere on the railway system for redundant men took preference over anybody else. He could have stayed at Tinsley but through the closure of Wath, he chose to go to Doncaster where he wanted to broaden his horizon; he had an ambition for the East Coast Main Line. Other men also opted to move from Wath to Doncaster. It wouldn't of course go down very well with the Doncaster men; they saw it as hindering their promotion prospects. It is going beyond the scope of this book, but I would like to foretell the remainder of Richard's career as an example that the closure of Mexborough with the passing of steam, opened up "new doors" and gave fruitful careers to those who stayed on the railways. A lot of the Doncaster men didn't have as much traction knowledge as Richard, by that I mean, they were not trained on as big a variety of locomotives. They were trained on the Deltics of course and Richard wasn't. He was then trained on the DMU, on local passenger work and finally he became a Top Link Driver going further afield to Lincoln, March, Peterborough and London. By 1985, the Deltics had been withdrawn, and Richard was then trained with the Deltic drivers on the HSTs. He initially worked the Doncaster to Kings Cross route, and this was later extended to Newcastle. In those days, all main line trains exceeding 100mph had to be double manned. When Doncaster MPD was broken up under the restructure; Richard became an Intercity Driver with ECML: this company having a very short reign before being succeeded by GNER.

The last class of locomotive he drove was the Class 91 electrics on intercity duties. In comparison to the HSTs, these were much lighter in weight and were very prone at high speed, to skidding when the brakes were applied. Richard would recall that it was not a very nice sensation for the driver, who could feel the wheels gliding; could see the speedometer drop back to zero and could see that sanding and keeping the brakes full on was having no effect. For a few seconds, a driver would be at the mercy of the rail condition, just sitting there with "everything crossed" and hoping for the welfare of his passengers. Had the brakes been taken off, a computer in the cab would have recorded this and linked this activity to the driver on duty.

Richard completed his last shift on the 9th December 03; finally retiring on 22nd February 04 after just 4 months short of 50 years service.

CHAPTER 20

THE WATH MANVERS RAIL DISASTER OF 1948

There is no relevance of this chapter being in this book other than it happened in the place of Mexborough. I wrote the story of this accident in 2000 because it happened in my trainspotting days; it was a very serious accident killing eight people yet an account of it seemed to be left out of so many books written on the subject of railway accidents. The only book I do remember giving an account of it was "Danger on the Line" by Stanley Hall. I hoped that my little book about this accident would share all that I had learned over the years with local people, and with young people, because Wragby Row, at the top of Highwoods Terrace is now totally transformed to what it was like 60 years ago, and also with people of my age and older, because it will help to prompt their memories of this terrible tragic day. My only reason for making mention of it again is that through writing the book, another story ensued which I will unfold in this chapter, but before I do, I will pen another paragraph summarising what did happen, for those who have perhaps forgotten.

It was Whit Tuesday, May 18th 1948 and the 11-45am express from London St Pancras to Bradford Forster Square was loaded up to 12 coaches. It was double headed with 2 engines ex L.M.R. Jubilee Class, numbers 5606 Cyprus

Ex LMS Jubilee Class locomotive No 45609 "Gilbert & Ellice Islands" taken in the early days of British Railways. This was the engine which overturned at Manvers.
National Rail Museum, York

and 5609 Gilbert & Ellice Islands. It was a busy end to the holiday period; the weather had been dry and warm and Whit Tuesday had been no exception; it was a fine hot spring day with temperatures approaching the eighties. Because so many people were travelling, British Railways decided to run an additional relief train 15 minutes ahead of the parent express.

The parent express arrived in Sheffield at 3-30pm and left at 3-35pm being 6 minutes late of its booked time. There were only now 194 passengers on the train since the bulk of the travellers had left 10 minutes earlier in the relief train. The distance to Wath Road Junction was 11 miles and this was covered in 16 minutes. As they were traversing the Junction at about 60 mph; the driver of the leading engine noticed the rails ahead were badly distorted. He immediately applied the brake but it was too late. The engine bucked into the air, derailed and came to a stop 30 yards away. The train engine ploughed through the soft ballast and overturned onto its side at the top of the embankment. The rapid deceleration undoubtedly led to the scene of chaos behind. The leading coach overturned and the next four coaches were thrown violently down the embankment towards the coke ovens, and were wrecked. The sixth coach mounted the wreckage and was held vertically in mid air by the restaurant coach which was lying at an angle with its leading end partly down the bank. The last four coaches stayed on the rails and were practically undamaged. Six passengers were killed in the accident; 55 people were admitted to the Montagu hospital. 34 were detained and two; a passenger and the train engine driver, died after admission. The official enquiry concluded that the cause of the accident was due to distortion of the rail resulting from the hot weather; whereby expansion in the rails had made the joints very tight. The relief express which had previously passed through, set up vibrations which the track ballast was unable to hold and the resultant forces thus caused the line to kink. Of course in

Wilson Belden in the foreground with his sleeves rolled up. He had been delivering minerals to the nearby Manvers Arms (now The Staithes) when the crash occurred. The 6th coach has mounted the restaurant car and has come to rest at a crazy uphill angle. Sheffield Telegraph & Star

1948, the railway infrastructure was still in a poor condition generally as it had suffered years of neglect in the 2nd World War. A memorial stone erected by R.M.B.C. was unveiled on the 18th May 1997 on the actual site where the accident happened. The driver of the train engine which overturned was Bertie Edwin Wilsher; age 53 of Middle Bank Terrace, Cricklewood. His depot was Kentish Town. Dr Lynch gave his cause of death as bronchial pneumonia following 2nd and 3rd degree burns to the face, upper and lower limbs, chest and abdomen.

NOW FOR THE UNTOLD STORY.

Some 3 years had passed since the book was published and then one day I received a letter from a Mr Alan Wilsher. He told me that it was his father who had been the fatally injured engine driver. A friend of his had seen the book and bought it for Alan. He said he read it "fifty times" over, he couldn't believe that someone had written about his father. He wanted to contact me but his immediate problem was how could he find out my address. One name mentioned in my book, was Ray Lambert, and I'd included his "address" – Tasmania; he was the train register lad in Wath Road Junction Signalbox when the accident occurred and had, since retiring, emigrated there. He sought the numbers from International Directories of all the Lamberts in Tasmania. On his second phone call he had contacted the right Lambert and Ray gave him my address. After I'd received his letter and rung him, he readily accepted my invitation to South Yorkshire and with his son Graham, we visited the memorial stone, the Montague Hospital where

Ray Lambert was a train register lad and was in the Wath Road signal box when he saw the accident occur. He emigrated to Tasmania but came back to see the memorial which RMBC erected, after facilitation by Ken Wyatt.

THE DAY I SHALL NEVER FORGET

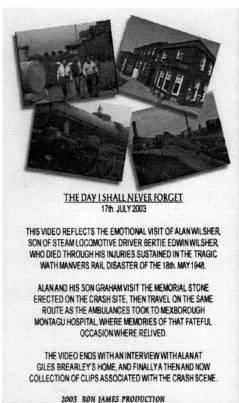

THE DAY I SHALL NEVER FORGET
17th JULY 2003

THIS VIDEO REFLECTS THE EMOTIONAL VISIT OF ALAN WILSHER, SON OF STEAM LOCOMOTIVE DRIVER BERTIE EDWIN WILSHER, WHO DIED THROUGH HIS INJURIES SUSTAINED IN THE TRAGIC WATH MANVERS RAIL DISASTER OF THE 18th. MAY 1948.

ALAN AND HIS SON GRAHAM VISIT THE MEMORIAL STONE ERECTED ON THE CRASH SITE, THEN TRAVEL ON THE SAME ROUTE AS THE AMBULANCES TOOK TO MEXBOROUGH MONTAGU HOSPITAL, WHERE MEMORIES OF THAT FATEFUL OCCASION WHERE RELIVED.

THE VIDEO ENDS WITH AN INTERVIEW WITH ALAN AT GILES BREARLEY'S HOME, AND FINALLY A THEN AND NOW COLLECTION OF CLIPS ASSOCIATED WITH THE CRASH SCENE.

2003 RON JAMES PRODUCTION

Left: This video was prepared by Giles Brearley, Ken Wyatt and Ron James and presented to Alan Wilsher. The photograph is Alan's father, the engine driver who died from his injuries.
Right: The back of the video cover detailing it's contents.

memories of that fateful occasion were relived and I was able to interview Alan in my brother's library to learn more about how this tragic accident had impacted upon his and his family's life.

Strangely, he thought dad had a premonition of the accident. Mum, Dad, Alan (Age 22 and just demobbed from the RAF) and his younger brother David (Age 6) were sitting at the breakfast table. Dad expressed dismay at the type of dream he'd had; not that he did dream much; but there was blood everywhere he said; and was going into some detail when there was a knock at the door. Mum answered it, but when she returned to the table, the conversation had changed.

Their house was less than 500 yards from the railway on which dad travelled; and in those days; trains nearly always ran to time, so it had been commonplace to go down to the track side precisely when they knew dad's train would be passing to give him a waive. On this day, it was David, the youngest son who went to waive. Dad would not normally have returned home that night; he would have lodged in Leeds and brought the return Carlisle or Manchester train back to London the following day. At teatime, Alan was sitting with his brother at the table, Mum was out, and on the 6 '0' clock news on the radio, they heard that the London to Bradford express had crashed in Yorkshire. Alan got straight onto his bike and cycled to the Kentish Town depot where he managed to find the Superintendent on duty and asked for more information. The Superintendent knew nothing about it. He immediately telephoned Leeds; who confirmed the accident and said that Dad had gone to hospital but was not badly injured. Alan left his bike at the depot and hurried across to Kings Cross station after having been told how to get to Wath. He had to travel to Doncaster but he didn't have enough money for the fare and so the police at Kings Cross gave him the money. Meanwhile the police had been informed of the accident and of the engine driver's critical condition and they went round to inform Mrs Wilsher. She made immediate arrangements with neighbours and left for Kings Cross station along with Gordon; Alan's second brother, in the police car. Of course in those days mum would have no transport and she would hardly have enough money to buy two rail tickets to Doncaster. The police loaned her the rail fare. Alan was sitting on the train at Kings Cross when he heard the station tannoy enquiring if there was an Alan Wilsher on the train. At this point, Mum and two of her three sons were united for the journey to Doncaster. They arrived just before midnight; Alan remembers it being quite foggy (after such a hot day) and they took a taxi to Mexborough Montagu hospital, that fare he recalls was 9s-6d. The little hospital seemed so overburdened; it was like a battlefield but a doctor called them to one side and explained the problem in the nicest possible way. Alan wasn't totally prepared for what he saw. Dad was bound from head to toe in bandages; he was like a mummy. The only words his father said, on Alan's arrival was "For Gods sake, put the lights on". The lights were on and Alan knew that his father was blind; whether temporary or permanent, he was never to know. About 4am, his father whispered to Alan, "look after your mother", and it wasn't long after that that he died. His injuries had been horrific; mainly 2nd and 3rd degree burns to a large part of his body following a rupture of the engine's boiler and the escape of steam.

Alan spoke of his father's qualities as an engine driver. He was apprehensive of the condition of rolling stock and the rails; and thus was scrupulous in observing speed restrictions; and there were a tremendous amount of them after the war when tracks had been hammered to the devil but very little had been done in the way of maintenance. He was a top link driver; proud of it and immaculate in appearance. Before leaving for work, he would always polish the steam proof top of his cap and his shoes. His overalls might be grubby after a long day on the footplate but they were never filthy dirty; and he would ensure that his fireman Alan Hubbard was turned out the same. One particular day, his father was due to drive the Prince of Wales' (Edward V111) train and his supervisor gave him some new overalls. He threw them back to the supervisor, refusing to wear them saying that his own overalls were clean. Alan said that he only really remembered seeing dad in overalls; his shifts were haphazard; could start at any time of the day and when he thought about it, he said that he couldn't ever recall dad sitting down at the table at lunchtime, with the family for Christmas dinner. The hours and working conditions were why his father didn't want either of his sons to follow him on the railway. Cleanliness didn't stop with overalls; if he took a loco out from the depot which wasn't in tip top condition; he would go mad and bring the cleaners back to finish the job properly. He would also have concern for his fireman and show such annoyance if his loco was not in prime condition causing him to shovel an extra ½ ton coal over the 3 tons he had shovelled from London to Sheffield.

The Railway Board paid for the funeral and Bertie Wilsher was cremated at Golders Green cemetery; his coffin having been conveyed by fellow engine drivers from Kentish Town who acted as pall bearers. At the coroner's inquest, a verdict of Act of God was reached. The footplatemen's union ASLEF offered Mrs Wilsher £2000 plus £800 for younger son David who was still a dependent. Alan felt this was not enough and wanted to take it further, but his mother was so upset, she didn't want to cause a scene. Of course, compensation was an unheard of word in those days; any money offered came really from fellow member's subscriptions.

Alan didn't go onto the railways; he went back to the bicycle trade he was in before he did his RAF service but by a strange quirk of coincidence; he was at Harrow in 1953 to experience the 3 train pile up when 112 people were killed. He was managing Buntings cycle shop just opposite the station; he had just opened up for the day when there was a massive eruption of noise as the three trains came to grief and pulled down the station bridge. The shop was taken over by the rescue authorities and used as an ambulance station. Alan is now 80; has been married over 50 years and he realises just how short a life together, his mother and father had enjoyed; just 23 years. It was an emotional ending to the interview; indeed we all felt sorry for Alan that South Yorkshire had left such a legacy.

I have not met Alan's younger brother, who was just 6 at the time of his dad's accident, but quite out of the blue, he sent me a stirring account of his own thoughts and views as he remembered them. With his permission, I have printed this.

"The date 18th May 1948. My brother was some 10 years older; we slept in the same room. I woke in the night and Gordon was not in his bed. I got up to see where he was and went into my mum's bedroom. Instead of mum being in the bed, I stirred the lady who lived next door, we called her Granny Sears. I asked her what was happening; where were my mum and brother. During the previous afternoon, my dad had called me to give him a kiss as he was off to work.

It was a very hot Whit Tuesday, I was busy playing with my friend Chris. I shouted to Dad that I would wave when he passed the house later in the afternoon. Dad was pulling the 11-45am St Pancras to Bradford train.

With my mum during the holidays, we would waive to dad as he passed the Cricklewood signal box with some cut up parachute silk, that my eldest brother Alan had "nicked" from the RAF. My mum called me to waive to dad, he would blow the engine whistle from almost Cricklewood station to the signal box, and he would also be waiving back to us. I lived in one of the railway cottages adjacent to the shunting line of Cricklewood Sidings. We were able to look across to the main lines from the back of the house. I never saw my dad again; I was 6 ½ years of age.

I remember mum sitting in an armchair, strange, it was not the normal chair, and in fact I hardly remember mum ever sitting down, dad always sat in the opposite chair. Mum told me that dad had been in a train crash and he would not be coming home. I do not have any other memories of that day. I lived in an unmade road; there were 105 homes in the road made up of groups of ten terraced cottages. We knew almost everybody by name. Dad was the only main line express driver in the road. All the families had fathers working for LMS; shunters, signalmen, gangers, firemen, cleaners, and goods drivers. Five houses had been bombed. There were 110 homes before the war. The road was in the process of having new drainage and being turned from a country track to tarmac. The only person who had a car in the road was a travelling salesman for Hoover, a son of a goods driver. The day I next remember, the road was full of cars; the press were after photographs and stories.

Dad was brought home to Cricklewood and a service at the local Baptist Church was standing room only. He was then cremated at Golders Green crematorium. For reasons best known to my mum and brothers, I was not allowed to go. This was a big mistake, as I really believed that Dad would one day walk back through the door. I missed him most when I was ill with those schoolday illnesses, because mum would let me sit in the front room where I could watch the trains go by. The funeral I believe, would have helped me to come to terms that my Dad had gone to heaven. Although I was a scout and frequented the local Baptist church, I am not a religious person, a childhood belief that people should not die in horrific circumstances.

The effect it has had on my life has certainly been one of bitterness and frustration. In today's world, Mum would have had enough compensation to live a comfortable life. One did not have solicitors; they were for the rich. Mum was given £2000 compensation, but no advice on investment. I guess it was spent over a period of time on holidays and items for the house. As the youngest and just started school, I was given £800; this was for my education and clothes etc. Mum had to attend court to apply for handouts from this. When I reached 21, the balance was just over £500; the money had not been put into any interest fund.

As I grew up learning more of the accident, I knew that if Dad had lived, he would have suffered from severe 2nd and 3rd degree burns from the steam of a burst boiler and he would also have been blind. Close friends and my brothers tell me that I have my dad's character, which I am proud about. He did not suffer fools and would stand his ground when things were not quite right. On occasions, he would not take an engine out if he knew it was not in at least a 90% condition. The war had taken its toll on the railways and maintenance was poor. The accident without doubt, was caused because the line was in a poor state, and on that day, there was a question mark over the maintenance that had been carried out, on the part of the line where the engine derailed.

As I have grown older and listened to the stories over again, it would seem that mum was befriended by the then General Secretary of ASLEF. From accounts, he talked mum in to not making a fuss and accepting the compensation payout. My eldest brother Alan who had just completed his national service in the RAF wanted mum to take solicitor's advice, but mum seemed complacent to accept what was on offer.

Many years later, I wrote to ASLEF to see if I could find out any more information about the accident. I was informed they had no record of the accident. Mum had to get a job to make ends meet. The rent still had to be paid to the LMS. I remember her getting a rise and she had to have a shilling (5p) cut from her widow's pension. Poor mum never got over the tragedy; I would come in from school, and later, when I was at work, where she would

David Wilsher, on duty on the Kent & Sussex private railway